Covert Relations

James Joyce
Virginia Woolf
and
Henry James

COVERT RELATIONS

James Joyce,
Virginia Woolf,
and
Henry James

DANIEL MARK FOGEL

University Press of Virginia
Charlottesville and London

THE UNIVERSITY PRESS OF VIRGINIA
Copyright © 1990 by the Rector and Visitors
of the University of Virginia

First published 1990

Library of Congress Cataloging-in-Publication Data

Fogel, Daniel Mark, 1948–
    Covert relations : James Joyce, Virginia Woolf, and Henry James /
Daniel Mark Fogel.
        p. cm.
    Includes bibliographical references.
    ISBN 0-8139-1280-6
    1. English fiction—20th century—History and criticism.
2. Joyce, James, 1882–1941—Knowledge—Literature. 3. Woolf,
Virginia, 1882–1941—Knowledge—Literature. 4. James, Henry,
1843–1916—Influence—Joyce. 5. James, Henry, 1843–1916—Influence—Woolf. 6. Modernism (Literature)—Great Britain. I. Title.
PR888.M63F64   1990
823'.91209—dc20   90-31097
                                                                              CIP

Printed in the United States of America

For my children

Nicholas
Rosemary
and
Emily

Contents

Acknowledgments

I am grateful to Professor Quentin Bell for permission to quote from unpublished reading notes and manuscripts by Virginia Woolf, materials now housed in the Alvin and Henry Berg Collection of the New York Public Library and at the University of Sussex. I am grateful also to Lola Szladits and her staff at the Berg Collection, and, for generous assistance, to the staffs of the three libraries where this book was researched and written: the British Museum; Olin Library, Cornell University; and Middleton Library, Louisiana State University. Quentin Bell also kindly has permitted me to quote from a letter he wrote me that included his recollection of comments his aunt Virginia Woolf made to him about Henry James.

Many friends and colleagues have encouraged and stimulated my work on *Covert Relations* over the past ten years; I hope that I will not inadvertently omit some who deserve my thanks here. First place among these acknowledgments must go to Leon Edel, who read the complete manuscript of *Covert Relations* with an eagle eye, providing detailed, illuminating, and highly instructive comments. The late Maurice Beebe gave me a heartening early response to the research on James Joyce and Henry James with which this study began; his invitation to prepare an essay on Joyce and James for the *Journal of Modern Literature* was a welcome spur to my work. (I am grateful to the *Journal of Modern Literature* for permission to use material that originally appeared in its pages, copyright Temple University, as "henryJAMESjoyce: The Succession of the Masters" [*JML* 11 (1984): 199–229). Morris Beja, Jane Ford, A. Walton Litz, and Mark Seltzer provided opportunities to present papers reporting on various aspects of my research on Joyce, Woolf, and James. The late Richard Ellmann kindly read my first essay on Joyce and James and provided an acute critique. For their encouragement, and for discussions that stimulated my research, I owe special thanks to Charles Caramello, Richard A. Hocks, John Carlos Rowe, and Adeline R. Tintner. During several summers spent reading and writing at Cornell, I benefitted greatly from conversations with Carol Dole, Jane Elizabeth Fisher, and Paula Vene Smith; as the notes to my three chapters on Virginia Woolf and Henry James make clear, I am especially indebted to Carol Dole and Paula Smith for their acute insights into the Woolf-James relation and for their generosity in sharing their work with me. At Louisiana State University, I have been very fortunate in my students and colleagues, and I would be remiss if I did not acknowledge—beyond the general, sustaining atmosphere of a rich and vital intellectual community—special debts of gratitude to Panthea Broughton, Carl Freedman, Debra Journet (now of the University of Louisville), J. Gerald Kennedy, Joseph Kronick, Michelle Massé, Patrick McGee (who provided an invaluable, late reading of the entire manuscript of *Covert Relations*), Herb Rothschild, James Olney, and Lewis P. Simpson. Thanks, too, to Marcus McAllister for his drawings of an Eton suit and of two styles of morning dress pertinent to the argument in the second of my two chapters on Joyce and James. My wife, Rachel, was the first—and for long stretches of time the only—reader of the successive drafts of this book; her support, love, and enthusiasm have been indispensable.

Anyone who writes on James Joyce and Virginia Woolf, not to mention Henry James, must of course build on vast bodies of scholarship and criticism. I have tried in the chapters that follow to acknowledge what I owe on particular points, and I want here only to recognize the most general and important debts. For the theory on which this study is based, I am especially indebted, of course, to Harold Bloom; to feminist revisionists and critics of Bloom, notably Sandra Gilbert and Susan Gubar, and Janice Doane and Devin Hodges; and generally speaking, to the whole remarkable enterprise of feminist criticism and scholarship over the past three decades. Without the volumes of Michael Groden's James Joyce Archive, I would probably still be several years from completing this study. For scholarship on Henry James, James Joyce, and Virginia Woolf, I am most indebted to their great biographers: Leon Edel on Henry James; Richard Ellmann on James Joyce; and Quentin Bell on Virginia Woolf.

To Louisiana State University I owe the opportunity to devote two sabbatical leaves and a summer (under a stipend from the LSU Council on Research) to my work on modernism and literary influence. For their essential support, I owe thanks to my department chairperson, John R. May (and his predecessor, Gale Carrithers, Jr.) and to my dean, David Baily Harned (and his predecessor, Henry L. Snyder). Had I not been able to take leave from my duties as editor of the *Henry James Review,* by placing the journal in the supremely capable hands first of Bainard Cowan and then of Veronica Makowsky, neither of the sabbaticals would have been possible. A Summer Stipend from the National Endowment for the Humanities was also of great importance in enabling me to complete this project. Special thanks, finally, to Nancy Essig, Director of the University Press of Virginia, and to her colleague, Cynthia Foote, an unsurpassed copy editor.

Key to Frequently Cited Works

BS—Henry James, *The Better Sort* (1903)

CE—*The Collected Essays of Virginia Woolf,* ed. Leonard Woolf, 4 vols. (1967)

DVW—*The Diary of Virginia Woolf,* ed. Anne Olivier Bell, 5 vols. (1977–84)

JJ—Richard Ellmann, *James Joyce: New and Revised Edition* (1982)

LJJ—*The Letters of James Joyce,* ed. Stuart Gilbert and Richard Ellmann, 3 vols. (1957, 1966)

LVW—*The Letters of Virginia Woolf,* ed. Nigel Nicolson and Joanne Trautmann, 6 vols. (1975–80)

MB2—Virginia Woolf, *Moments of Being,* ed. Jeanne Schulkind, rev. ed. (1985)

MD—Virginia Woolf, *Mrs. Dalloway* (1925)

ND—Virginia Woolf, *Night and Day* (George Doran, 1920)

OR—Virginia Woolf, *Orlando* (1928)

PL—Henry James, *The Portrait of a Lady* (1881; rpt. in *Novels 1881–1886*)

PL2—Henry James, *The Portrait of a Lady,* 2 vols. (1908).

SH—James Joyce, *Stephen Hero* (1960)

TL—Virginia Woolf, *To the Lighthouse* (1927)

U—James Joyce, *Ulysses,* ed. Hans Walter Gabler (1986)

VO—Virginia Woolf, *The Voyage Out* (1915; rpt. George Doran, 1920)

WV—Virginia Woolf, *The Waves* (1931)

Covert Relations

James Joyce
Virginia Woolf
and
Henry James

Introduction

In *Covert Relations: James Joyce, Virginia Woolf, and Henry James,* I want to present substantially new accounts of the artistic development of James Joyce and Virginia Woolf, working for the most part under terms established by the new movement in influence study that is concerned far less with sources and allusions than with the psychodynamics of the transmission of literary tradition and authority.

The modern theory of literary influence originates in a series of books by Harold Bloom, beginning with *The Anxiety of Influence* (1973). Although Bloom's theory is often elaborate, and even esoteric in its Kabbalistic terminology, its chief premises are elegantly simple. Poems, says Bloom, are written about—and in response to—other poems. Therefore, the critic must dispense with the task of seeking the meaning of a poem in and of itself, for meaning lies in the relations between texts, in intertextuality. Every strong poet, moreover, is a strong misreader, whose misreadings (or, as Bloom terms them, *misprisions*) of a precursor allow the later writer to swerve away from the work of the powerful predecessor, thus establishing, in the departure, autonomy and originality as an artist. In this process, direct traces of the predecessor's influence will be repressed (hence the title of another major exposition of Bloom's theory, *Poetry and Repression* [1976]). Bloom's model for the dialectic of influence is Freudian and, specifically, oedipal: poets must in some sense murder their poetic fathers in order to come into their own, to achieve their own identities and authority.

Bloom has been powerfully and ably attacked for the phallocentrism of his model, which presumes that strong poets are necessarily males, sons battling poetic fathers, and which provides no basis for understanding the predicament of the female author or of the feminine generally except as an object—say, the Muse— to be possessed by the victors in an all-male contest for authority.[1] In addition, as my study of the relation between James Joyce and Henry James suggests, the "anxiety" of Bloom's Freudian model may be less apt for some influence relations than others: less apt for the Joyce-James relation, typified by Joyce's aggressive, playful, virtuoso mockery, satire, and parody, than for the Woolf-James relation, in which Henry James may be read as a leading symptom of the pervasive patriarchy by which Woolf knew herself to be both oppressed and obsessed. *Covert Relations* nevertheless shows that both Joyce and Woolf conceptualized their relations with precursors in terms remarkably like Bloom's. The book also shows that for each of these writers a hitherto largely concealed struggle with a strong precursor was critical in the development of literary identity. I hope, moreover, that *Covert Relations* will help, with similar studies, to form a sufficiently large sample to allow us to generalize with some confidence on an empirical basis about the ways in which gender inflects influence relations. At all events, we are considerably past the point when influence study can be disparaged a priori as mere "source-hunting." After Harold Bloom's work and after the work of the post-Freudian psychoanalytical critics (notably feminist critics and theorists), we can no longer take the author at her or his word or rest content to deal with explicit literary references or allusions. What is left out, what is ignored, what is repressed—these elements have come to assume perhaps even a greater importance than the conscious influences apparent in a literary work.

My focus throughout the five chapters of *Covert Relations* is on the works of Joyce and Woolf, but the pivot around which my discussions of both authors revolve is Henry James. In general terms, James's role as a founder of modernism is long and well established. Ford Madox Ford, Joseph Conrad, Ezra Pound, and T. S. Eliot all acknowledged James's importance as a model and as a pioneer of the modern. These acknowledgments by leading modernists were matched early on by similar recognitions on the part of scholars of literature. Leon Edel, for instance, had never heard of Henry James when, in 1927, he was told by Professor George W. Latham of McGill University that he could not write an M.A. thesis on Joyce's *Ulysses* because "[a] writer has to die before we write dissertations about him" and that, as for "these moderns [Edel had spoken to Latham of Dorothy Richardson and Virginia Woolf as well as of Joyce], I suppose some of them will survive, but you know I have always had a hunch—they all go back to Henry James."[2] In recent years, a variety of critics and theorists have pointed to James's anticipations of modernism and of the distinctive artistic and philosophical predilections of the twentieth century.[3] No one, however, has shown in detail the working out of the influence of Henry James in the development of any of the major modernists. In particular, moreover, no one has shown James's central importance for the development of James Joyce, who scarcely acknowledged the existence of Henry James, or for the development of Virginia Woolf, who wrote copiously and ambivalently on James while concealing in her novels—and in unpublished and until now apparently unremarked notes and manuscripts—his vital role in her imaginative life.

My first two chapters are devoted to the James Joyce–Henry James relation. In chapter one, "*Ulysses*: Henry James in the Carpet," I show how a complex network of allusions to Henry James operates throughout Joyce's masterpiece, particularly in the concealment of Henry James within the figure of Philip Beaufoy in "Calypso" and "Circe," in the debate about Shakespeare in "Scylla and Charybdis," and in the prose of "Eumaeus." In chapter two, "henryJAMESjoyce: The Succession of the Masters," I seek to develop the full meaning of the Henry James trope in *Ulysses* by setting forth an account of the early development of James Joyce from *Stephen Hero* through *A Portrait of the Artist as a Young Man* as a series of responses to, and evasions of, Henry James. The argument returns thereafter to *Ulysses* in order to draw out meanings made salient by the analysis of Joyce's early career and to show that Joyce used the Henry James material in *Ulysses* to make a covert statement about his own relation to literary tradition and at the same time to eliminate, as it were, the concealed precursor.

Until I drafted this book from copious notes accumulated over a number of years, I thought that the sections on Virginia Woolf and on James Joyce would be approximately equal in length. But the three chapters on Woolf have come to be about twice as long as the two on Joyce, and in retrospect this disproportion seems inevitable because of the much greater mass of material, published and archival, on Woolf's literary and personal relations with Henry James. In chapter three, "Who's Afraid of Henry James?—Virginia Woolf/ Influence/Influenza," I begin in the first section with a vignette of Woolf and James eyeing each other in 1907 and proceed in the second section to examine their relation up to that year. In the third section of the chapter, I explore the ways in which Woolf repeatedly connected James with disease and with the Freudian family romance, anticipating the central metaphors in Harold Bloom's theory of influence. Chapter four, "'Partners in Merit': Virginia Woolf on Henry James," explores Woolf's comments on Henry James in published essays and reviews, and in her diary entries, her letters, her reading notes, and her unpublished manuscripts. Chapter five, "A Stew of One's Own: Virginia Woolf's Fiction and the Burden of Henry James," traces Woolf's emulation of James and her resistance to him throughout her nine novels. Here I propose that Henry James played a considerable part in the artistic self-creation of Virginia Woolf and in her self-destruction as well. Finally, in the Conclusion, I offer some observations about the role of gender in the two influence relations, Joyce-James and Woolf-James.

I believe that the principal points in the argument of *Covert Relations* rest on strong conjunctions of external and internal evidence. When, however, one is working on the presumption that the authors one is treating have been engaged in conscious and unconscious deception, in covering their own tracks, and in repression, one must have recourse at times to the conjectural and the circumstantial. I have tried to avoid the dubious, fail-safe technique of asserting influence both when it is obviously there and when it is conspicuously absent. I hope, moreover, that readers will agree with me that the main lines of the arguments made in *Covert Relations* are amply supported by a variety of kinds of evidence and that the more speculative points gain in plausibility as they are drawn into the context those main lines define. Above all, I aim to convince readers that in their strikingly different ways James Joyce and Virginia Woolf recognized the extent to which Henry James was an indispensable forerunner; that there was something of a mythic, tribal element in their veneration and destruction of James as master; that, indeed, we may find in the whole course of literary history that we consume the towering innovators in the process of further creation; and that Harold Bloom's focus on the particular "anxiety of influence" has, in this perspective, wider and deeper meanings.

Chapter One

Ulysses:
Henry James
in the Carpet

I

Few topics in literary studies are as intriguing or as deeply mysterious as the question of how major authors make the quantum leap from apprentice work to their first masterpieces. We are better able, for example, to trace the progress of Keats from such richly achieved works as *The Eve of St. Agnes* to the great odes of spring 1819 than to account for his breakthrough when he first evidenced the characteristic power and tone of his mature voice in "Upon First Looking into Chapman's Homer." Between the firm assurance and authority of that opening salvo of Keats's greatness and the uncertain, soft, self-consciously poetic verse that came before it there lies a vacancy, a silence, that challenges and affronts the critical imagination. Baffled, we may be tempted to rest content with the mere evocation of the mystery, to say of Keats in this instance, as Yeats says of Caesar, Helen of Troy, and Michelangelo, "*Like a long-legged fly upon the stream,/His mind moves upon silence*" ("Long-Legged Fly").

The challenge to literary history is even greater when the leap to artistic mastery entails not only the writer's discovery of a mature voice but also the foundation of a new mode and style of literature. The mystery in the case of James Joyce, one of the great founders of modernism, is compounded, moreover, by the tendency of critics to locate the formative influences on his art in the work of writers in other genres and languages and often in remote periods as well: Homer, Dante, Shakespeare, Flaubert, D'Annunzio, and Ibsen are the most frequently cited—and not a single writer of novels in English! The gulf between the modes of these writers and Joyce's in *Dubliners* and *A Portrait of the Artist as a Young Man,* not to mention *Ulysses* and *Finnegans Wake,* yawns wide. Only in the cases of Flaubert and D'Annunzio is there a traceable general influence on the specific literary form of Joyce's work. Now, however, analysis of a complex, wide-ranging, and hitherto unnoticed network of allusions to Henry James in *Ulysses* makes it possible to place the American novelist practically at the head of the list of major influences on Joyce and to present thereafter a new account of Joyce's development as a writer of novels and tales.

The critical episodes of the Joyce-James story lie in 1904. But since the key to unlocking their meaning lies in *Ulysses,* it is there our quest must begin. I want to start with three assertions and then go on to make the case for each in its turn: (1) the figure of Henry James can be clearly discerned beneath that of Philip Beaufoy, who wrote the tale Leopold Bloom reads in the outhouse in "Calypso" (the first chapter in which Bloom appears in *Ulysses*) and who also appears in "Circe" (the hallucinatory Nighttown episode) to accuse Bloom of plagiarism; (2) in the argument about Shakespeare's life and art in "Scylla and Charybdis" (the National Library episode) Joyce created an elaborate response to James's tale about the curator of the Bard's boyhood home, "The Birthplace"; and (3) the prose of "Eumaeus" (the post-Nighttown chapter set in the cabman's shelter) not only expresses the exhaustion of Stephen Dedalus and Bloom after their Circean adventures but also unmistakably burlesques the late style of Henry James, which Joyce thought had exhausted the traditional resources of fiction.

Philip Beaufoy first comes into *Ulysses* in one of the most striking of the early incidents in the novel. "Calypso," the fourth chapter in the novel, details Leopold Bloom's preparation of his breakfast kidney, his excursion to the shop of Dlugacz, the pork butcher, and his service of breakfast in bed to his wife, Molly—along with the note to her from Blazes Boylan that, as poor Bloom surmises, fixes an adulterous tryst for that very afternoon. In the preceding chapter, we have become familiar with Stephen Dedalus's snot and have witnessed his urination, but when Joyce follows Bloom to the "jakes" in the garden at 7 Eccles Street we arrive at the memorable zenith of the naturalistic depiction of bodily functions in the novel in English: "Quietly he read, restraining himself, the first column and, yielding but resisting, began the second. Midway, his last resistance yielding, he allowed his bowels to ease themselves quietly as he read, reading still patiently that slight constipation of yesterday quite gone. Hope it's not too big bring on piles again. No, just right. So. Ah!" (*U* 56). What Bloom has been reading is "Matcham's Masterstroke," the "prize titbit" in his paper (*Titbits*), "written by Mr Philip Beaufoy, Playgoers' Club, London." Bloom's response to the story is mixed:

> It did not move or touch him but it was something quick and neat. Print anything now. Silly season. He read on, seated calm above his own rising smell. Neat certainly. *Matcham often thinks of the masterstroke by which he won the laughing witch who now.* Begins and ends morally. *Hand in hand.* Smart. He glanced back through what he had read and, while feeling his water flow quietly, he envied kindly Mr Beaufoy who had written it and received payment of three pounds, thirteen and six.

Bloom thinks that he himself "might manage a sketch." Shortly thereafter, "he tore away half the prize story sharply and wiped himself with it" (*U* 56–57).

Who is Philip Beaufoy, and why is he a worthy object of the investigation upon which we are about to embark? According to Stanislaus Joyce, the words Bloom reads in the prize story echo a tale that James Joyce wrote while still a schoolboy at Belvedere.[1] Philip Beaufoy, a real and apparently egregious writer for *Titbits*, is therefore a mask for the young James Joyce.[2] Stanislaus does not say, however, that his brother's early story was called "Matcham's Masterstroke" or even that the name *Matcham* appeared in it. In fact, *Matcham* is the first in a series of clues that there is a mask beneath the mask: Beaufoy masks young James Joyce, and Joyce in turn masks Henry James.

Matcham—readers of the late Henry James will recognize this as the name of a great English country house featured prominently in James's last great novels, *The Wings of the Dove* and *The Golden Bowl*. In *The Wings of the Dove*, Matcham is the great house where Milly Theale has her most splendid sense of the fullness of life—making the occasion of her visit there "a high-water mark of the imagination"—but where, at the same time, she poignantly realizes how sharply curtailed her own life will be. At Matcham, Milly views a Bronzino portrait of a young woman who strikingly resembles her and who is, to her own intense consciousness, "dead, dead, dead." [3] In *The Golden Bowl*, Matcham plays a role more germane, perhaps, to the immediate context in *Ulysses*. In "Calypso," just before going out to the jakes, Bloom brings Molly the letter from Blazes Boylan setting up their adulterous assignation at four o'clock that afternoon. In *The Golden Bowl*, Matcham is the site of a weekend party attended by Prince Amerigo and Charlotte Verver without their spouses: from there they go to Gloucester, where they become lovers in act and in fact at a discrete inn.

There are other details besides the word *Matcham* in the "Calypso" defecation passage that become extremely telling once Beaufoy is identified with Henry James, but since the identification depends on data in two other episodes of *Ulysses*, I will consider them first. Two clues in "Circe"—the fifteenth chapter of *Ulysses*, the hallucinatory Nighttown episode in which Bloom is transformed into a woman at Bella Cohen's brothel and in which Philip Beaufoy appears again—are particularly important. First, in accusing Bloom of plagiarism, Beaufoy calls his own works "the Beaufoy books of love and great possessions." In whatever sense the word *possessions* is understood (whether as obsessions, as property, or even—as may be plausibly argued for *The Turn of the Screw*—as *demonic* possessions), there could be no apter description of the works of Henry James and particularly of the novels running from *The Spoils of Poynton* through *The Golden Bowl*. What is especially striking here, furthermore, is Joyce's direct verbal echo of Henry James's description of his theme in the "Notes for The Ivory Tower," published posthumously with that unfinished novel in 1917. The hero of *The Ivory Tower*, James wrote, would come "face to face with . . . the black and merciless things that are behind the great possessions."[4] Second, to the court in which Bloom imagines himself in the dock, Beaufoy declares, "My literary agent Mr J. B. Pinker is in attendance" (*U* 374), and Pinker was of course agent for Henry James.

Pinker was of course, one might well rejoin, agent for many of the major writers of the day. And as to the echo of Henry James's "great possessions" in James Joyce's "Circe," it consists of just two words. Is there any evidence that Joyce associated Henry James and Pinker and that he even knew of, let alone read, the "Notes for The Ivory Tower"?

J. B. Pinker had written to Joyce proposing to represent him in March of 1915. Joyce then asked Ezra Pound to interview Pinker for him. Late in March, Pound wrote to Joyce: "Also I saw Pinker. I enclose his draft of agreement. It is straight and fair enough. He is agent for Conrad and Henry James etc. etc. and I think he will probably do better for you then [*sic*] any one else could."[5] Joyce had special reason, therefore, to associate Pinker with Henry James as well as with Conrad and also with H. G. Wells, who had encouraged Pinker's overture to Joyce (*JJ* 384). But neither the Polish mariner nor the Fabian Wells, who carried his below-stairs origins as a chip on his shoulder, could conceivably be embodied in the fastidiously correct Philip Beaufoy, who appears in "Circe" in "*accurate morning dress*" invoking the code of the "born gentleman" (*U* 374) and who, as we have noticed in "Calypso," has a fashionable London address, the Playgoers' Club. (Henry James's London club address would have been at the Athenaeum or at the Reform). Nor by any stretch of the imagination could the works of Conrad or of Wells be characterized as "books of love and great possessions." Finally, both Conrad and Wells were married, and Bloom's last words about Beaufoy in "Circe" are the fragmentary "and he, a bachelor, how . . ." (*U* 375). In short, only one of these writers fills the bill: punctilious, Anglicized, celibate Henry James, with his sympathy for a hierarchic, aristocratic social order and his predilection to write almost exclusively about the people whom he called "the better sort."

Was Joyce aware of Henry James's "Notes for The Ivory Tower"? He nowhere mentions having read James's "project" for his novel, and his use of James's phrase "great possessions" might only be coincidence. But given the Jamesian matrix of the Beaufoy figure, there is a high probability that Joyce was intentionally echoing James, for Joyce could scarcely have helped being aware of the publication and importance of James's plan for his novel. In August 1918, the serialization of *Ulysses* was interrupted after the first five episodes so that an issue of *The Little Review* could be devoted to Henry James. The Henry James number, organized by Ezra Pound—the impresario of the serial publication of *Ulysses* as well—contained essays by several hands, most notably two by T. S. Eliot and three by Pound himself. The third of Pound's contributions, "The Notes to 'The Ivory Tower,'" closed out the special issue and was continued into the number for September 1918, which included "Ulysses, Episode VI" ("Hades"). Pound's essay begins with the statements that "the great artists among men of letters have occasionally and by tradition burst into an *Ars Poetica*" and that "various reviewers have hinted obscurely that some such treatise is either adumbrated or concealed in the Notes for *The Ivory Tower;* . . . but no one has set forth the gist or the generalities which are to be found in these notes." Pound then goes on to set forth, in outline, "the formula for building a novel (any novel, not merely any 'psychological' novel)" and "the things to have clearly in mind before starting to write it" as "enumerated in *The Ivory Tower* notes." Having concluded the outline, Pound marches toward the conclusion of his essay (in the issue that included Joyce's "Hades") with the remark that "I give this outline with such fulness because it is a landmark in the history of the novel as written in English. It is inconceivable that Fielding or Richardson should have left, or that Thomas Hardy should leave, such testimony to a comprehension of the novel as a 'form.'"[6] Joyce, who was working on *Ulysses* with the aid of his own precompositional notes (apparently far more fragmentary but no less serviceable than James's), would have found Pound's precis of Henry James's notes of abundant interest. That Pound's discussion of the "Notes for The Ivory Tower" was printed in *The Little Review* with *Ulysses* in any case significantly increases the likelihood that Joyce's "great possessions" directly and intentionally echoes James's.

That probability—along with the identification of Philip Beaufoy as Henry James—seems to me to rise to a virtual certainty when we correlate the passages in "Calypso" and "Circe" with the one explicit mention of Henry James in *Ulysses*. It occurs in the concluding words of the following sentence from the last section of "The Wandering Rocks" (the tenth chapter of the novel, subdivided into nineteen sections that detail the activities of numerous minor characters throughout Dublin, and of Stephen Dedalus and Leopold Bloom as well, for a period of about an hour in the mid-afternoon): "The Right Honourable William Humble, earl of Dudley, G.C.V.O., passed Micky Anderson's alltimesticking watches and Henry and James's wax smartsuited freshcheeked models, the gentleman Henry, *dernier cri* James" (*U* 208). I will return to this sentence later, but I want to make two points right away. First, in the last nine words of the "Wandering Rocks" sentence, strategically located at nearly the precise midpoint between the "Calypso" and "Circe" passages with which I have so far been concerned, Joyce packs direct echoes of the two Philip Beaufoy episodes: "smart" in "smartsuited" picks up Bloom's thoughts on "Matcham's Masterstroke"—"Begins and ends morally. *Hand in hand*. Smart."—and "gentleman" looks forward to Beaufoy's twice using the same word in his first speech in "Circe" (*U* 374). Thus, Henry James, openly named, is twice linked to Beaufoy.[7] Second, Joyce's revisions of the placards (galleys) and page proofs of the first edition of *Ulysses*, along with the dated stamps placed by the printer on these materials, show that Joyce worked on all three passages at about the same time. In "Calypso," one of the details most apposite to Henry James, Bloom's thought that Beaufoy's tale "begins and ends morally," was added in Joyce's hand to the first version of gathering five of the page proofs, a version dated "30 Juin 1921."[8] In "The Wandering Rocks," the entire sentence naming Henry James was written in by Joyce on the second version of gathering sixteen of the page proofs, dated "12 Octobre 1921." [9] And in "Circe," the key phrase "of love and great possessions" was added by Joyce on placard 50, dated "3 Decembre 1921." [10] To be sure, nearly three and a half months separate the addition to "Calypso" and the one to "Wandering Rocks," and seven and a half weeks intervene between the latter and the addition to "Circe." But these are small spans of time measured against the seven-year composition of *Ulysses,* and in each of the last two cases, in "The Wandering Rocks" and in "Circe," Joyce seized the first available opportunity after June 30, 1921, to reinforce the Henry James trope in these episodes, providing crucial clues to the Beaufoy-James identification and forging in the sentence about "Henry, *dernier cri* James" the remarkable link between the two Beaufoy episodes. The timing—with the publication date of *Ulysses,* February 2, 1922, fast approaching—suggests that Joyce was working in this final round of revisions with the significant, sustained intention of coordinating the three passages and of strengthening the covert identity of Beaufoy and James.

To return to "Calypso" to pick up other elements in the passage there that seem especially telling now that Beaufoy has been shown to be a mask for Henry James, one notes first of all the name *Beaufoy,* literally "good faith" or "beautiful word," and how apposite it is to the integrity and high polish with which Henry James consecrated his labors at the altar of art. Second, it now seems possible that the "Masterstroke" of the title of Beaufoy's tale has Jamesian resonances no less than the "Matcham." From the 1890s on, Henry James was known to his acolytes as "the Master." James liked the appellation. When Hugh Walpole wondered how to address his distinguished older friend (circa 1909), James replied that "for the present" Walpole could call him "my very dear Master." The title was not just private, moreover, but public—how much so is perhaps best indicated by the headline in the New York *Evening Journal* for January 4, 1906, which proclaimed the false rumor that Henry James was smitten with the notorious and wealthy Emilie Grigsby, who had been Charles T. Yerkes' companion when the tycoon died at the Waldorf and who was wrongly supposed by the

Hearst press (on the basis of a rumor propagated by Grigsby herself) to have been the model for Milly Theale in *The Wings of the Dove:* "Heroine in Master's Novel: Grigsby in Language of Love."[11] The whole word *masterstroke,* furthermore, was a favorite of Henry James, and Joyce would have found it more than once in the pages of *The Better Sort,* a collection of Henry James's stories that, as I will argue in the next chapter, was critically important in Joyce's early development.[12] Doubtless more speculatively—would one offer such a conjecture with any writer but Joyce?—one might note the appositeness of *masterstroke* to Henry James, the master who died following a stroke early in 1916. Also more speculatively, here is Stanislaus Joyce's account of the plot of the early story by James Joyce that "Matcham's Masterstroke" recalls: "The plot concerned a man who gets to a masked ball disguised as a prominent Russian diplomat, and, when returning home on foot, narrowly escapes assassination at the hands of a Nihilist outside the Russian Embassy."[13] In the late 1890s, when Joyce first wrote this story, the most notable model in English for a tale concerning an abortive assassination attempt was, I would suggest, Henry James's *The Princess Casamassima* (1886), whose hero fails in his mission to kill a duke, a pillar of the establishment who is called a "master . . . worth your powder."[14] Finally, Mr. Bloom's epithet for the author of "Matcham's Masterstroke," "kindly Mr Beaufoy," is remarkably like Joyce's exclamation about Henry James in a letter of 1905 to Stanislaus: "O that nice old Henry James!"[15]

I want to make three additional points about the Beaufoy passage in "Circe." The words *great possessions* may not be the only echo of James's "Notes for The Ivory Tower." When Beaufoy refers to his own works as "really gorgeous stuff, a perfect gem" (*U* 374), Joyce may be burlesquing the superlatives Henry James deploys in discussing his novel and the effects he wants to aim for in it: for example, "to the last perfection," "a Joint of the first water," "absolutely precious," and "the great beauty."[16] Furthermore, when Beaufoy offers "damning evidence" of Bloom's alleged plagiarism, "the *corpus delicti,* my lord, a specimen of my maturer work disfigured by the hallmark of the beast" (*U* 375), Joyce is perhaps alluding not only to the mark of the beast in Revelation 13:16–17 but also to the greatest short example of Henry James's "maturer work," "The Beast in the Jungle," a tale on which Joyce drew, as we shall see, for his central theme in "The Dead." Thus, in the nightmare world of "Circe," Bloom/Joyce might plausibly be accused of having "cribbed" that particular tale by Beaufoy/James. And if, finally, Joyce associated Henry James with Shakespeare (a possibility we are about to consider), then Beaufoy's echo in the phrase "the most inherent baseness" of *Coriolanus* (an allusion apparently unnoticed hitherto) (*U* 374; *Coriolanus* 3.2.123) is another link between Beaufoy and James.[17] Given the context in *Coriolanus*, moreover, the allusion may be taken to comment ironically on Henry James's ambivalent relation to the mass market, which James aspired to command though, like the editors of *The Little Review*, he would make no compromise with the public taste. For the phrase "most inherent baseness" appears in Coriolanus's empassioned refusal to pander to the citizenry gathered in the marketplace. Incidentally, the speech in *Coriolanus* begins, before the dramatic reversal of Coriolanus's refusal, with these lines, "Well, I must do't./Away, my disposition, and possess me/Some harlot's spirit!" (3.2.110–12). Thus the allusion in *Ulysses* should remind us of a Shakespearian context beautifully apt for the Nighttown setting in Bella Cohen's brothel.

II

There is, moreover, another episode in *Ulysses* that Joyce may be said to have cribbed, in part at least, from Henry James. In having Stephen Dedalus set forth in "Scylla and Charybdis" an elaborate, factitious account of the relation between Shakespeare's life and art, Joyce provided a model for understanding the transaction between his own biography and work: if for Shakespeare the mundane and sordid facts of Stratford could become the transcendently great art produced in London, then for Joyce the facts of Dublin, no less mundane and sordid, could become the transcendent myth of *Ulysses* forged in Trieste-Zurich-Paris. "Scylla and Charybdis," the ninth chapter of *Ulysses,* which presents Stephen's debate with the Dublin literati in the National Library, is itself a triumphant demonstration of the theory Stephen expounds. But Joyce transformed art as well as life to create his own work. As Richard Ellmann remarks, "inspired cribbing was always part of James's [Joyce's] talent; his gift was for transforming material, not for originating it." [18] No one seems to have pointed out before that Joyce's inspired cribbing probably included at least one, and possibly two, texts by Henry James that are concerned with Shakespeare and that provide the central concept of "Scylla and Charybdis." Joyce himself may have planted a clue to the Shakespeare–Henry James nexus in *Ulysses* in the allusion to *Coriolanus* that Joyce puts, as we have just seen, in Beaufoy's mouth in "Circe."

In "The Birthplace," first published in 1903 in Henry James's *The Better Sort,* the protagonist, Morris Gedge, is put in charge of "the early home of the supreme poet, the Mecca of the English-speaking race" (*BS* 247)—of Shakespeare's birthplace, in other words, though the "supreme poet" is never named in James's tale. Gedge discovers in himself a conscientious revulsion against the phony spiel—of the "here-his-little-feet-often-pattered" variety—that he is expected to deliver as he guides visitors through the house. He himself knows, as one of two visitors who become his confidants says, that "abysmally little" is known about the poet of the shrine: "'That's the interest; it's immense. He escapes us like a thief at night, carrying off—well, carrying off everything'" (*BS* 279). Gedge is convinced, moreover, that the poet is to be found in his work:

> It was as if, in deep, close throbs, in cool after-waves that broke of a sudden and bathed his mind, all possession and comprehension and sympathy, all the truth and the life and the story, had come to him, and come, as the newspapers said, to stay. "It's absurd," he didn't hesitate to say, "to talk of our not 'knowing.' So far as we don't it's because we're donkeys. He's *in* the thing [the set of the poet's works in which Gedge immerses himself before taking up his custodial post at the birthplace], over His ears, and the more we get into it the more we're with Him. I seem to myself at any rate," he declared, "to *see* Him in it as if He were painted on the wall." (*BS,* 253)

But when Gedge falls "into the habit of sailing, as he would have said, too near the wind, or in other words—all in the presence of the people [visitors to the birthplace]—of washing his hands of the legend" (*BS* 286), he is threatened with dismissal by the trustees of the shrine. To protect his income, not so much for his own sake as for that of his wife, less conscience-stricken than he because of a less fine sensibility, he becomes a master entertainer. His spell-binding pitch soon becomes a transatlantic sensation. When the couple in whom Gedge has confided return, after an interval and having last seen Gedge before his flights of Barnumesque show-manship, he does his act for them. "'You're really a genius,'" the wife in the couple responds (*BS* 297). Transcending the demeaning elements in his situation, Gedge triumphs by becoming an artist. Or, in a competitive reading, Gedge is lampooned, sent up by Henry James for becoming a vivid embodiment of the philistinism from which he had earlier recoiled, for making "the Show" "the Biggest on Earth" (*BS* 290). James, I think, wants us to revolve both readings in our minds and to hold them there as opposing faces of the same medal.[19] James's temper in this respect is not unlike Joyce's in "Scylla and Charybdis," for Joyce has "Judge Eglinton" sum up the debate on Shakespeare, "—The truth is midway, he affirmed" (*U* 174).

The argument that "Scylla and Charybdis" is in part a compli-cated response to "The Birthplace" rests primarily on the similar situations in the two works and secondarily on some verbal paral-lels and on one item of external evidence. Stephen Dedalus relates, as does Gedge, an account of Shakespeare's life that he freely admits he does not believe. In telling his tale, Stephen is no less concerned with showmanship than Gedge: "Local colour," Stephen tells him-self. "Work in all you know. Make them accomplices" (*U* 154). Stephen's relation to his audience is like Gedge's: by the brilliance of his performance, Stephen proves his superiority to Eglinton, Best, and company, exercising, at the same time, an artistry that they and the Dublin literary world they represent have proved (so far at least) incapable of appreciating, as witness Stephen's exclusion from Russell's anthology and from Moore's soirée (*U* 157–58).

Stephen triumphs, but, like Gedge, he is also ironically undercut, particularly when Mulligan enters the scene and casts some hilarious highlights on Stephen's portentous solemnity. And Stephen believes, with Gedge, that the artist is to be found in his work, so that throughout his exposition he draws on the plays to develop the "facts" he presents about Shakespeare's life. Stephen is not concerned, as is Gedge, with Shakespeare's physical birthplace but with the birthplace of myth in the womb of imagination that an androgynous artist-God—a Shakespeare or a Joyce—impregnates with himself and with "all his race": "When Rutlandbaconsouthamptonshakespeare or another poet of the same name in the comedy of errors wrote Hamlet he was not the father of his own son merely but, being no more a son, he was and felt himself the father of all his race, the father of his own grandfather, the father of his unborn grandson who, by the same token, never was born, for nature, as Mr Magee understands her, abhors perfection." "Himself his own father, Sonmulligan told himself. Wait. I am big with child. . . . Let me parturiate!" (*U* 171). Shakespeare fathers himself in the ghost in *Hamlet,* his son in Prince Hamlet, his faithless wife in Gertrude, and his brothers in the villains Richard III and Edmund; and Joyce fathers a youthful version of himself in Stephen Dedalus and fathers Stephen's spiritual father (a maturer version of himself) in Leopold Bloom, not to mention his own biological father in Simon Dedalus.

The verbal parallels between "The Birthplace" and "Scylla and Charybdis" are not exact, but they are nevertheless suggestive. A statement by Eglinton—"of all great men he is the most enigmatic. We know nothing but that he lived and suffered. Not even so much" (*U* 159)—recalls the statement from "The Birthplace" about "the fact of the abysmally little that, in proportion [to what there must have been], we know" (*BS* 279). Russell tries to check Stephen's discourse early on with the rebuke that "this prying into the family life of a great man" is "interesting only to the parish clerk. I mean, we have the plays. . . . We have *King Lear:* and it is immortal" (*U* 155), recalling a speech by Gedge: " 'It's all I want—to let the author alone. . . . There are all the immortal people—*in* the work; but there's nobody else" (*BS* 283). Perhaps more tellingly for my argument, there is the following enigmatic non sequitur in a letter of December 1906 from James to Stanislaus Joyce: "Kick in the arse for the following. G. K. C.: G. B. S.: S. L.: H. J.: G. R." Ellmann glosses the initials thus: "G. K. Chesterton, George Bernard Shaw, Sidney Lee, Henry James, Grant Richards."[20] Now this list contains the names of two persons whom Joyce introduces in connection with Shakespeare in "Scylla and Charybdis." Mr. Lyster, hoping that "Mr Dedalus will work out his theory for the enlightenment of the public," adds that "we ought to mention another Irish commentator, Mr George Bernard Shaw," whose irreverent pieces on Shakespeare began to appear in the *Saturday Review* in the nineties (*U* 161). When Stephen says that *Pericles* is "the first play of the closing period," Best names one of Joyce's principal sources on Shakespeare in asking, "What does Mr Sidney Lee, or Mr Simon Lazarus as some aver his name is, say of it?" (*U* 160). To find "H. J." in sequence, therefore, with "G. B. S." and "S. L"—Sidney Lee was a major biographer and editor of Shakespeare—might be sufficient grounds for one's supposing that Joyce, having read Henry James's "The Birthplace," was linking him with others who had written about "the supreme poet." But what of the other two sets of initials on the list? G. K. Chesterton wrote very little on Shakespeare, but by December 1906, he had published essays on *Love's Labour Lost* and *A Midsummer Night's Dream*, both in 1904, the year in which *Ulysses* is set.[21] Grant Richards is the only person on the list who does not have an obvious Shakespeare connection and the only one against whom Joyce had a genuine personal grudge (for 1906 was the year in which Richards accepted *Dubliners* for publication, then demanded alterations in the text [e.g., the removal of six uses of the word *bloody*, five of which Joyce grudgingly deleted], and finally reneged on the acceptance). Possibly Joyce's list merely brought together enviably successful authors with the man who had just barred him from the success of publication. But the hypothesis that the consistency of the list lies in Joyce's association of the persons indicated with views and accounts of Shakespeare competitive with his own gains credence in the light of three considerations. First, Grant Richards had published W. E.

Henley's ten-volume *Works of Shakespeare* (known as the Edinburgh Folio) from 1901 through 1904. Second, the consistency of Shakespearian reference in the list makes it at least possible that "G. R." is not Grant Richards but the prominent historian G. W. Rudsen, whose *William Shakespeare: His Life, His Works, and His Teaching* was published in 1903. And, third, yet another possible identity of "G. R."—indeed, in my analysis the most probable—is George Russell, who after all appears in "Scylla and Charybdis" as one of Stephen's chief adversaries in the debate about Shakespeare.[22]

In any case, Henry James is linked in the letter with two (and, if the Russell possibility is accepted, with three) persons who figure as Shakespearians in "Scylla and Charybdis." That James follows "S. L." on the list is especially curious since in 1906 Sidney Lee began to issue the volumes of his *Complete Works of William Shakespeare* (the Renaissance Edition), which included an Introduction to *The Tempest* by Henry James. Possibly Joyce had seen an advertisement or prospectus of the collection listing James among authors of the introductions; yet, since the volume containing *The Tempest* was not published until 1907, he could not have read James's essay when he wished a "kick in the arse" to "G. B. S.: S. L.: H. J." et al. The only Shakespeare-James association to date in December 1906 would have been "The Birthplace."[23] But Joyce's interest in James's Introduction would have been primed by "The Birthplace" and abetted by his interest in Lee as an authority on Shakespeare. And Joyce would have found support for the Joyce-Dedalus theory about Shakespeare in Henry James's defense in the *Tempest* Introduction of an abiding interest in the man who wrote the plays and of the idea that any line drawn between the artist and the life will be merely arbitrary. To pursue Shakespeare the man, says James, is to engage in "a quest of imaginative experience" that "has itself constituted one of the greatest observed adventures of mankind; so that no point of the history of it, however far back seized, is premature for our fond attention." Early in the Introduction, James says that though we cannot touch the man himself directly in the plays, we touch the artist, and it is "as if, thereby, in meeting *him,* and touching him, we were nearer to meeting and touching the man." James's conclusion reiterates: "The secret that baffles us being the secret of the Man, we know, as I have granted, that we shall never touch the Man *directly* in the Artist. We stake our hopes thus on indirectness, which may contain possibilities." Incidentally, Henry James envisions Shakespeare as a rather Joycean artist, one whose universe is language, whose genius lies above all in his "power of constitutive speech." For most artists, "life itself, in its appealing, overwhelming crudity, offers itself as the paste to be kneaded. . . . whereas we see Shakespeare working predominantly in the terms of expression, *all* in the terms of the artist's specific vision and genius." Finally, like Morris Gedge, and like Dedalus/Joyce in "Scylla and Charybdis," Henry James in his Introduction to *The Tempest* dramatizes the Shakespeare he imagines, as when he envisions the composition of *The Tempest* by "a divine musician who, alone in his room, preludes or improvises at close of day":

> He sits at the harpsichord, by the open window, in the summer dusk; his hands wander over the keys. They stray far, for his motive, but at last he finds and holds it; then he lets himself go, embroidering and refining: it is the thing for the hour and his mood. The neighbours may gather in the garden, the nightingale be hushed on the bough; it is none the less a private occasion, a concert of one, both performer and auditor, who plays for his own ear, his own hand, his own innermost sense, and for the bliss and capacity of his instrument.[24]

The possibility that Joyce read Henry James's Introduction to *The Tempest* must be assigned a somewhat lower probability than my main contention here, that in James's Gedge of 1903 Joyce found the inspiration for developing, in 1904 (in all probability, according to Ellmann), for the sake of his own art, an artful, factitious account of Shakespeare's life. The conjecture that Joyce read James's Introduction is, however, lent some further plausibility by the extent to which Joyce provides an answer to what James takes to be the supremely baffling question of Shakespeare's retirement: "*How* did the faculty so radiant there contrive, in such perfection, the arrest of its divine flight?"[25] A possibility that the bachelor Henry James did not imagine ("And he, a bachelor, how," Bloom asks of

Beaufoy), that a man might wish simply to retire and to enjoy his grandchildren, is sketched out in Stephen's Shakespeare biography. Stephen sees Shakespeare as creating throughout his early and middle periods under the impetus of a deep wound to his self-esteem dealt him by Anne Hathaway and then as achieving in his late plays a reconciliation, a resolution of the turmoil expressed throughout his earlier work, having been enabled to do so by the birth of a grandchild, "a girl, placed in his arms, Marina. . . . —Marina, Stephen said, a child of storm, Miranda, a wonder, Perdita, that which was lost. What was lost is given back to him; his daughter's child. *My dearest wife,* Pericles says, *was like this maid.* Will any man love the daughter if he has not loved the mother?" (*U* 160–61). Henry James's Introduction to *The Tempest* is, in my view, one of the great ignored foundational documents of modernism. James's brilliant analysis of Shakespeare's universe of language, his unparalleled power of "constitutive speech," may have been among the clearest calls challenging Joyce to rival Shakespeare in the profuse creation of an imaginative world of discourse, a world that in Joyce's case is embodied in (and almost consumed by) its own increasingly radical constitutive speech.

III

If Joyce caricatures Henry James in Philip Beaufoy and cribs from James's "The Birthplace" in "Scylla and Charybdis," does he also parody James's distinctive prose style? James of course does not appear in Joyce's famous sequential imitation of the historical development of English prose in the fourteenth chapter of *Ulysses*, "The Oxen of the Sun," for the authors whose styles are mimicked there are all English, as were all of the writers surveyed in the two books on English prose that Joyce consulted when writing the episode.[26] Shakespeare, the most important English author for Joyce, is not among those whose style Joyce reproduces in "Oxen"; Shakespeare gets a chapter to himself, "Scylla and Charybdis." Similarly, Joyce incorporated parody of Henry James throughout the sixteenth chapter of *Ulysses,* "Eumaeus," the episode in which Bloom and Stephen recover at the cabman's shelter from their ordeals in Nighttown.

That James Joyce parodies Henry James in "Eumaeus," I will readily concede, is not a provable contention; indeed, the parody seems to have gone almost unremarked by readers of *Ulysses.*[27] It is scattered in phrases, sentences, and paragraphs here and there throughout the episode, particularly in the first two-thirds. In the James parodies one finds some typically Jamesian phrases, but the argument that Joyce is parodying James rests less on precise verbal echoes than on Joyce's generally caricaturing the rhythm, shape, and diction of James's late prose: its endemic qualifying phrases and clauses; its fastidious parentheses; its mixture of elaborately formal English diction with English and American slang, reworked clichés, and French words and phrases (remember that in "The Wandering Rocks" James is "the gentleman Henry, *dernier cri* James"); its late identification of pronouns (as in the opening words of *The Wings of the Dove,* "She waited, Kate Croy"); its posing of alternative, antithetical descriptions of things; its elaborate circumlocutions; and its prolixity.[28] I leave it to readers of Henry James to decide whether they feel a shock of recognition in the following representative samples of what I take to be the Henry James parody in "Eumaeus." I begin here with the first words in "Eumaeus" and move chronologically through the episode, interpolating occasional comments of my own in square brackets:

> Preparatory to anything else Mr Bloom brushed off the greater bulk of the shavings and handed Stephen the hat and ashplant and bucked him up generally in orthodox Samaritan fashion which he very badly needed. His (Stephen's) mind was not exactly what you would call wandering but a bit unsteady and on his expressed desire for some beverage to drink Mr Bloom . . . hit upon an expedient by suggesting, off the reel, the propriety of the cabman's shelter, as it was called, hardly a stonesthrow away near Butt Bridge where they might hit upon some drinkables in the shape of a milk and soda or a mineral. (*U* 501)

En route to his taciturn and, not to put too fine a point on it, not yet perfectly sober companion . . . (*U* 502)

The guarded glance of half solicitude half curiosity augmented by friendliness which he gave at Stephen's at present morose expression of features did not throw a flood of light, none at all in fact on the problem. (*U* 507)—["flood of light" is a favorite James phrase, as in the Preface to *The Ambassadors,* where he speaks of "a flood of such light," and also as in the text of that novel—of which there are several possible echoes in "Eumaeus"—where Strether acquires "an amount of light that affected him . . . as flooding the scene," "an inexorable tide of light." See the Bodley Head *Ambassadors* (London, 1970), 28, 375, and 379].

—Now touching a cup of coffee, Mr Bloom ventured to plausibly suggest to break the ice, it occurs to me you ought to sample something in the shape of solid food, say, a roll of some description. (*U* 508)

Mr Bloom was all at sea for a moment. (*U* 509)

. . . culminating in an instructive tour of the sights of the great metropolis [London], . . . our modern Babylon [a recurrent James metaphor for London and, in *The Ambassadors,* for Paris]. (*U* 512)

He drank needless to be told and it pointed only once more a moral when he might quite easily be in a large way of business if—a big if, however—he had contrived to cure himself of his particular partiality ["it pointed only once more a moral" seems especially Jamesian]. (*U* 522)

From inside information extending over a series of years Mr Bloom was rather inclined to poohpooh the suggestion as egregious balderdash for, pending that consummation devoutly to be or not to be wished for, he was fully cognisant of the fact that their neighbours across the channel, unless they were much bigger fools than he took them for, rather concealed their strength than the opposite. (*U* 524)

With a touch of fear for the young man beside him whom he furtively scrutinised with an air of some consternation remembering he had just come back from Paris . . . [Bloom here fears that Paris has corrupted Stephen in a way reminiscent of Strether's initial apprehensions about Chad Newsome in *The Ambassadors*]. (*U* 527)

This gratuitous contribution of a humorous character occasioned a fair amount of laughter among his *entourage*. (*U* 531)

The vicinity of the young man he certainly relished, educated, *distingué* and impulsive into the bargain, far and away the pick of the bunch though you wouldn't think he had it in him yet you would. (*U* 534)

As these examples perhaps indicate, Joyce is not merely imitating Henry James, as he imitates the styles of diverse writers in "The Oxen of the Sun," but is more pointedly burlesquing him. For if Joyce felt, as I have already suggested, that Henry James had exhausted the traditional resources of fiction, "Eumaeus" was the appropriate point at which to show Jamesian prose dissolving into the general exhaustion of language throughout the episode, an exhaustion that reflects the post-Nighttown fatigue of the two main characters. My contention that Henry James is parodied in "Eumaeus," moreover, seems to me to be strengthened by our finding this to be one of the few episodes aside from "Calypso" and "Circe" in which Philip Beaufoy is mentioned: "To improve the shining hour he [Bloom] wondered whether he might meet with anything approaching the same luck as Mr Philip Beaufoy if taken down in writing suppose he were to pen something out of the common groove (as he fully intended doing) at the rate of one guinea per column. *My Experiences,* let us say, *in a Cabman's Shelter*" (*U* 528). In other words, when Bloom thinks of writing up the experience of exhaustion at the cabman's shelter narrated in "Eumaeus," it is under the inspiration of Philip Beaufoy, Joyce's mask for Henry James. Bloom's "Eumaeus" would be—and is, in part, in Joyce's "Eumaeus"—Beaufoy-Jamesian, something to be penned, like the works of Henry James, "out of the common groove."

Chapter Two

henryJAMESjoyce: The Succession of the Masters

I

The full meaning of the Henry James trope in *Ulysses* can only be set forth in the context of the long foreground constituted by James Joyce's pre-*Ulysses* relations with Henry James. I want to trace Joyce's knowledge and use of Henry James as Joyce evolved beyond the premodernist mode of *Stephen Hero,* through the transitional, protomodernist modes of *Dubliners* and *A Portrait of the Artist as a Young Man,* toward the fully formed modernism of *Ulysses.* Although my account of this literary relation is very far from the full story of Joyce's early development, it is, I believe, not only a new chapter in that story but also a central chapter, and indeed an essential one. As for Henry James himself, Kenner remarks in *The Pound Era* that James during his American tour of 1904–5 neither met nor intuited the proximity of any of the coming generation of modernists—Pound, Williams, Stevens, Moore, and Eliot, and, for that matter, Hemingway (who was five) and Louis Zukofsky ("who had just been born"). Although Kenner takes James to be practically the father of modernism, he observes, "yet when we collect 1904's memorabilia it is James who seems to be absent."[1] Kenner's *seems* is a happy qualification.

For there is irrefutable evidence that Joyce read considerable amounts of Henry James during his annus mirabilis of 1904. In January of that year, Joyce wrote the essayistic character study "A Portrait of the Artist," the germ, as Henry James would have put it, for *Stephen Hero* and *A Portrait of the Artist as a Young Man.* His brother reports that Joyce had "asked me to give him some titles for essays. I made out a list of half a dozen or so, of which I remember 'Revellers,' 'Athletic Beauty,' 'A Portrait of the Artist' (I was then reading *The Portrait of a Lady* with boundless admiration)."[2] Henry James's novel indeed interested both Joyce brothers. Crucial to my argument about Henry James's early influence on James Joyce are the following statements by Joyce's friend Constantine P. Curran, recollections of the summer of 1904:

> Of Henry James, who was new to me, he spoke admiringly, and in connexion with the same draft of *Stephen Hero* turned me to *The Portrait of a Lady*. . . .
>
> Meredith's stylized obscurity, his *boutades* at the expense of the English character and the conventions of English society, and what long afterwards I have seen characterized in him as "oracular allusiveness" all seemed to me to have some equivalent in what I was reading of Joyce [*Stephen Hero* in manuscript]. Anyway, Joyce did not seem to think so, and it was then he mentioned Henry James's *Portrait of a Lady* where indeed there is some resemblance to Joyce's endeavour to render, though with less detachment, an inner life in conflict with circumstance. I found much hard going in his involution of the inner and outer action—if action is the right word—and James has not escaped the same charge of obscurity.[3]

Mary and Padraic Colum also testify to Joyce's interest in James's *Portrait of a Lady,* recalling that Joyce once spoke to them of his admiration for James's presentation of his heroine, Isabel Archer.[4] Not long after Joyce spoke to Curran about *The Portrait of a Lady* (probably at the North Bull or Bewley's Cafe), Stanislaus Joyce set down in a diary entry for early October 1904 an essay comparing George Meredith, on the whole unfavorably, to Henry James, remarking that "Jim considers Daisy Miller silly, I am sure he is mistaken . . . Jim says he cannot understand how any woman could prefer Winterbourne to Giovanelli."[5] From Stanislaus's comment we know that Henry James had emerged as a topic of discussion and debate between the Joyce brothers. To *The Portrait of a Lady* and *Daisy Miller,* we can add with certainty three other works by

James that Joyce read at about this time, all mentioned in letters of 1904 and early 1905: the tale "The Madonna of the Future" (or the collection of tales of the same title), which Joyce found "very pleasant reading"; James's essay on Baudelaire—"damn funny," Joyce wrote—in *French Poets and Novelists* (and therefore perhaps the other essays in the volume); and the early James potboiler *Confidence* (1879), which, Joyce complained, "bores me dreadfully."[6] With *Confidence,* Joyce was scraping, as it were, the bottom of the Jamesian barrel, but there is reason to suppose that he had first gone through most, if not all, of its voluminous contents, both because Stanislaus records that "he read quickly, and if the book or the author did not appeal to him he forgot them both" but that "if a book did . . . make some impression on him, he tried to read as many by the same writer as he could lay his hands on" and, more explicitly (and as if in confirmation of Stanislaus's statement), because Joyce wrote to his brother on March 15, 1905, "I have read H. J. consecutively and am now hesitating between De Amicis, A. France and Maupassant for a plunge."[7] Joyce only mentions Henry James in three other letters. In two letters of December 3 and 7, 1906, he finds himself "outrageously, illogically sick" of "Italy, Italian and Italians," and he derides James's "tea-slop about" Italy and "subtle Romans" (the second of these letters also contains the list of initials discussed in chapter 1). The third letter is perhaps more suggestive for my argument. On January 19, 1905, Joyce tells Stanislaus, "I find your letters dull only when you write about Nora or Henry James but no doubt both of these subjects bore you as you have no special affinity for either of them" (*LJJ* 2:201, 198, 81). This is the rebuke of a person who feels that he himself is the one who has a special affinity for, and intimacy with, the subjects in question. Implicitly, Joyce claims in Henry James, as in Nora, a lover's exclusive property: Stanislaus has nothing to tell him about "either of them." Aside from the remarks recalled by the Colums and by Gilbert Seldes, the mention of Henry James at the end of "The Wandering Rocks," and a few allusions to Henry James in *Finnegans Wake,* no open references to Henry James by Joyce are recorded after 1906, a circumstance on which I will comment shortly.[8]

Here, then, is my reconstruction of Henry James's role in the early development of James Joyce. As we have seen, in the earliest form of what would become his fictional autobiography, the "Portrait of the Artist" essay, Joyce echoes the title of a novel that he had read with intense admiration, *The Portrait of a Lady*, the masterpiece crowning the first third of Henry James's long career. In *Stephen Hero*, the next stage toward Joyce's *Portrait*, Joyce closely emulated James's novel in fictional technique and in theme. Unlike the subjective drama of *A Portrait of the Artist*, the drama of *Stephen Hero* is played out on an objectively rendered stage, as is the action of James's novel. *Stephen Hero* and *The Portrait of a Lady* are both bildungsromans about the clash between freedom-seeking youth and a world of circumstance downright naturalistic in its power to determine character and destiny. James's Isabel Archer must suffer the spreading, swelling savor of the truth in Madame Merle's warning to her about the inescapable confines of the "envelope of circumstances" (*PL* 397) in which one must live. And the "fine words" and "fine oaths" of Stephen's youth are cried "bravely and passionately even in the teeth of circumstance," "for not infrequently in the pauses of rapture Dublin would lay a sudden hand upon his shoulder, and the chill of the summons would strike to his heart" (*SH* 38). In *Stephen Hero*, one can detect Joyce trying to capture James's very tricks of phrasing in weaving around a protagonist a tone of urbane yet sympathetic irony. Witness, for instance, how Joyce's attribution to Stephen of "a certain crude originality of expression" (*SH* 27) imitates James's attribution to Isabel of "a certain nobleness of imagination which," James goes on to say, "rendered her a good many services and played her a great many tricks" (*PL* 241). The essential character of both Isabel Archer and Stephen Dedalus has two faces, an idealism that evokes admiration and tenderness and an egotism that invites irony and criticism. Joyce's attempt to develop a worldly irony akin to that of James's narrator does not quite come off in *Stephen Hero*, but one of James's remarks about

Isabel Archer seems an apt statement of what Joyce was aiming for there and as clear a one of what he at last achieved in *A Portrait of the Artist* as any we have heard in the long debate about the tone of that novel: Isabel, James wrote, "would be an easy victim of scientific criticism, if she were not intended to awaken on the reader's part an impulse more tender and more purely expectant" (*PL* 242). Concluding his recollection of Joyce's having pointed to *The Portrait of a Lady* in connection with *Stephen Hero*, Curran says, "In mentioning Henry James I do not suggest that Joyce regarded him as his model but rather that, if anyone had to be dragged in, he would think him a stronger candidate than Meredith and a writer at least equally worth his consideration." [9] But the titles of the earlier and later versions of Joyce's work, his preference for a *Stephen Hero–Portrait of a Lady* link to the Meredith link Curran had proposed, and internal evidence all argue that Henry James *was* a model. And that he was perhaps explains why in *Stephen Hero* Joyce transforms the death of his brother George into the fictional death of Stephen's sister Isabel and has Stephen think that "he could not go in to his sister and say to her 'Live! live!'"—a perfect echo of Strether's famous exhortation to live in *The Ambassadors* (1903) (*SH* 161).

Fragmentary, rough, and rejected by its author, *Stephen Hero* is nevertheless of very special interest because it is the earliest sustained work of imagination we have from Joyce. Harry Levin follows T. S. Eliot in thinking that early on "Joyce's two masters in prose were Newman and Pater"; and Levin suggests that "their alternating influence would account for the oscillations of style in the *Portrait of the Artist*." [10] The occasional purple prose in *A Portrait of the Artist as a Young Man* may well be thought Pateresque, as Levin, particularly irked by Joyce's overfondness for the word *swoon*, goes on to suggest; but the style of *Stephen Hero* is only infrequently so, and the one stage of Joyce's fiction that seems on the whole to be modeled in style on Newman and Pater is the essay "A Portrait of the Artist." Already in *Stephen Hero* there is much that is authentically Joycean: in the finished *Portrait* and even in *Ulysses* and *Finnegans Wake*, there are bits of *Stephen Hero*, ranging from big chunks of the aesthetic theory and fragmentary snatches of dialogue to various images—Joyce's first attempt at a long fiction is loaded with inert raw material, sometimes in big verbatim lumps, that would come to life when assimilated to a context in which Joyce had found a genuine voice of his own. Find it he did, through a disciplined concentration of point of view in Stephen Dedalus, through rigorous selectivity, and through the structural redisposition of his materials to accommodate them to a very pure form of bildungsroman (which meant making the joyous embrace of the artist's vocation at the end of part 4 the climax of the book and which also meant playing down to a considerable extent what had been a protracted and melodramatic portrayal of Joyce's rebellion against Catholicism). But in *Stephen Hero* Joyce is groping toward the enigma of a manner that Stephen himself assiduously cultivates, and his attempt is redolent of Henry James as it is of no one else.

The elements in *Stephen Hero* that seem drawn from James's *The Portrait of a Lady* stand out in particularly high relief against a backdrop of the very substantial differences between the two novels: the much greater depth to which autobiographical sources are sunk in James, for example, not to mention the striking discrepancies between the subject matter and milieux of the two writers or the elder's immeasurably more authoritative control of the form of his work in terms of the dramatic structure of incident and episode and of the overall relation between character and plot. The similarities are all the more striking. Isabel Archer wants to be very special; she even fantasizes being in an exposed, "a difficult position, so that she might have the pleasure of being as heroic as the occasion demanded" (*PL* 242). Stephen Dedalus relishes his studied aloofness as "not without a satisfactory flavour of the heroic" (*SH* 29). Isabel frightens young men: "they had a belief that some special preparation was required for talking with her. Her reputation of reading a great deal hung about her like the cloudy envelope of a goddess in an epic" (*PL* 224–25). Stephen is "an enigmatic figure in the midst of his shivering society where he enjoyed a reputation" (*SH* 35), and "very few had ever heard of the writers he was reported to read" (*SH* 39). In their transcendentalism (Isabel seeing "the world as a place of brightness, of free expansion, or irresistible action" [*PL* 241]; Stephen exalting in "a temperament ever trembling towards its ecstasy" and "a soul . . . over which the image of beauty had fallen as a mantle" [*SH* 193–94]), both protagonists insist on their autonomy and uniqueness: Isabel "was resolutely determined not to be superficial" (*PL* 243) and Stephen was "determined to fight with every energy of soul and body against any possible consignment to what he now regarded as the hell of hells—the region, otherwise expressed, wherein everything is found to be obvious" (*SH* 30); Isabel may not "know whether I succeed in expressing myself, but I know that nothing else expresses me" (*PL* 398) and Stephen "above all things . . . hated to be compared with others" (*SH* 66). For souls such as these, convention is a potentially stifling nemesis: because "he wished to express his nature freely," Stephen "was determined no conventions of a society . . . should be allowed to stand in his way" (*SH* 146–47). "You wanted," the dying Ralph Touchett tells Isabel Archer, "to look at life for yourself—but you were not allowed. . . . You were ground in the very mill of the conventional" (*PL* 785). Here Ralph echoes Henry James's own notebook entry: "The idea of the whole thing is that the poor girl, who has dreamed of freedom and nobleness, who has done, as she believes, a generous, natural, clear-sighted thing, finds herself in reality ground in the very mill of the conventional." [11]

Stephen aspires to the life of art, and insofar as he is the author of *Stephen Hero,* a necessary prelude to the finest *Künstlerroman* (a narrative about the protagonist's calling to a life in art) in English prose, Joyce's *Portrait,* we are privileged to know that his pretences to genius are not baseless. Isabel wants to make her life an art, and—at great cost to her own happiness but with an immense gain in knowledge of the world and of herself—she does so. Beyond such parallels as we have noted in the basic conceptions of the all-important title characters, *The Portrait of a Lady* and *Stephen Hero* share a number of subtexts concerning such topics as feminism, imperialism, and Catholicism. But it is the voice that Joyce projects in the narrative descriptions in *Stephen Hero* that betrays most of all the young writer's apparently enraptured immersion in

Henry James. Consider, for example, how much the following satiric description of Simon Dedalus is reminiscent of *The Portrait of
a Lady*. Mr. Dedalus is reacting here to his wife's unexpected cham-
pionship of Ibsen:

> He listened to her praises with a somewhat startled air, observing no
> feature of her face, his eyeglass screwed into an astonished eye and
> his mouth poised in naïf surprise. He was always interested in novel-
> ties, childishly interested and receptive, and this new name and the
> phenomena it had produced in his house were novelties for him. He
> made no attempt to discredit his wife's novel development but he re-
> sented both that she should have achieved it unaided by him and that
> she should be able thereby to act as intermediary between him and
> his son. He condemned as inopportune but not discredited his son's
> wayward researches into strange literature and, though a similar
> taste was not discoverable in him, he was prepared to commit that
> most pious of heroisms namely the extension of one's sympathies late
> in life in deference to the advocacy of a junior. (*SH* 87)

The witty, worldly, analytic aphorisms smack of James's satiric portraits of such figures as Mrs. Touchett, Henrietta Stackpole, and the
Countess Gemini. Here, for example, is a description of Ralph
Touchett's piquantly eccentric mother: "She flattered herself that
she was a very just woman, and had mastered the sovereign truth
that nothing in this world is got for nothing. She had played no social part as mistress of Gardencourt, and it was not to be supposed
that, in the surrounding country, a minute account should be kept
of her comings and goings. But it is by no means certain that she did
not feel it to be wrong that so little notice was taken of them, and
that her failure (really very gratuitous) to make herself important
in the neighbourhood, had not much to do with the acrimony of
her allusions to her husband's adopted country" (*PL* 250). Mrs.
Touchett "masters" a "sovereign truth"; Mr. Dedalus is "prepared
to commit that most pious of heroisms namely the extension of
one's sympathies late in life in deference to the advocacy of a ju-
nior." Would any sensitive reader of James not endowed with a
photographic memory doubt, were he or she so misinformed, that

this last description of Simon Dedalus is an account of Daniel Touchett's acceding to Ralph's suggestion that Daniel should leave Isabel money (the bequest that makes her in short order a target of opportunity for Madame Merle and Gilbert Osmond)? The longer one looks at them, the more Jamesian such phrases of Joyce's become. The pitch of Joyce's satire and the level of its diction, not to mention the periodic complexity of his sentences, may well be judged a precociously talented appropriation of Henry James's manner in the first edition of *The Portrait of a Lady*. Similarly, here is a much later description of Mr. Dedalus that, in the conjectural hypothesis of a point of view ("he would not have been wrong if he had imagined") closely resembles the occasionally tentative conjectures of Henry James's narrator in *The Portrait of a Lady* ("But it is by no means certain that she did not feel it to be . . ."): "His son's notion of aristocracy was not the one which he could sympathise with and his son's silence during the domestic battles no longer seemed to him a conveyed compliment. He was, in fact, sufficiently acute to observe here a covert menace against castellar rights and he would not have been wrong if he had imagined that his son regarded [these] assistance at these tortuous and obscene monologues as the tribute exacted by a father for affording a wayward child a base of supplies" (*SH* 111).

Even as Joyce was struggling to complete *Stephen Hero* on the model of *The Portrait of a Lady,* he was, I believe, reading Henry James's late fiction and working to absorb its lessons. James's late work helped Joyce to learn the shift to an interior narrative perspective accomplished in the development from *Stephen Hero* to *Dubliners* and *A Portrait of the Artist*. Henry James's career had been a progressive enlargement and application of his discovery that fiction might gain in dramatic power, psychological insight, verisimilitude, and richness of rendering insofar as the objective grounds of reality were subsumed in and mediated by the subjectivity of characters in whom narrative perspectives might be centered. James had moved, moreover, from realism in the sixties and seventies, through naturalism in the eighties and early nineties, into an increasingly dense fusion of these modes with the poetic symbolism of his work from the mid-nineties on, a fusion wrought to its highest pitch in 1902 in the symbolist prose-poetry of Milly Theale's death in Venice in *The Wings of the Dove*. Thus Henry James spanned the seemingly antithetical literary schools that James Joyce looked forward to uniting as early as his 1902 essay on Mangan. James's fusion of naturalism and symbolism, moreover, is precisely the synthesis of romanticism and classicism that has been seen as characteristic of modernism from the birth of the movement down to the present day.[12] In addition, the moments of sudden illumination that mark crucial points in the histories of Henry James's characters are strikingly like Joyce's epiphanies. And Joyce may well have detected other affinities between James's work and his own literary predilections. For example, the dialectics of Jamesian and Joycean fiction are very similar. As Homer Brown writes, "the simplest way of describing the dialectical process of Joyce's writing is the rather Hegelian explanation Joyce gave of his use of the philosophy of Giordano Bruno, in a letter to Harriet Shaw Weaver: 'His philosophy is a kind of dualism—every power in nature must evolve an opposite in order to realise itself and opposition brings reunion.'" For a detailed, parallel description of Henry James's use of a Hegelian dialectic throughout his fiction, see my *Henry James and the Structure of the Romantic Imagination*.[13] Also, in the pages of his brother's diary devoted to Meredith and James, which James Joyce read, Joyce would have found this description of a rather Joycean Henry James (a description in which, incidentally, Stanislaus Joyce anticipates Ezra Pound's eloquent view of James as a champion of freedom): "Henry James's mind is socialistic; there are years of sanely reasoned disapproval behind the convent episode in *A* [sic] *Portrait of a Lady*. Writing of a nun's voice, he says, 'It fell with a leaden weight upon Isabel's ears; it seemed to represent the surrender of a personality, the authority of a Church.' . . . The emotion Meredith harps loudly on is love, in Henry James it is freedom."[14]

There are strong indications that James's collection of tales *The Better Sort*, published in February 1903, was of particular importance for James Joyce. *The Better Sort*, I believe, gave Joyce both general and specific cues for his work on *Dubliners*. Although

Jamesians seem not to have noticed this, *The Better Sort* belongs in the same rare genre as *Dubliners* as a progressive, thematically unified series of stories. The first story in James's collection, "Broken Wings," treats the late reunion of two lovers, their relation having been in abeyance for many years because each thought the other too much more successful in a career as an artist for them to have a genuinely reciprocal relation; in the end, having discovered their mirror illusions (each having been in fact not nearly so successful as the other imagined; each having been, really, a failure), they renew their relation and their love, a bittersweet resolution chastened by their joint consciousness of failure and disciplined by their commitment nevertheless to art: "'Let us at least be beaten together! . . . And now to work!'" (*BS* 23). The stories that follow—"The Beldonald Holbein," "The Two Faces," "The Tone of Time," "The Special Type," "Mrs. Medwin," "Flickerbridge," "The Story in It," and "The Beast in the Jungle"—develop a series of recurrent themes: the appropriation and exploitation of others for selfish purposes; the consequent sense in the victim of entrapment and of abuse, which may even lead to death (as it does in "The Beldonald Holbein" for Mrs. Brash, who turns her face, like Milly Theale, "to the wall" [*BS* 48]); vanity; jealousy; and the chilling monstrosity of egotism developed to the point at which the humanity and reality of the Other cannot be acknowledged. All of these concerns converge on a sense that increases from story to story of the inevitability of failure in human relations; that and that precisely, the failure of relation, emerges as Henry James's overriding theme in the first nine tales in *The Better Sort*. In "The Story in It," eighth in this sequence, James has a set of characters debate whether or not art always represents a relation of some kind; the story itself concerns an unrealized, unreciprocated relation, a relation confined to a single party, whose "consciousness . . . *was,* in the last analysis, a kind of shy romance" (*BS* 188). In the ninth tale, "The Beast in the Jungle," this theme is deepened, pitched in a more somber (and undoubtedly more major) register, with the unrealized, unreciprocated love of May Bartram for John Marcher counterpointed and even overshadowed by Marcher's great climactic recognition that he had never seen her "but in the chill of his egotism and the light of her use" (*BS* 243). In the next story, "The Birthplace," an ambivalently redirectional tale so far as the development of the volume as a whole is concerned, Gedge's partial failure of relation with his wife (to whom he is devoted but from whom he is in a sense estranged by her inability to share the fineness of his scruples) is in some sense offset by the arguably triumphant artistry with which he becomes the Barnum of the shrine to "the supreme poet." The last tale in *The Better Sort*, "The Papers," completes the resolution of James's themes and brings him round to where he began, with a compact between lovers, now with a different mixture of elements than in "Broken Wings" and on a higher level: for unlike the aging artist-lovers in the first story, those in the last are young, fresh, and full of faith in each other and in the artistic careers on which they are about to embark. The possibility of relation, we might say, emerges triumphant in the end.

There have been a number of sound analyses of the unity of Joyce's *Dubliners:* suffice it to say here that the lyric curve of Joyce's collection is very similar to that of James's, for the stories in *Dubliners* progressively deepen one's sense of the spiritual paralysis of the Irish people and of the failures of relation among them until, at the climax of the final tale, "The Dead," Gabriel Conroy transcends the narrow, patronizing egotism that has hitherto emprisoned him in misapprehension and achieves a vast imaginative empathy, not only with his wife Gretta and her long-dead beau Michael Furey, who had been touched by the deep passion Gabriel himself has never felt, but also with his aged aunts and, indeed, with "all the living and the dead." In a sense Joyce, too, returns to his starting point on a higher level, for the first story in *Dubliners* had concerned a death unredeemed by the empathy that suffuses and elevates Gabriel Conroy as his soul travels west toward the cemetery where "poor Michael Furey" lies buried.[15]

James Joyce writes about the people of a city, Dubliners. Henry James might have titled his collection *Londoners,* for with the exceptions of "The Birthplace" and of "The Story in It" (which deals with Londoners off on a country weekend) all of the stories in *The Better Sort* take place in the first city of the British empire. "When you remember," Joyce wrote in 1905, "that Dublin has been a capital for thousands of years, that it is the 'second' city of the British Empire, that it is nearly three times as big as Venice it seems strange that no artist has given it to the world." [16] In *Dubliners,* Joyce develops themes closely allied to James's in *The Better Sort:* moral, spiritual, and psychological paralysis; the pathos of the missed opportunity and the unlived life; manipulation, exploitation, and indifference. Some of the tales in *The Better Sort* played into chapters that Joyce would write much later on for *Ulysses.* A case in point (in addition to "The Birthplace" and "The Beast in the Jungle," which I have already mentioned in connection with *Ulysses*) is "The Papers," a tale about two Fleet Street journalists that, in Bloom's words about "Matcham's Masterstroke," "begins and ends morally"; "The Papers" concludes with the hero and heroine arm in arm, not unlike the "*hand in hand*" Bloom reads at the end of Beaufoy's tale (*U* 56). What I think Joyce may have taken for *Ulysses* from "The Papers" is the wind imagery of his newspaper episode, "Aeolus." Witness, for instance, this sentence in "The Papers" describing a man who is constantly written up by the press: "He comes in, he breaks out, of himself; the letters, under the compositor's hand, form themselves, from the force of habit, into his name—any connection for it, any context, being as good as any other, and the wind, which he has originally 'raised,' but which continues to blow, setting perpetually in his favour." And this, of the same person: "one quite regrets there's no one . . . to do the thing better, . . . to— having raised the whirlwind—really *ride* the storm." And witness also Henry James's frequent references to the "roar" and "howl" of Fleet Street and the Strand (*BS* 323, 390, 423). At least one of the tales in *The Better Sort* proved more immediately useful for Joyce, with a utility that was perhaps not solely literary: as we have seen, "The Birthplace" may not only lie behind "Scylla and Charybdis" but is also likely to have been a leading inspiration for Joyce's own working out, as early as 1904, of the theories about Shakespeare set forth in *Ulysses* by Stephen Dedalus more than a decade later (but in fictional time, to be sure, also in 1904).

The Henry James tale that seems most strongly to have influenced Joyce, however, is "The Beast in the Jungle," the most celebrated of the stories in *The Better Sort*. Henry James's great narrative about John Marcher, who realizes in a climactic epiphany set in a cemetery that "no passion had ever touched him" (*BS* 242), is a clear prototype for James Joyce's greater—indeed his own greatest— short story, "The Dead." "The Beast in the Jungle" may also have connections with another of the deeply poignant stories in *Dubliners*, "A Painful Case." [17] Marcher's discovery about himself is virtually the same as Gabriel Conroy's in "The Dead." Gabriel contemplates the image of the dead boy who had long ago loved his wife, and, as his imagination carries him toward the cemetery where poor Michael Furey lies buried, Gabriel thinks that though it is better to "pass boldly into that other world, in the full glory of some passion" "he had never felt like that himself towards any woman." [18] Joyce follows James in working here with a set of simple equations: to love is to live, and to fail to love is to suffer a living death. The stories share one other odd similarity: readers of "The Beast in the Jungle" and "The Dead" are divided about whether the last paragraphs of these tales depict the deaths of the protagonists. The first name of Mr. Duffy, the central figure in "A Painful Case" (who resembles Stanislaus Joyce in a number of particulars), is James, perhaps a nod at the literary lineage of Joyce's tale as well as a private joke inspired by Stanislaus's fierce though passing admiration of Henry James, about which James Joyce enjoyed ribbing his brother. [19] Mr. Duffy, in any case, egotistically ignores, and thus utterly fails to reciprocate, the love of a woman, thereby precipitating her into her grave—just what John Marcher does to May Bartram in "The Beast in the Jungle." Again Joyce follows a typically Jamesian equation: to fail to give love can be to kill. This equation lies not only at the heart of "The Beast in the Jungle" but also notably in Henry James's late fiction (it is prominent in his earliest fiction too) at that of *The Wings of the Dove*. One might also note, incidentally—to depart from *The Better Sort*—that in "The Dead" Joyce was writing in the tradition of the Christmas ghost story, a tradition in which he had two distinguished literary precursors, Charles Dickens in *A Christmas Carol* and, more recently (1899), Henry James in *The Turn of the Screw*. Also incidentally, Henry James's ghostly tales may provide a general precedent for James Joyce's use of ghosts, particularly in *Ulysses,* where the ghosts of Hamlet's father and of Stephen's mother figure largely. Indeed, I find some additional reinforcement for my idea that Joyce read the Henry James number of *The Little Review* in the affinity between a remark there by A. R. Orage, writing on "Henry James and the Ghostly," and Stephen Dedalus's definition of a ghost in "Scylla and Charybdis." Arguing that in "his stories of the unembodied" James "examined the subconscious, as it were, face to face," Orage says, "No student of his works can fail to observe how imperceptibly his method of dealing with real persons shades into his dealing with ghosts."[20] "What is a ghost?" Stephen asks. "One who has faded into impalpability through death, through absence, through change of manners" (*U* 154). Finally, in addition to the influence of *The Better Sort,* there may also be some imprint of *The Portrait of a Lady* on *Dubliners.* Compare, for example, the description of Isabel Archer's feelings at the moment of her final rejection of Caspar Goodwood—"The world . . . seemed to open out, all around her, to take the form of a mighty sea . . . in which she felt herself sinking and sinking. . . . She clasped her hands; her eyes were streaming with tears" (*PL* 798–99)—with the description of Eveline's feelings at the moment of her rejection of Frank: "All the seas of the world tumbled about her heart. He was drawing her into them: he would drown her. . . . Her hands clutched the iron in frenzy. Amid the seas she sent a cry of anguish!"[21]

Hugh Kenner notes in passing that "Eveline" "follows James's rule about the unified point of view," and he is right, with the proviso that Henry James, his mind never violated by an idea, was not in his own practice strictly subject to the rule attributed to him in a widespread truism of criticism, as witness the variety of perspectives from which James narrates *The Awkward Age* (no central intelligence), *The Turn of the Screw* (two first-person narratives, one introductory to the other), *The Ambassadors* (third-person but limited to one character's point of view), and *The Wings of the*

Dove (third-person with a succession of central intelligences: Kate's, Densher's, Susan Stringham's, Milly Theale's, Densher's again). Kenner errs, consequently, in my view, in going on to suggest that "James does not expect that we may imagine the other tellings" (versions of the same events from perspectives other than that of his central intelligence character).[22] Like Henry James in *The Better Sort,* Joyce uses both first- and third-person narration in *Dubliners,* moving from first person in the first three stories to third in the rest. Conversely, in *A Portrait of the Artist,* the movement is from third person to first. But in either narrative mode, Joyce by and large follows James in centering his story in a center-of-consciousness character. Sometimes, like James in *The Wings of the Dove* (where, within single paragraphs, there are alternating interior views of Kate and of Densher), Joyce moves from center to center, as he does at the beginning of "The Dead" in shifting from Lily's point of view to Gabriel's. Insofar as the first-person diary entries in *A Portrait of the Artist* contain major clues to their own unreliability and to Stephen Dedalus's capacity for self-deception, thus ironizing retrospectively the entire text that they close (as Zack Bowen cogently argues in showing the discrepancy between the diary account of Stephen's last talk with Cranly and the talk itself), Joyce is following a trail blazed by Henry James's controversial first-person narrators in such works as *The Aspern Papers* and *The Turn of the Screw.*[23]

Because *A Portrait of the Artist as a Young Man* derives from *Stephen Hero,* we may see in it much the same relation to Henry James's *The Portrait of a Lady* (whose title it echoes)—thematically, at least, if not so much technically. Technically, by the time of the composition of *A Portrait of the Artist,* Joyce would seem to have mastered the lessons of Henry James's later fiction. In *Dubliners,* as just noted, Joyce had already learned to exploit the opportunities for drama and irony inherent in Henry James's method of rigorously restricting point of view to a central intelligence. James's longer fictions, of course, suggest themselves as more fitting models than James's short stories for Joyce's first novel. In two of James's last three novels there is more than one center of consciousness, for

The Golden Bowl, like *The Wings of the Dove,* is built upon shifting centers. In *The Ambassadors,* however, Joyce might have found in Lambert Strether a close precedent for his anchoring his novel solely in the subjectivity of Stephen Dedalus, and an even closer one perhaps in Maisie Farange, James's central intelligence in *What Maisie Knew,* whose development is followed through several years of childhood (from age five to age eight or perhaps nine). Characters other than Stephen Dedalus have very little existence in *A Portrait of the Artist*—in contrast to other characters (e.g., Maurice) in *Stephen Hero*—for they only figure to the extent that they influence or counterpoint Stephen's development; such a minimizing of secondary figures, who are brought in only as they affect the process of consciousness in the central-intelligence character, is typical of Henry James's late fiction. Also typical of late Henry James is Joyce's suppression in *A Portrait* of critical scenes (fully dramatized in *Stephen Hero*), scenes that we only learn about in retrospect: compare, for instance, the elimination from Joyce's *Portrait* of the long, painful conversation in which Stephen tells his mother that he will not do his Easter Duty (a refusal we learn of only after the fact, in Stephen's conversation with Cranly) to James's elimination from *The Wings of the Dove* of Densher's last interview with Milly Theale (an interview portrayed for us only in its aftereffects in Densher's consciousness and in Kate's sense of the change Densher has undergone).

The dialectic of *A Portrait of the Artist* is much like that of such James novels as *The Ambassadors.* Strether moves from a thesis (the inadequate innocence of the hidebound morality of Woollett, Massachusetts) through its antithesis (the worldly sophistication of his European experience as epitomized in Gloriani and Madame de Vionnet) to a higher innocence, a resolution that at once unites, annuls, and transcends these extremes (the blend of appreciation and criticism with which he views Madame de Vionnet in the end). Similarly, Stephen moves from a thesis (the body of chapter 2 of *A Portrait*) through its antithesis (the spirit of chapter 3) to a resolution (Stephen's commitment to art and to life that resolves, annuls, and transcends the body-spirit opposition). For both Strether and

Stephen, the fall, whether immersion in Parisian worldliness or in "the swoon of sin," is a fortunate one. In addition, the imagery of Joyce's novel seems resonant with James's, especially with that of *The Wings of the Dove*. As Richard Ellmann observes, from the beginning of *A Portrait of the Artist*, Stephen's "soul is surrounded by liquids, urine, slime, seawater, amniotic tides, 'drops of water' (as Joyce says at the end of the first chapter) 'falling softly in the brimming bowl'. . . . Then at the end of the fourth chapter the soul discovers the goal towards which it has been mysteriously proceeding—the goal of life. It must swim no more but emerge into air, the new metaphor being flight" (*JJ* 297). In Henry James's novel, it is only through flight, flight on the wings of the dove, that Milly Theale escapes, in death, the perilous water-worlds of London and Venice.[24] When Stephen Dedalus is catalyzed into his resolve "to fly by those nets" "of nationality, language, religion," it is through his vision of the dovelike girl on the shore: "Her slate-blue skirts were kilted boldly about her waist and dovetailed behind her. Her bosom was as a bird's, soft and slight, slight and soft as the breast of some dark-plumaged dove."[25] Above all, in Joyce's novel, as in Henry James's works from *The Portrait of a Lady* through *The Wings of the Dove*, the paramount concern is the protagonist's quest for experience and freedom, for an autonomy constantly threatened by the world of circumstance.

Dubliners and *A Portrait of the Artist* do not *sound like* Henry James the way *Stephen Hero* and parts of "Eumaeus" do. In *Stephen Hero*, the young Joyce, enamored of James, seeks to resurrect James's manner as the worldly realist of *The Portrait of a Lady* in the vain hope of thereby purchasing some much-needed distance on his subject. In *Dubliners* and *A Portrait of the Artist* Joyce applies the distancing and ironizing techniques of James's later fiction to achieve an authority that frees him from the need to appropriate the Master's voice directly. We might conjecture that such liberation was a precondition for the concealment of James that Joyce undertook as he was writing these first truly Joycean books. Joyce's Jamesian voice in *Stephen Hero* bears out Harold Bloom's idea that "the true ephebe, the potentially strong poet" sounds "in his first voices what is most central in the precursors' voices. . . . For the revisionary ratios that will be employed as means-of-defense by the maturing poet do not manifest themselves in the ephebe." [26]

II

By the time James Joyce came of age, a lean and hungry young man about Dublin in the first few years of the twentieth century, Henry James was in many ways very much the Master of the legend— orotund, cerebral, baroque in his personal and literary manner, and as enormous in reputation as he was disappointing (most of all to himself) in sales. James was something of an oracle or guru for an important set among the avant-garde of fiction. Joseph Conrad called him "cher maître." Ford Madox Ford both idolized and bur-lesqued James, as he does in his suspect anecdotes about the Master. H. G. Wells was stung by James's critiques of his work, and he sought revenge in the cruel caricature of James's fiction in *Boon.* Edith Wharton exposed herself to James's criticism, knowing full well that he was constitutionally unable to withhold it, even for the sake of friendship.

James Joyce, then, was au courant with other serious practi-tioners of the art of fiction in looking much to Henry James during 1904, a watershed year in Joyce's early artistic development as well as in his personal life and in his fictionalized self-portrait in *Ulysses.* In 1904, James Joyce went out of his way to speak highly of Henry James. At the same time, he emulated James artistically in a variety of ways, so that his development from *Stephen Hero* through *Dub-liners* and *A Portrait of the Artist as a Young Man* to *Ulysses* can be seen as a progressive application of lessons learned (assimilated, too, to be sure, and in the process often disguised) from Henry James. Impelled by the internal pressures of his imagination to dis-tinguish himself from James and even to eradicate any trace of the origins of his art in Jamesian soil, Joyce took on the camouflage of artistic strategies antithetical to those of his mentor, and, within a few years of 1904, he seems to have practically stopped referring to

James. But if he was in some sense denying the memory of his indebtedness to Henry James, Joyce became aware of the denial, and
also of the symbolic resonance between his (or any male writer's)
relation to a literary father and the universal relation of fathers and
sons generally. This awareness came to him during the composition
of *Ulysses*, leading him to encode in that novel a covert record of his
recognition that also served as a means of mastering what had been
denied. In so doing, Joyce not only provided crucial evidence for the
reconstruction of his artistic development; he also anticipated the
biological, psychological, and literary analogies at work in one of
the most widely discussed theories of literary influence now current,
Harold Bloom's.

In a sense there were two Henry Jameses available to the generation of high modernists that includes Eliot, Pound, Joyce, Stevens,
Williams, et al., and both Jameses are admirably evoked in the
opening pages of Hugh Kenner's great excursion into the period
Kenner calls *The Pound Era*. One Henry James is the portly, waist-
coated "lord of decorum," representative of "not only a life" but
also of "a tradition" that "seemed over, that of effortless high civil-
ity"; this Henry James became, for Ezra Pound, a "synecdoche for
'custom indicating high culture.'" The other Henry James is the
protomodernist whose "great sensibility brought in a generation":
"But for that sensibility *Prufrock* is unthinkable, *Mauberley* and
the *Cantos* are unthinkable." This avant-garde Henry James who
fathers the modernist sensibility is the magician of nuance, of irresolution, of finely attuned responsiveness to things (as opposed to
the "Ideas" that Eliot felt had never violated James's "mind so fine")
and "to impalpabilities—tones and airs, surfaces and absences,"
thus inaugurating "a poetic of the mute ('And sawdust restaurants
with oystershells'), a poetic of eschewals and refrainings, working
round the margins of a voiceless theme."[27] We might say that as
James Joyce pushed out of his own sight and out of that of his readers his indebtedness to the second Henry James, he magnified the
attributes of the first, the stodgy, decorous, fastidious, overly genteel
figure. If there was a massive misprision of James entailed in this

maneuver, it is precisely the sort of misreading that Harold Bloom would prompt us to look for in a writer who should have been able to gauge better than virtually anyone else the extent of the error.

Thus my new account of Joyce's relation to James not only belongs to the story of how the major modernists drew on immediate predecessors but also bears upon one of the cruxes of literary theory now. In *Ulysses*, of course, James Joyce moved far beyond the influence of Henry James that I have been suggesting helped to shape Joyce's previous fiction. Having traced some of the likely contours of that earlier influence, we are now in a position to explore the implications of the Henry James trope in *Ulysses*. On one level, Joyce is making an implicit statement about his relation to literary tradition. For Joyce, Henry James was the last word, the *dernier cri*, in smart fiction. As a darling of the literary establishment, James represented cultural law and order—the Egyptian high priest to Joyce's outlaw Moses—as he does when Beaufoy/James accuses Bloom/Joyce of cribbing his "books of love and great possessions." Joyce's broad statement is that the whole novel whose individual episodes are intended to leave the cultural territory they cover smouldering similarly makes scorched earth (and soiled toilet tissue) of the work of Henry James and of the whole literary tradition culminating in "*dernier cri* James." "The word *scorching*,"Joyce wrote to Miss Weaver, "has a peculiar significance for my superstitious mind not so much because of any quality or merit in the writing itself as for the fact that the progress of the book [*Ulysses*] is . . . like the progress of some sandblast. . . . and each successive episode, dealing with some province of artistic culture (rhetoric or music or dialectic), leaves behind it a burnt up field." [28] That is why Joyce has the viceregal cavalcade pass "the gentleman Henry, *dernier cri* James" at the end of "The Wandering Rocks," the episode that separates the traditional narrative art of the first half of *Ulysses* (complicated, to be sure, in typically Joycean ways) from the radical technical experiments of the second half. On another level, the Henry James figure in the carpet of *Ulysses*—coupled with the analysis I have outlined of Henry James's early lessons for James Joyce—suggests that James was no less important a model for Joyce than Homer, Dante,

Shakespeare, and Ibsen, literary ancestors whom Joyce could more openly acknowledge because as poets and dramatists—and, except for Shakespeare, as writers in other tongues—they were not such close and threatening competitors as the nearly contemporary Anglo-American (and, incidentally, ancestrally Irish) novelist. Thus the salient items observed in the window of Henry and James clothiers at the end of "The Wandering Rocks" are the *models* there: that Henry James served a critical function as a *model* in Joyce's career explains why Joyce, in denial and repudiation of his indebtedness, created in Philip Beaufoy a stuffy, old-hat simulacrum of Henry James.

I am suggesting, then, that the James trope in *Ulysses* embodies James Joyce's awareness of James's powerful influence. Three additional lines of internal evidence reinforce this theory. First, Bloom several times confuses, and associates, the names of the author of "Matcham's Masterstroke," *Beaufoy,* and of the woman who gives birth in "The Oxen of the Sun," Mina *Purefoy.* In "Lestrygonians," Bloom asks Mrs. Breen, "Do you ever see anything of Mrs Beaufoy":

—Mina Purefoy? she said.
  Philip Beaufoy I was thinking. Playgoers' Club. Matcham often thinks of the masterstroke. Did I pull the chain? Yes. The last act.
—Yes.
—I just called to ask on the way in is she over it. She's in the lying-in hospital in Holles street. Dr Horne got her in. She's three days bad now.
—O, Mr Bloom said. I'm sorry to hear that. (*U* 130)

Thus the seed is sown for Bloom's meeting with Stephen at the lying-in hospital. Bloom thinks of going there just after his masturbatory orgasm in "Nausicaa": "Mrs Beaufoy, Purefoy. Must call to the hospital" (*U* 305). Earlier, in "Sirens," Bloom makes the same association of Beaufoy and Purefoy when his stratagem to keep Richie Goulding from seeing his letter to Martha Clifford suggests an idea for a story: "Blot over the other so he can't read. There. Right. Idea prize titbit. Something detective read off blottingpad. Payment at the rate of one guinea per col. Matcham often thinks the

laughing witch. Poor Mrs Purefoy" (*U* 230). Given Bloom's association of the two names and their similar sounds and meanings, are
we not justified in concluding that Joyce has designed a telling parallel, that Bloom's ideas and anxieties about biological procreation
revolve around the figure of Mrs. Purefoy just as Bloom/Joyce's
anxieties about literary creation revolve around the figure of Beau-
foy/James?

Second, the same nexus of Beaufoy with procreation and paternity is suggested in the hitherto unremarked resemblance of Beaufoy as he appears in "Circe" and the apparition of Rudy Bloom at
the end of the same episode. Beaufoy is "*palefaced*"; Rudy has "*a
delicate mauve face*" (*mauve:* "bright but delicate pale purple,"
says the *Concise Oxford Dictionary*).[29] Beaufoy "*carries a large
portfolio labelled* Matcham's Masterstrokes"; Rudy appears "*holding a book in his hand.*" Beaufoy is attired in "*accurate morning
dress*"; Rudy is "*dressed in an Eton suit.*" The close resemblance
between their outfits can be seen in illustrations A–C: figure A
shows an Eton suit worn with a waistcoat; figure B, morning dress
of 1896, also worn with a waistcoat; and figure C, a dress coat of
1899, shown here because after 1898 the morning coat had its
fronts cut away like those of the dress coat.[30] With Rudy facing
Bloom (he "gazes, unseeing, into Bloom's eyes"), the one particular
in which the outfits are sharply distinguishable, the absence in the
Eton suit of the long tails of the dress coat, would be obscured.
Moreover, Beaufoy and Rudy seem to be color-coded together, with
Beaufoy's "*lavender trousers*" matched by Rudy's "*mauve*" com-
plexion and by the "*violet bowknot*" of Rudy's "*slim ivory cane.*"
(One notes, incidentally, the cane held by the gentleman in figure
B). Also, the "*white lambkin*" that "*peeps out of his* [Rudy's] *waistcoat pocket*" seems to echo Beaufoy's "*outbreast pocket with peak
of handkerchief showing*" (*U* 374, 497). When Rudy appears,
Bloom is standing over the drunken form of his spiritual son,
Stephen Dedalus. Rudy reads his book from right to left, as Bloom
remembers his own father reading Hebrew. Father and son are
fused in the Rudy figure, the most luminous symbol in *Ulysses* affir-
mative of a possible atonement of father and son, and Rudy is

An Eton suit.

Morning dress of 1896.

A dress coat of 1899.

Drawings by Marcus McAllister

dressed, as we have just seen, so as to recall key details of the clothes worn by Beaufoy/James—the literary father of James Joyce!

Third, in "Ithaca"—the seventeenth chapter of *Ulysses,* a catechism of seemingly objective questions and answers—Bloom's thoughts on Stephen's anecdote *A Pisgah Sight of Palestine,* or *The Parable of the Plums,* are recorded as follows: "It, with the preceding scene and with others unnarrated but existent by implication, to which add essays on various subjects or moral apothegms (e.g. *My Favourite Hero* or *Procrastination is the Thief of Time*) composed during schoolyears, seemed to him to contain . . . certain possibilities of . . . success, whether specially collected and selected as model pedagogic themes . . . or contributed in printed form, following the precedent of Philip Beaufoy" (*U* 561). *My Favourite Hero* is not only Stephen's schoolboy theme; it was Joyce's, too, and the subject was Ulysses.[31] In other words, Bloom thinks that Stephen's early narrative efforts—including Stephen/Joyce's earliest prototype for *Ulysses* itself—will follow "the precedent of Mr Philip Beaufoy." Thus, both versions of James Joyce in *Ulysses,* Stephen Dedalus and Leopold Bloom, are tagged as followers of Philip Beaufoy, Stephen in the passage just quoted, Bloom in various musings about his own prospective literary efforts and in Beaufoy's accusation of plagiarism. In addition, the "Ithaca" passage marks another Beaufoy/James connection, the word *model* in this seventeenth episode ("model pedagogic themes . . . following the precedent of Philip Beaufoy" [*U* 561]) echoing the word *models* in the tenth episode, "Wandering Rocks" ("Henry and James's wax smartsuited freshcheeked models, the gentleman Henry, *dernier cri* James" [*U* 208]).

Given what I have taken to be James Joyce's acknowledgment to C. P. Curran of Henry James's literary paternity, it is hard indeed to dismiss the idea that the concealment of Henry James in *Ulysses* as a symbolic antagonist to the author was a powerful attempt to overthrow—or, with respect to the defecation passage in "Calypso," to eliminate—his literary father. I would suggest, furthermore, that the overthrow was successful, so that Henry James is subsumed—or, perhaps better, sublated—in *Finnegans Wake* in the allusions in that work to James that have been identified by Adeline Glasheen.

The hypothesis of intentional concealment would help to explain Joyce's virtual silence about Henry James after 1906. And for Joyce to create in Beaufoy a version of his literary father would be to parallel his fathering, as the artist-God of *Ulysses,* of himself (in Bloom and Stephen) and of his biological father (in Simon Dedalus)—a brilliant stratagem for reversing the priorities of literary succession. If so, my argument represents a revisionist extension of the literary theory of another Bloom, the formidable Harold, who has generally maintained that his oedipal model for literary influence does not apply to novelists but only to strong poets (who need not be writers of verse, to be sure, at least if they are among the strong theorists in Bloom's pantheon, notably Emerson, Nietzsche, and Freud).[32] Surely, Professor Bloom notwithstanding, here is a case that justifies the extension of Harold Bloomian reading from "strong poets" in Bloom's inclusive sense of the term to an even more inclusive one comprising such strong poets of the novel as Henry James and James Joyce. In *Ulysses,* furthermore, Joyce posits strong oedipal conflicts as universal, particularly when Stephen asks, "Who is the father of any son that any son should love him or he any son?" And, Stephen adds, "the son unborn mars beauty: born, he brings pain, divides affection, increases care. He is a new male: his growth is his father's decline, his youth his father's envy, his friend his father's enemy" (*U* 170).

In saying that the Henry James trope in *Ulysses* embodies James Joyce's response to the influence of Henry James, I have meant to indicate the many ways in which the Joyce-James relation corresponds to major elements of Harold Bloom's "anxiety of influence" theory. I want to recall, however, a qualification that I offered in the Introduction to this book, that the "anxiety" of Bloom's Freudian model seems less apt for Joyce's feelings about James than it does for the Woolf-James relation to which we shall turn in the next three chapters. Joyce seems in the end to have put to rout any fear he may conceivably have had of Henry James. In this regard, we might compare and contrast Joyce's stance toward the strong precursor with Henry James's. As Adeline Tintner argues, Henry James's possession of the great writers who preceded him expressed, not an anxiety, but a serene drive to power. His serenity may be exemplified in his remark that "the authors and the books that have . . . done something for us . . . exist for us, with the lapse of time, as the substance itself of knowledge: they have been intellectually so swallowed, digested and assimilated that we take their general use and suggestion for granted, cease to be aware of them because they have passed out of sight. But they have passed out of sight simply by having passed into our lives. They have become a part of our personal history, a part of ourselves, very often, so far as we may have succeeded in best expressing ourselves."[33] James's drive to power led him to be a critic as well as a creator, one who "rewrote" his literary forebears in his own fiction as an act of intelligent appreciation. Joyce, on the other hand, did not want to rewrite: he took the road of aggression, of virtuoso mockery, parody, and satire. What we may feel above all in James Joyce's stance toward Henry James is not so much anxiety as a highly aggressive playfulness.

Finally, I want to suggest two last possible motives for the concealment of Henry James in *Ulysses*. First, Joyce had too much respect for Henry James to have such fun openly at his expense as he clandestinely does in *Ulysses*. In this regard, one might say that Joyce's barbs at Henry James are deflected on Philip Beaufoy in much the same way that his shafts at Yeats find their mark in *Ulysses* in the figure of George Russell—and for the similar reason of Joyce's deep, abiding, grudging respect for both Yeats and James. Second, during the composition of *Ulysses,* Ezra Pound proposed in two letters to Joyce and in a published review a trio of modern novelists worthy of attention: Hardy, James, and Joyce. For example, in a letter to Joyce of September 1915, Pound wrote, "In english I think you join on to Hardy and Henry James (I don't mean a resemblance, I mean that there's has [sic] been nothing of permanent value in prose in between)."[34] Joyce's critique of Hardy in a conversation recalled by Arthur Power may well have been a rejoinder of sorts to Pound's judgment.[35] In making covert use of Henry James in *Ulysses,* Joyce perhaps was supplying the other half of the rejoinder, in a private joke at Pound's expense and without risking offense to the unsuspecting Pound, who was as much under the influence of Henry James as the young Joyce had been, but who never deconstructed or transcended the James influence as Ireland's supreme novelist did so cunningly. Joyce's indebtedness to, and joking about, Henry James have in any case long remained Joyce's private affair; but if the arguments I have set forth here are correct, then we find ourselves at last enabled to share with Joyce the triumphant liberation of his secret laughter.

Chapter Three

Who's Afraid of Henry James: Virginia Woolf/ Influence/Influenza

I

We have seen that James Joyce covertly recognized Henry James as the father of literary modernism and that Joyce's tropes for literary influence conform in many important respects to the biological and psychological models of Harold Bloom's theory of influence. My aim in the next three chapters of this book is to describe the parallel relation between Virginia Woolf and Henry James in order to develop a new account of Woolf's development as a writer.

Although much of what follows will be an exploration of Virginia Woolf's awareness of Henry James and of the effect of that awareness on her art, I want to begin with a vignette that shows the precursor's awareness of his literary successor—an awareness that so far as I know is without parallel in the Henry James–James Joyce relation. The scene is Rye, East Sussex. Writing to Sara Norton Darwin on September 11, 1907, Henry James reports, "Leslie's Stephen's children three of them—the three surviving poor dear mild able gigantic Thoby, gathered in his flower—have taken two houses near me (temporarily) and as I write the handsome (and most loveable) Vanessa Clive-Bell sits on my lawn (unheeded by me) along with her little incongruous and disconcerting but apparently very devoted newly acquired sposo. And Virginia, on a near hilltop, writes reviews for the *Times*—and the gentle Adrian interminably long and dumb and 'admitted to the bar,' marches beside her like a giraffe beside an ostrich—save that Virginia is facially most fair. And the hungry generations tread me down!" [1] Here we have Henry

James, the Master, who in 1907 was immersed in revising and prefacing his novels and tales for the New York Edition of his works and whose latest novel, *The Golden Bowl,* had already been reviewed, quite critically, by Virginia Stephen (as we shall see shortly) —here we have Henry James declaring that "Virginia . . . writes reviews for the *Times*. . . . And the hungry generations tread me down!" Similarly, some months earlier, James spoke of the Stephen children's "hungry *futurity*":

> She [Vanessa] and Clive are to keep the Bloomsbury house, and Virginia and Adrian to forage for some flat somewhere—Virginia having, by the way, grown quite elegantly and charmingly and almost "smartly" handsome. I liked being with them, but it was all strange and terrible (with the hungry *futurity* of youth); and all I could see mainly was the *ghosts,* even Thoby and Stella, let alone dear old Leslie and beautiful, pale, tragic Julia—on all of whom these young backs were, and quite naturally, so gaily turned.[2]

Clearly (though in jest to be sure), James saw in his relation to the "most fair" daughter of his old friend Leslie Stephen the germs of rivalry, literary succession, and generational conflict.

Virginia Stephen's contemporaneous comments on Henry James complete the vignette. That summer of 1907, according to Quentin Bell, Woolf and her brother Adrian rented a cottage at Playden, a little north of Rye. Vanessa and Clive Bell came down a bit after them, taking a place in Rye itself. Vanessa had written to Woolf, hoping that "old Henry James won't be too monumental and difficult."[3] In the event, James was both. During August, Woolf was reading James's *The American Scene,* and her comments typify the ambivalence we shall see her expressing again and again about Henry James. James holds her, entraps her, and elicits at the same time her critical reserve. Thus she writes to Lady Robert Cecil on August 16, "I am embalmed in a book of Henry James: The American Scene: like a fly in amber. I dont expect to get out; but it is very quiet and luminous." The image of being embalmed is repeated two days later in a letter to Clive Bell, with the addition of a sharply critical thrust, as though she were trying to kick her way out of the amber prison: "I am reading Henry James on America; and feel myself as one embalmed in a block of smooth amber: it is not unpleasant, very tranquil, as a twilight shore—but such is not the stuff of genius: no, it should be a swift stream" (*LVW* 1:304, 305). Such may not be "the stuff of genius," but Woolf feels herself made small ("like a fly"), and the amber that metaphorically holds her is a "block," suggesting the monumentality that Vanessa had hoped would not be too much a feature of "old Henry James."

Woolf's most famous account of Henry James at this time was delivered a week later in a letter to Violet Dickinson (August 25, 1907):

> Well then, we went and had tea with Henry James today, and Mr and Mrs [George] Prothero, at the golf club; and Henry James fixed me with his staring blank eye—it is like a childs marble—and said, "My dear Virginia, they tell me—they tell me—they tell me—that you—as indeed being your fathers daughter nay your grandfathers grandchild—the descendant I may say of a century—of a century—of quill pens and ink—ink—ink pots, yes, yes, yes, they tell me—ahm m m—that you, that you, that you *write* in short." This went on in the public street, while we all waited, as farmers wait for the hen to lay an egg—do they?—nervous, polite, and now on this foot now that. I felt like a condemned person, who sees the knife drop and stick and drop again. Never did any woman hate "writing" as much as I do. But when I am old and famous I shall discourse like Henry James. We had to stop periodically to let him shake himself free of the thing; he made phrases over the bread and butter "rude and rapid" it was, and told us all the scandal of Rye. "Mr Jones has eloped, I regret to say, to Tasmania; leaving 12 little Jones, and a possible 13th to Mrs Jones; most regrettable, most unfortunate, and yet not wholly an action to which one has no private key of ones own so to speak." (*LVW* 1:306)

We will return to this passage later; there is really, for this preliminary vignette, too much to say. Again we see Henry James's awareness of Woolf as a writer. Again we see the ambivalence of her response to him. He makes her "nervous." He prompts her to declare that she hates "'writing.'" He makes her feel "like a condemned person, who sees the knife drop and stick and drop again." He provokes her to ridicule his elephantine sentences and elaborate circumlocutions. But at the same time, she aspires to emulate him: "when I am old and famous I shall discourse like Henry James." And he shares some important traits with what will come to be the paradigm of ideal artistry for Virginia Woolf. He is sexually ambiguous, tending toward androgyny, not a cock of the walk, let us say, but a gossipy hen who lays eggs. His eye "like a childs marble" will appear years later in Woolf's writing, in the description in *Orlando* of the eyes of her ideal androgynous artist, Shakespeare.[4]

So Virginia Woolf and Henry James eyed each other in 1907— with a mixture of pleasure, amusement, and dis-ease on each side. This moment has a prologue that I would like to review before moving on to the considerable complications of its sequel.

II

Three years before Woolf was born, Leslie Stephen, by publishing *Daisy Miller: A Study* in the *Cornhill Magazine,* had had a hand in Henry James's first big success. Throughout Virginia Stephen's childhood, James was one of "father's friends." In "A Sketch of the Past," she calls them "old men, sitting round the tea table talking . . . Henry James, Symonds."[5] The intellectual life of the late Victorian age represented by her father's circle was remote to Woolf, but she always associated Henry James with that life, with her parents, and with the idea of greatness.

> Nor indeed was there any close connection between ourselves and the world of intellect. The great figures were of course on the horizon: Meredith, Henry James, Henry Sidgwick, Symonds, Haldane, Watts, Burne-Jones: they were figures in the background. But the kind of memory I have of them is of figures only, looming very large, but far away.
> . . . I remember not what they said, but the atmosphere surrounding them. I remember the ceremony of being taken to see them and the way in which both father and mother conveyed that a visit to Meredith was something altogether out of the way. Both shared a

reverence for genius. The reverence impressed me. And the eccentricity, the individuality: how Meredith dropped rounds of lemon into his tea. . . . I remember the hesitation and qualification, the humming and hawing of Henry James' voice. So that no doubt I was supplied very early with a vision of greatness and great men. Greatness still seems to me booming, eccentric, set apart; something that we are led up to by our parents and is now entirely extinct.[6]

In another, recently discovered and apparently more finished version of this passage, the image of James is enhanced:

Great figures stood in the background. Meredith, Henry James, Watts, Burne-Jones, Sidgwick, Haldane, Morley. But with them again we had no close connection. My memories of them are strong; but only of figures looming large in the distance. . . . I remember still more clearly the ceremony of our visits to great men. For father and mother were equally respectful of greatness. And the honour and the privilege of our position impressed themselves on us. I remember Meredith dropping slices of lemon into his tea. . . . and I remember the hesitations and adumbrations with which Henry James made the drawing room seem rich and dusky. Greatness still seems to me a positive possession; booming; eccentric; set apart; something to which I am led up dutifully by my parents. It is a bodily presence; it has nothing to do with anything said. It exists in certain people. But it never exists now. I cannot remember ever to have felt greatness since I was a child. (*MB2* 158)

The final sentence adds further support to the view of Phyllis Rose, set forth before the discovery in 1980 of this version of "A Sketch of the Past": "She had known great writers in her childhood, with the result that literary greatness seemed a thing of the past, just as mountains one sees as a child remain in the memory higher and more majestic than any seen in later years. . . . Though she was the center of the literary life of London, she was never again to be conscious of greatness as in the days when Henry James or George Meredith walked through the door of the house in Hyde Park Gate."[7] Since Woolf wrote this memoir in 1940, we can conclude that toward the end of her life her sense of the belatedness that Harold Bloom ascribes to writers who suffer from the anxiety of influence was acute. That sense of belatedness, moreover, was directly associated with Henry James.

And James and greatness were linked, as we have noted, with her parents, especially with her father. Seeking to explain Woolf's mixed feelings about James, Carol Dole suggests that "James may well have come in for some of the hostility she felt toward her father and toward the Victorians."[8] *Ambivalence* is the word that Woolf herself uses for her feelings toward Leslie Stephen in the new version of "A Sketch of the Past," in a passage inspired by her recent reading of Freud. "But in me," Woolf writes, ". . . rage alternated with love. It was only the other day when I read Freud for the first time, that I discovered that this violently disturbing conflict of love and hate is a common feeling; and is called ambivalence" (*MB2* 108). What follows, some seventeen pages new to the second edition of *Moments of Being*, is by far the most important newly discovered material in the volume. Woolf anatomizes her father into several identities: "the sociable father" whom "I never knew," "the writer father" whom "I can get of course in his books"—"I always read *Hours in a Library* by way of filling out my ideas, say of Coleridge, if I'm reading Coleridge; and always find something to fill out; to correct; to stiffen my fluid vision"—and, apparently above all, "the tyrant father" (*MB2* 115–16).

Yes: "it was the tyrant father—the exacting, the violent, the histrionic, the demonstrative, the self-centered, the self pitying, the deaf, the appealing, the alternately loved and hated father—that dominated me then," *then* being 1897, "when Nessa and I inherited the rule of the house" after Stella Duckworth's death and two years after the death of Julia Stephen, Woolf's mother (*MB2* 116). This Leslie Stephen was the Victorian patriarch that Jane Marcus and others have identified in Virginia Woolf's father.[9] He presided over a household where "nailed over the fire place" in the front hall was "a long strip of chocolate coloured cardboard on which was written: 'What is to be [*sic*] a gentleman? It is to be tender to women,

chivalrous to servants . . . [Woolf's elipsis]'—What else I cannot remember; though I used to know it by heart. What innocence, what
incredible simplicity of mind it showed—to keep this cardboard
quotation—from Thackeray I think—perpetually displayed, as if it
were a frontispiece to a book—nailed to the wall in the hall of the
house" (*MB2* 117). When Virginia Woolf struck out at the patriarchy in *A Room of One's Own* and *Three Guineas,* she did so
with a force that had been gathering at least since the girlhood
when she had felt herself to be "a nervous, gibbering, little monkey"
who was "shut up in the same cage" at Hyde Park Gate with her
father, "the pacing, dangerous, morose lion; a lion who was sulky
and angry and injured; and suddenly ferocious, and then very
humble, and then majestic; and then lying dusty and fly pestered in
a corner of the cage" (*MB2* 116).

Still, as Virginia R. Hyman has suggested in an important essay,
in many ways Leslie Stephen was a model for his literary daughter.
In the end, the "writer father" may have been more important for
her than the "tyrant father." "Very early," Hyman observes, "Virginia indicated her preference for her father (as Vanessa had indicated her preference for her mother) and also determined very early
to emulate him by becoming a writer." [10] Lyndall Gordon presents a
similar analysis of Woolf's relation to her father; and both Hyman
and Gordon draw on Vanessa Bell's report that on the whole she
preferred her father to her mother. [11] This reading of Woolf's view of
her parents directly contradicts the view set forth in Ellen Bayuk
Rosenman's recent, highly illuminating discussion of Woolf and the
mother-daughter relationship. Rosenman points to Woolf's twice
calling "Julia Stephen the 'centre' of her childhood existence" in "A
Sketch of the Past." [12] But Rosenman does not cite—and maybe did
not have available to her—the new version of "A Sketch," where
the references to Julia Stephen as a center remain but where Woolf
describes her father's study thus: "His old rocking chair covered in
American cloth was the centre of the room which was the brain of
the house. He had written all his books lying sunk in that deep
rocking chair. . . . Across it lay his writing board; with the sheets of
foolscap always folded down the middle so that he could make cor-

rections in the margin. And there was his fine steel pen and the curious china inkpot, with a well, lidded, out at the side" (*MB2* 119).

If Julia Stephen was the center of Woolf's childhood, Leslie Stephen, the parent Woolf preferred, worked at "the centre of the room which was the brain of the house." Every night five-year-old Virginia told her literary father a story. Hyman sees Woolf as following her father not only in her vocation as a writer but also in her "preference for intellect over convention, for asceticism over sexuality, for the world of the Stephens over the world of the Duckworths."[13] Two factors greatly complicated her relation to her father. First, there was the full-blown emergence of "the tyrant father" in Woolf's adolescence, after Stella's death. He was for a time an embodiment in spades of the Victorian patriarchy against which the mature Woolf would take her stand. Second, there was her literary rivalry with Leslie Stephen. Leonard Woolf's view that both Vanessa and Virginia "exagerrated his [Leslie Stephen's] exactingness and sentimentality and, in memory, were habitually rather unfair to him owing to a complicated variety of the Oedipus complex" and that there was "a faint streak of this in the drawing and handling of Mr. Ramsey [*sic*]" in *To the Lighthouse* suggests the aptness of Harold Bloom's oedipal model of the anxiety of influence for understanding Virginia Woolf's relation *as a writer* to her father.[14] It is in this light that we must read her famous diary entry of November 28, 1928, which would have been her father's ninety-sixth birthday. What if he *were* still alive? "His life would have entirely ended mine. . . . No writing, no books;—inconceivable" (*DVW* 3:208). Even after his death, Woolf referred her writing to her father with melancholy results: "I dreamt last night," she writes in 1908, "that I was showing father the manuscript of my novel; and he snorted, and dropped it on to a table, and I was very melancholy, and read it this morning, and thought it bad" (*LVW* 1:325).

We are now in a better position to understand the provocation represented by Henry James's remarks to Virginia that day in 1907 in Rye. Not only does James affix his beam on Woolf's fragile identity as a writer; he does so specifically by tying that identity to her father—she is a writer by virtue of "being your fathers daughter . . .

the descendant I may say of . . . ink—ink—ink pots." With "ink pots," James strikes (unwittingly to be sure) at Woolf's private image for her father's literary potency: "And there was his fine steel pen and the curious china inkpot, with a well, lidded, out at the side. All his books were dipped out of that well on the point of Joseph Gillott's long shanked steel pens" (*MB2* 119). Is it any wonder that, in this context, Woolf hates "writing"? We recall that in the new portion of "A Sketch of the Past" Woolf speaks of continuing to rely on "the writer father" for "filling out my ideas, say of Coleridge, if I'm reading Coleridge." The reference to Coleridge is a pregnant one for two reasons, the second of which connects with Henry James. First, Coleridge's relation to his daughter, Sara, encapsulates Woolf's anxieties about her relation to Leslie Stephen, so that the mention of Coleridge in these post-Freudian pages about her own father in "A Sketch of the Past" is by no means accidental. Woolf penned them as she was preparing to write her essay "Sara Coleridge"; the Leslie Stephen passage is dated "a hot summer day, July 1940" (*MB2* 115), and "Sara Coleridge" was written—according to Leonard Woolf's footnote to its publication in *The Death of the Moth* (1942)—in September 1940. Read as a palimpsest of Woolf's relation to Leslie Stephen, the opening of "Sara Coleridge" doubles its poignancy:

> Coleridge also left children of his body. One, his daughter, Sara, was a continuation of him, not of his flesh indeed, for she was minute, aetherial, but of his mind, his temperament. The whole of her forty-eight years were lived in the light of his sunset, so that, like other children of great men, she is a chequered dappled figure flitting between a vanished radiance and the light of every day. And, like so many of her father's works, Sara Coleridge remains unfinished.[15]

In the draft of this essay, Virginia Woolf wrote, "she was a poem he had written in the flesh. . . . He would have liked her to remain unfinished, his own fragmentary masterpiece."[16]

We can now set up an analogy: Coleridge is to Sara as Virginia feared Leslie Stephen might be to her. The Henry James connection emerges in Woolf's association of James and Coleridge, and in her apparent confusion of the two, in a review of *Coleridge the Talker*. Also written in September 1940, the review contains this fancy:

> Dickens would need to be doubled with Henry James, to be trebled with Proust, in order to convey the complexity and the conflict of a Pecksniff who despises his own hypocrisy, of a Micawber who is humiliated by his own humiliation. He is so made that he can hear the crepitation of a leaf, and yet remains obtuse to the claims of wife and child. An unopened letter brings great drops of sweat to his forehead; yet to lift a pen and answer it is beyond his power. The Dickens Coleridge and the Henry James Coleridge perpetually tear him asunder. The one sends out surreptitiously to Mr. Dunn the chemist for another bottle of opium; and the other analyses the motives that have led to this hypocrisy into an infinity of fine shreds.[17]

The "Henry James Coleridge" does not appear again in the published version of the review but figures much more largely in the surviving typescript drafts (e.g., "Dickens provides the leading note, but Henry James seizes it: catches it up & develops & embellishes & expands & expounds it until the sentence [illegible interlinear interpolation] enpocketed with parentheses breaks down into incoherency under the strain").[18] Woolf does, however, seem momentarily to confuse James and Coleridge in the next paragraph of the essay as published. It begins, "Thus often in reading the 'gallop scrawl' of the letters from Highgate in 1820 we seem to be reading notes for a late work by Henry James. He is the forerunner of all who have tried to reveal the intricacies, to take the faintest creases of the human soul." Woolf means the "He" at the beginning of the second sentence to refer to Coleridge; grammatically, of course, it refers to Henry James. Indeed, the last appearance of *Coleridge* (without a possessive apostrophe or a prefatory *Dickens* or *Henry James*) as a possible antecedent is more than two pages before this pronoun, and the confusion is not resolved until the end of the third sentence of the paragraph: "The great sentences pocketed with parentheses, expanded with dash after dash, break their walls under the strain of including and qualifying and suggesting all that Coleridge feels, fears, and glimpses."[19] Given the association and confusion of James and Coleridge at roughly the same time that Virginia Woolf was writing both "Sara Coleridge" and the "Sketch of the Past" passage about her reliance on her father for filling out her ideas about Coleridge—and also given the Leslie Stephen–Henry James association we have posited—we can amplify the analogy suggested at the beginning of this paragraph, thus: Coleridge/Henry James is to Sara as Virginia Woolf feared Leslie Stephen/Henry James might be to her.

There are five more evidential threads upon which we must tug, at least briefly, in order to complete the story of the Woolf-James relation up to the summer of 1907. The first of these is the latest, Woolf's remark about James in a letter of 1935 thanking Stephen Spender for a copy of *The Destructive Element:* "He loomed up in my young days almost to the obstruction of his works" (*LVW* 5:392). She did not, in her young days, know James primarily as a writer, but as her father's familiar—and as a portentous, almost threatening figure, who "loomed up" as an "obstruction." The second is the first record we have of her literary acquaintance with James, a mention in her 1897 diary that she is reading him—what we do not know.[20] A few years later, however, she was not only reading James but also reviewing him. The sixth of the nearly four hundred contributions to periodicals recorded in Kirkpatrick's *Bibliography of Virginia Woolf* is Woolf's review, published in February 1905, of *The Golden Bowl.* And S. P. Rosenbaum has recently brought to light her review in 1906 of James's *English Hours.*[21]

Both reviews were published in the women's pages of *The Guardian,* a church newspaper. The editor of the women's section, the Honourable Mrs. Arthur Lyttleton, gave Woolf the first of her many unhappy experiences with editorially mandated cutting and pasting in calling for the review of *The Golden Bowl* to be halved. Woolf was properly upset: having spent "5 days of precious time toiling through Henry James' subleties [*sic*] for Mrs Lyttleton" and having written "a very hardworking review for her," she hurriedly "cut two sheets to pieces, wrote a scrawl to mend them together, and so sent the maimed thing off—with a curse." Relating the incident in a letter to Violet Dickinson, Woolf concludes: "It was quite good before the official eye fell upon it; now it is worthless, and doesn't in the least represent all the toil I put into it—and the book deserved a good, and careful review" (*LVW* 1 : 178). That the experience of reading *The Golden Bowl* was "precious time toiling" suggests the impatience with James that Woolf expresses in the review, and it very nearly lends credibility to her remark of 1921 to Roger Fry—after she had already published four major essays on James in the *Times Literary Supplement!*—that "I have never read his [James's] great works; but merely pretended" (*LVW* 2:478). From her extensive chapter-by-chapter reading notes on *The Golden Bowl*, however, we can be certain that Woolf did read the novel from cover to cover.[22] She tells Fry in the same letter of 1921, "I am too feeble minded to finish"—"too feeble minded to finish" either the novel itself or an analogy Woolf develops briefly between *The Wings of the Dove* and a deserted museum, "vast and silent and infinitely orderly and profoundly gloomy." She did, however, finish *The Wings of the Dove*, a feat she reported with pride later on to Ottoline Morrell: "I . . . actually *read through* the Wings of a [*sic*] Dove" (*LVW* 2:548; italics added).

Since it appears that no manuscript of the *Golden Bowl* review survives, we must be content with the "maimed thing" as it was printed. From the absence of any reference to the particulars of James's plot and from Woolf's failure to even name the characters, one might wrongly conclude that she did not read "its all but 550 closely printed pages" through. But such detail is just what she might have dropped in cutting "two sheets to pieces." Her comments on the novel are in some respects wonderfully astute, though also quaintly euphemistic. The adulterine theme of *The Golden Bowl* is not named directly; it is merely "a certain natural difficulty which must frequently occur outside Mr James's novels, but which can hardly ever, one would imagine, produce such an amount of thinking and analysing and hair-splitting as it does within them." Woolf's insight that "the book, indeed, might be called a study in the evils of unselfishness, so much pain does their [the characters'] care for each other inflict" lucidly anticipates several of the best modern commentaries on *The Golden Bowl*. The complaint against James running throughout the review is against the "surfeit of words" expended on "a slight theme." The characters are not "live people" but "so many distinguished ghosts." There is too much detail: "the portrait would be greater as a work of art if he were content to say less and suggest more." [23]

Years later, Woolf was to think of James as a master of nuance and suggestion, as we will see. But though she differs in this regard from her later views, her first essay on Henry James is characteristic of her divided reaction to him. She opens and closes with superlative praise: thus her first sentence—"Mr Henry James is one of the very few living writers who are sufficiently great to possess a point of view"—and thus her last—"There is no living novelist whose standard is higher, or whose achievement is so consistently great." The second sentence of the review asserts great familiarity with James: "We know by this time what that point of view is, and when we read a new book by him we do not expect to make discoveries, but to look once more at familiar sights through the old spectacles." From this point on the essay is highly critical. Though there is not a page "that has not its own exquisite felicity of word or thought which alone would illumine a whole chapter of an ordinary novel," James's "gifts . . . fail very little of first-rate quality," for, while genius would have avoided the overburdening of the novel with detail, "genius . . . is precisely what we do not find: and it is for this reason that we do not count Mr James's characters among the creatures of our brains, nor can we read his books easily and without conscious effort. But," Woolf adds in the penultimate sentence of the review, "when we have made this reservation our praise must be unstinted." Woolf at twenty-three was already what she called herself some thirteen years later, one of the "fickle Jacobeans." [24]

In an introductory paragraph on Woolf's 1906 review of *English Hours*, Rosenbaum notes that the "whole admiring, slightly mocking attitude" of her remarks is characteristic. [25] Woolf praises James, concluding that his portrait of the English is "so charming and so true." She asks, "Who, then, of living writers can present upon his page a spectacle so tremendous [as that of "the psychology of the land"], with such memories and emotions and experiences seething and blending beneath the placid face that we know so well? If any one is fit for the task, it must be the same writer who has made such astonishing discoveries beneath other tranquil surfaces." And "indeed, it is possible to read Mr. Henry James upon various aspects of the English countryside not only with pleasure, and possibly with profit, but also certainly with amusement." Here, with "amusement," a defensive element seems to enter Woolf's discourse, explicable perhaps in view of her next sentence, where she pronounces that "it is really entertaining to find that we ourselves are part of the show. Indeed, we may be said to be the flower of it." What she is reacting against, I think, is particularly James's treatment of young Englishwomen in his essay on Warwickshire, the chapter of *English Hours* on which Woolf dwells in her review. English girlhood is marked by what James calls "an intimate salubrity" (Woolf quotes this phrase), a "rosy absence of a morbid strain"; when such an air is found with "real perfection of feature and colour the result is the most delightful thing in nature." James reifies the young Englishwoman. She is a "delightful *thing*." She is an object, part of nature, and not an active subject. And what must have irked Woolf all the more was James's extension of this linguistic sexism almost immediately into the realm of sexual politics: "Such as the woman is," James writes, "she has here, more than elsewhere, the look of being completely and profoundly, without reservation for other uses, at the service of the man she loves. This look, after one has been a while in England, comes to seem so much a proper and indispensable part of a 'nice' face, that the absence of it appears a sign of irritability or of shallowness. Latent responsiveness to the manly appeal—that is what it means; which one must take as a very comfortable meaning." [26] For Henry James, coincidentally, Woolf's mother was the epitome of the woman commendably and "without reservation . . . at the service of the man she loves"; James's idealization of Julia Stephen, may, as Paula Smith suggests, have led him to use her, after her death, as the model for the idealized Lady Julia in *The Awkward Age*.[27] Woolf twits Henry James in the review for being deflected from the Shakespearian associations of Warwickshire into a discussion of "the temperaments and appearances of certain young English women." And she repeats again and again the advantages James has in writing about England because he is an American—a repetition that begins to smack of Marc Antony's "so are they all honorable men." As we will see later, Woolf's often sniffish snobbery toward Americans enters several times into her responses to James. She is evidently having a kind of perverse fun, at any rate, when she presents herself, because of her ancient English lineage, as senior to old Henry James: "We are, according to him, enormously old. . . . We were not conscious, perhaps, of the extreme richness and complexity—to use two favourite adjectives—of our temperaments, and it is not altogether pleasant to be treated with such respect by the young." It is almost as if Woolf already sees herself as standing in an oedipal relation to James and seeks, if only through wordplay, to reverse James's priority.

The final one of my five threads of evidence for reconstructing Woolf's sense of Henry James before 1907 is drawn from her letter of August 19, 1909, to Vanessa Bell. Remarking that the conversation of Saxon Sydney-Turner "is still odd," she quotes him as having asked her, " 'What did you mean, Virginia, when you said, about three years ago, that your view of life was that of a Henry James novel, and mine of a George Meredith?' I had to invent a meaning, and he actually told me that he thought me a very clever young woman—which is the highest praise I have ever had from him" (*LVW* 1:409). "Three years ago"—in 1906, then, or thereabouts, in the wake, in all probability, of her begrudging review of *The Golden Bowl*—Woolf was declaring that her own "view of life was that of a Henry James novel"! Curiously, it was Leonard Woolf's retrospective view that of all the Cambridge undergraduates who lionized Henry James in the early years of the century and who tried to talk like characters in his novels, Saxon Sydney-Turner most of all "was a character in an unwritten novel by Henry James."[28] James was such a fad in Leonard Woolf's crowd (which included, of course, Lytton Strachey and Virginia Woolf's brother

Thoby as well as Sydney-Turner) that Virginia Woolf was probably aware of their adulation of the American novelist at the time; she may even have been playing to the Cambridge group's James-mania when she told Sydney-Turner of her Jamesian "view of life."[29] Leonard Woolf wrote to Strachey from Ceylon in 1905, "I have just finished *The Golden Bowl* & am astounded. Did he invent us or we him? He uses *all* our words in their most technical sense & we cant have got them all from him."[30] Liberated by her father's death into free association with the young men of her brother's set, Woolf found Henry James at the center of their imaginative life. If her remark to Saxon Sydney-Turner was playing up to the group's idolizing of James, the barbed review of *The Golden Bowl* marked her strong need to resist the Master. If she did not resist James, then her new freedom might be social, it might be to a large degree intellectual as well, but it could hardly be creative. We recall her speculation about Leslie Stephen's surviving to age ninety-six: "no writing, no books;—inconceivable."

By 1907, Virginia Woolf's twenty-fifth year, the basic contours of her response to Henry James were already set: she associated him with her father, she praised him, she criticized him, and she even mocked him. He was monumental. He loomed. He was a block in which she was entrapped. He was the greatest of living novelists, but he was so hard to read that she denied him the accolade of genius. James, though he almost certainly did not know of Woolf's criticisms of his work (unsigned as they were, and published in a church paper to boot), nevertheless felt mixed with his admiration and affection for Woolf some sense of generational rivalry and unease in her presence, the feeling that evoked his Keatsian cry, "The hungry generations tread me down!" But the really active and productive dis-ease was Virginia Woolf's in the presence of Henry James.

III

For Harold Bloom, influence is an affliction as well as a necessary condition for poesis. "A poem is not an overcoming of anxiety,"

Bloom writes, "but is that anxiety." And, he adds in the typographi-
cally and figuratively spaced-out "Interchapter" of *The Anxiety of
Influence*, "Influence is *Influenza*—an astral disease. If influence
were health, who could write a poem? Health is stasis." [31] Virginia
Woolf also described influence as a disease, and associated it with
influenza. Repeatedly, furthermore, she linked Henry James with
the sickness of influence. Several times in her letters, diaries, and essays the word *influenza* appears in conjunction with Henry James.
One might almost think that, as the first serious modern student of
literary influence, she had invented Harold Bloom. Given Bloom's
commitment to a patriarchal story of warfare between literary fathers and sons and to a patriarchal canon for which the story provides a rationale, it is amusing to think that he might thus be urged
as a strong critic to think back through his mother, reversing the
sexual terms of his model. [32] In any case, the confluence of Woolf's
terms and Bloom's is striking.

Written in the late summer of 1928 and published in 1929,
Woolf's monograph-length essay "Phases of Fiction" looks like an
anatomy of the novel, but it may be read more fruitfully as the book
on influence that Woolf dreamed of writing. In the draft of an unpublished, fictionalized version of the essay, titled "Notes of a Days
Walk," she writes, "an interesting book might be written upon influence how some writers are far more infectious than others. They
[*sic*] young can hardly read ~~Meredith~~ Henry James or Mere[d]ith
without copying them; but they are influenced not by the more profound qualities of the writers they admire; but by the rythm [*sic*] of
the sentences, first; then by the actual words. Nor is it any proof of
excellence in Meredith and Henry james; only that each was highly
mannered." [33]

"Some writers are far more infectious than others." The equation
of disease and influence, along with the linkage of the equation to
Henry James, was by 1928 an old one for Woolf. In 1920, she protested too much, one thinks, to the criticism, published in the *Times,*
that her unsigned *TLS* review of Percy Lubbock's *The Letters of
Henry James* fell into some of "H.J.'s worst mannerisms. . . . I sup-

pose its the old matter of 'florid gush'—no doubt a true criticism, though the disease is my own, not caught from H. J., if thats any comfort" (*DVW* 2 : 29). (When we return to that review, in the next chapter, we will see that Woolf's critic had good reason to see Woolf's prose as infected by James's.) In 1922, in the same letter that announced she had "actually read through" *The Wings of the Dove,* Woolf adds that she "thought it such an amazing acrobatic feat, partly of his, partly of mine, that I now look upon myself and Henry James as partners in merit. I made it all out. But I felt very ill for some time afterwards" (*LVW* 2 : 548). The linkage of James and illness continued late in Woolf's life as well. In a diary entry of 1939, she criticizes Dickens for not being "*highly* creative: not suggestive," for lacking what really constitutes "Literature—that is the shading, suggesting, as of Henry James. . . . But these are influenza musings" (*DVW* 5 : 215).

Lest we misunderstand the latent force of the word *influenza* in Virginia Woolf's world, there are several points we should recall. The first great blow in Woolf's life, the loss of her mother, was laid to influenza. Quentin Bell tells us that Woolf announced the onset of her mother's final illness on March 4, 1895—two months before her of course unforeseen death—in her newspaper, the *Hyde Park Gate News:* "For the last fortnight Mrs Leslie Stephen has been in bed with the influenza." Virginia Woolf herself, as Stephen Trombley observes, "suffered incessantly from influenza." And, Leon Edel notes, "all of Virginia's later breakdowns were ushered in by bouts of this illness." [34]

At the end of the second decade of this century, moreover, no one could take influenza as lightly as we generally do today, when the term is often used improperly for severe varieties of the common cold. The influenza pandemic of 1918–19 was one of the great scourges of humanity, a plague unequalled in lethal virulence since the Middle Ages. Believed to have been a type-A influenza, the outbreak was unusual in the severity of its symptoms (enormous blood blisters, three-week comas, complete loss of hair, regurgitation through the mouth and nose of up to a pint of blood at a time), in the rapidity of its onset, and in its taking about half its toll of deaths in the twenty- to forty-year age group (whereas most influenza outbreaks are fatal chiefly for the aged). The toll was tremendous: Richard Collier reports 21,000,000 deaths during the most virulent, so-called "second wave" of the pandemic, from September 1 to December 31, 1918 (the first wave was in spring 1918; the third, spring 1919). This figure agrees with the ones given by W. I. B. Beveridge: "The total deaths throughout the world were estimated at between 15–25 million—the greatest visitation ever experienced by the human race." Upwards of 1 percent of the world population at the time was lost to the influenza, which struck one out of every two human beings. Schools and theaters were closed all over the planet. Trolley cars carried the dead in major American cities. The total mortality in the United States was over 500,000; in England and Wales, 200,000; in India, 5,000,000. Twenty-five percent of the people of Samoa died. In Nome, Alaska, so did 176 of the 300 Eskimoes there.[35]

Health authorities were slow to react to this modern plague. The World Health Organization and the World Influenza Center did not exist; they were founded in large part as a response to the pandemic of 1918. To read through the pages of the London *Times* for late summer and autumn of 1918 is to witness the slow public dawning of a great horror, beginning with obscure paragraphs on outbreaks of influenza in Spain, in North Africa, and in Istanbul, rising into the chilling, more detailed accounts of reported cases and deaths in various English cities and counties, and culminating on October 28 in a long, grim leading article that recognized the disease as the greatest plague to afflict humanity since the Middle Ages.

Virginia Woolf took note of the *Times* leading article. In her diary for Monday, October 28, 1918, she writes, "Lytton [Strachey] is probably moving in to Mary in a day or two, avoiding London, because of the influenza—(we are, by the way, in the midst of a plague unmatched since the Black Death, according to the *Times*" (*DVW* 1:209). In her very next diary entry (Wednesday, October 30), Woolf remarks parenthetically, "How I dislike writing directly after reading Mrs H. Ward!—she is as great a menace to health of mind as influenza to the body" (*DVW* 1 : 211). This is Woolf's most explicit analogy between influence and influenza; it is also the one not simply literal use of *influenza* I have found in her letters, diaries, and essays that is not linked with Henry James. What is most telling, at all events, is that Woolf identified influence and influenza just when she had become aware of the devastating calamity represented by the influenza pandemic. A menace as great to the mind as influenza to the body would have been a very fearful menace indeed.

The role of influenza in Woolf's family history, in her own life, and in the larger world around her give a profound resonance to her mentions of the disease in Jamesian contexts. In January of 1920 she told a correspondent, "My next work will be on Henry James' letters, I think—unless someone else has done it for me during the influenza. I shan't be sorry, since I'm stuck in the Ambassadors" (*LVW* 2:411). (The phrase "stuck in the Ambassadors" seems reminiscent of her image of being a fly embalmed in amber when she was reading *The American Scene*.) In an essay of 1930, "On Being Ill," Woolf says that long novels are too much for an invalid, that poems are preferable for sickbed reading: "*The Decline and Fall of the Roman Empire* is not the book for influenza, nor *The Golden Bowl* nor *Madame Bovary*" (*CE* 4:199). This essay, incidentally, contains comments on influenza that become fascinating when read in the light of Woolf's influence/influenza analogy. For example, after writing that "it becomes strange indeed that illness has not taken its place with love and battle and jealousy among the prime themes of literature," Woolf observes, "The public would say that a novel devoted to influenza lacked plot; they would complain that there was no love in it—wrongly however, for illness often takes on the the [*sic*] disguise of love, and plays the same odd tricks" (*CE* 4:193–94).

We began this section by noting the trope of disease and influenza in Harold Bloom's theory of the anxiety of influence. The central paradigm for Bloom's approach to influence is of course the Freudian family romance. In one key passage, Woolf moves rapidly from a comparison of influenza and literary genius, to a discussion of influence in which Henry James represents the endpoint of a development that begins with Sir Walter Scott, to a description of literary history as family history:

> And why should a family, like the Shelleys, like the Keatses, like the Brontës, suddenly burst into flame and bring to birth Shelley, Keats, and the Brontës? . . . Since we have not yet discovered the germ of influenza, how should we yet have discovered the germ of genius. . . . The genealogists say that certain stocks, certain families, breed writers as fig trees breed figs—Dryden, Swift, and Pope they tell us were all cousins. . . .
>
> But let us always remember—influences are infinitely numerous; writers are infinitely sensitive; each writer has a different sensibility. . . . Read a page of Scott; then of Henry James; try to work out the influences that have transformed the one page into the other. . . . Books descend from books as families descend from families. Some descend from Jane Austen; others from Dickens. They resemble their parents, as human children resemble their parents; yet they differ as children differ, and revolt as children revolt." [36]

Commenting on the last image, Harold Bloom himself remarks, "A critic of literary influence learns to be both enchanted and wary when such a passage is encountered," and I suppose the wariness arises in part here from the belatedness Bloom may feel in the face of this Woolfian formulation. [37]

Woolf's ambivalence about literary tradition parallels her ambivalence about family. One must break with the past in order to make something new. One is condemned to do so, moreover, by one's historical situation, by one's sense that "when the crash came in 1914" history changed, human life changed, and therefore literary art, taking life as its model, must perforce change as well. [38] The literary tradition, moreover, is patriarchal, and "in life and in art the values of a woman are not the values of a man. Thus, when a woman comes to write a novel, . . . she is perpetually wishing to alter the established values." [39] But "books descend from books as families descend from families," and Woolf as a reader "is tormented by the suspicion that reverence for the dead is vitally connected with understanding of the living" and that we must consult "the masterpieces of the past. We feel ourselves indeed driven to them, impelled not by calm judgment but by some imperious need to anchor our instability upon their security."[40] Even if the woman writer rejects the patriarchal canon—which Woolf never, finally, does—she must create a countertradition as the basis of her art, must "think back through our mothers."[41] Woolf's own mother, Julia Stephen, is a continuing presence for Woolf at least until her ghost is allegedly laid to rest in the idealized portrait of Mrs. Ramsay in *To the Lighthouse*. But she is also the paradigm of "the Angel in the House" who had to be slain, for "if I had not killed her, she would have killed me—as a writer."[42] On the other hand, Leslie Stephen is not just the remote, self-involved patriarch drawn as Mr. Ramsay, and not just the father whose survival would have made Woolf's writing "inconceivable"; he is also "the writer father" on whom she still relies, in 1940, "to stiffen my fluid vision" (*MB2* 15–16).

Virginia Woolf's response to Henry James mirrors her divided response to family and to the family romance of literary tradition. Even the imagery of sickness and health is divided with respect to James. For if, as we have seen, James was often associated with disease, he was also enjoyed and invoked as a remedy. In the summer of 1897, the season of Stella Duckworth's death, Woolf "read Macaulay and Henry James because she found that they soothed her nerves."[43] And at the end of her life, she turned to James for solace. In her penultimate diary entry (March 8, 1941), she wrote, "I mark Henry James's sentence: Observe perpetually. Observe the oncome of age. Observe greed. Observe my own despondency. By that means it becomes serviceable" (*DVW* 5:357–58). A few days later, in a similar vein, she wrote, "I remember a saying of Henry James— all experiences are of use to a writer. I think he was talking about a nervous breakdown" (*LVW* 6:478). But as Dole suggests, even these statements embody the division of Woolf's mind and spirit: to "mark Henry James's sentence" may be to feel oneself *sentenced,* condemned, just as, listening to James discourse on the street in Rye many years before, Woolf had "felt like a condemned person, who sees the knife drop and stick and drop again."[44] In order to explore the meaning of Virginia Woolf's complex relation to Henry James, we must first examine, in the next chapter, her substantial writings and many comments about him (picking up the story from 1907 on), before turning, in chapter five, to a new account of the development of her fiction as a saga of response and resistance to the lessons of the Master.

Chapter Four

"Partners in Merit": Virginia Woolf on Henry James

I

So far as we know, Virginia Woolf said very little about Henry James between 1907 and 1915, the year that her first novel, *The Voyage Out,* was published. We have already cited her mention, in 1909, of her having told Saxon Sydney-Turner, a few years before, that her "view of life was that of a Henry James novel." But in two letters of the same year, Woolf referred to James with apparent disparagement, once in a typically anti-American statement—"I never envisaged (as the French have it) anything so ghastly. Think of the long white roads, and the dusky inns at night, and the intelligent American with her guide Henry James"—and once in decrying the state of the literary scene: "Now Swinburne is dead, Meredith dumb, and Henry James inarticulate, things are in a bad way" (*LVW* 1:379, 390). Woolf is divided as ever on Henry James, implying that things would not be so bad if James were still voluble.

We find that in 1915 she was still trying to disabuse the men of Bloomsbury of Henry James—but that she was, at the same time, reading James herself. "Please tell me," she asked Strachey, "what merit you find in Henry James. I have disabused Leonard of him; but we have his works here, and I read, and can't find anything but faintly tinged rose water, urbane and sleek, but vulgar, and pale as Walter Lamb. Is there really any sense in it? I admit I can't be bothered to snuff out his meaning when it's very obscure" (*LVW* 2:67). Despite the complaints about James, "we have his works here, and I read."

We might pause a moment to detail Woolf's reading of Henry James. According to the selective catalogue of books in Virginia and Leonard Woolf's library, the following James volumes were found after Leonard Woolf's death: *Daisy Miller* (including also "An International Episode" and "Four Meetings"), *Portraits of Places, Tales of Three Cities* ("A New England Winter," "Lady Barberina," and "Impressions of a Cousin"), *The Golden Bowl, The Real Thing & Other Tales* (including also "Sir Dominick Ferrand," "Nona Vincent," "The Chaperon," and "Greville Fane"), *The Reverberator, Hawthorne, The Art of the Novel, The Aspern Papers, The Ivory Tower, The Sacred Fount,* and *Within the Rim.* Only the last five of these twelve titles would have come into the Woolf library after 1915.[1] But that catalogue is, as I just said, highly selective. It includes only those books still in the library after Leonard's death that were acquired by Holleyman & Treacher, Ltd., in 1970; another major portion of the library, acquired at the same time by Bow Windows Bookshop, Lewes, is not catalogued. The introduction to the catalogue specifically mentions, moreover, that among the additional uncatalogued books were nearly four hundred consigned to sale at Sotheby's in 1970, including signed presentation copies of the works of Henry James (probably inherited by Virginia Woolf from her father). Other sales also diminished the library before cataloguing. Only 2,617 items, in any case, appear in the published catalogue, while its compilers cite evidence that in 1928–29 the number of books the Woolfs owned was considerably in excess of 15,000.[2] From Woolf's published reviews and essays and from her letters, diaries, and reading notes, we know that she read *The American Scene, The Ambassadors, The Wings of the Dove, What Maisie Knew, The Turn of the Screw, The Sense of the Past, The Middle Years,* "The Great Good Place," "The Friends of the Friends," "Owen Wingrave," "The Private Life," *The Tragic Muse,* "Sir Edmund Orme," Percy Lubbock's two-volume edition of *The Letters of Henry James,* and the Preface to *The Portrait of a Lady.* (She probably also read *The Portrait of a Lady* itself as well as the other New York Edition prefaces, and also *Notes of a Son and Brother,* to which she refers in her review of *The Middle Years*). Of the works catalogued from her library, we know that she read *The Golden Bowl, Within the Rim, The Sacred Fount,* and *Hawthorne.* In addition, she read several books about (or largely about) James, including Joseph Warren Beach's *The Method of Henry James,* Percy Lubbock's *The Craft of Fiction,* and Stephen Spender's *The Destructive Element.* Doubtless incomplete as a list of Woolf's Jamesian reading, this is nevertheless a major portion of James's oeuvre—a formidable list, indeed, for one who asked, "Is there really any sense in it?"

When James died early in 1916, Woolf sardonically noted the event: "Henry James is dead. His last words, according to Sydney [Waterlow], were to his secretary, whom he sent for. 'I wish to dictate a few faint and faded words—' after which he was silent and never spoke again" (*LVW* 2:84). The tone of this report may seem continuous with that of the disparaging remarks to Strachey the year before, but a year and a half later Woolf was reading James again. As usual, her view of James was two-sided. In September of 1918, she wrote to Saxon Sydney-Turner, "What is there to say about The Sense of the Past? I'm afraid my old image must still hold good as far as I'm concerned—the laborious striking of whole boxfulls of damp matches—lovely phrases of course but—but—but. Sydney Waterlow sat on me with all the solemn weight (which is after all so light) of his portentous haystack for saying this" (*LVW* 2:181). The next month, she discussed Henry James with Katherine Mansfield ("& K. M. was illuminating I thought" [*DVW* 1:58]). The following week there appeared the first of six on-the-whole highly favorable reviews that Woolf published on James and James criticism in *TLS* in the years 1917–22.

Before we take up these important *TLS* essays, I want to consider some of the constraints that Woolf was working under when she put her views on Henry James before the public. Paula Smith astutely points to the pressure Woolf felt to praise Henry James.[3] In part the problem was that the *Times Literary Supplement* was very much an official organ of the patriarchy; in addition, its editor, Bruce Richmond, was stodgy and in fact downright prissy in the worst, patriarchal Victorian way. But even more than pressure from male censors, Woolf felt the internalized pressure of the expectation that young women be restrained, sympathetic, and unselfish, that they embody a "Victorian manner" that militated against the freedom and the authority vital to a reviewer and, generally, to a writer. In "A Sketch of the Past," she wrote that "the Victorian manner is perhaps—I am not sure—a disadvantage in writing. When I read my old *Literary Supplement* articles, I lay the blame for their suavity, their politeness, their sidelong approach, to my tea-table training. I see myself, not reviewing a book, but handing plates of buns to shy young men and asking them: do they take cream and sugar?" (*MB2* 150). In Woolf's speech of January 21, 1931 (the germ of *The Pargiters* and of *The Years*), she says that

> when I came to write reviews the Angel in the House stole behind me and said "You have got yourself into a very queer position. You are young and unmarried. But you are writing for a paper owned by men, edited by men—*whose chief supporters are men;* you are even reviewing a book that has been written by a man—one Mr Arnold Bennett— Therefore whatever you say let it be pleasing to men. Be sympathetic; be tender; flatter; use all the arts and wiles which I Heaven help me have used till I am sick of the whole thing (The Angel did sometimes speak like this to women ⟨when she was alone⟩) but believe me it is absolutely necessary. Never disturb them with the idea that you have a mind of your own. And above all be pure." With that she made as if to guide my pen.

Shortly thereafter Woolf writes of having had to slay the Angel, for otherwise "she would have killed me—as a writer."[4] Woolf's manuscript notes for the speech make it clear that she had Henry James especially in mind:

> And so when I came to write, there was little to prevent me. I doubt whether I ever suffered much obstacle. A few. I began simply as a reviewer: Novels were sent to me. I was paid a guinea a thousand words. . . . What an easy and unheroic lot, compared with Dame Ethel's! I suppose of all ways to earn a living, this is the easiest. But wait. I think there were barriers. Let me put it in this way. Editors used to send me lives of Dickens, and Jane Austen. . . . But before I

began my review, I always knew what I was expected to say. I felt some pressure on me to say what was agreeable. Dear old Henry James—he must be praised.[5]

That Henry James was connected with the Angel's threat to kill Woolf "as a writer" indicates, as Smith suggests, that James was a focal point for her anxiety of authorship as well as for the anxiety of influence he aroused in her.[6] In addition, Woolf had run up against Bruce Richmond's refusal to let her use the word *lewd* in her *TLS* piece on James's ghost stories, and her record of a talk with him on the matter shows that her "Dear old Henry James" in the notes for the speech of January 21, 1931 was an echo of his stricture, for she has Richmond say, "But you know the usual meaning of the word? It is—ah—*dirty*—Now poor dear old Henry James— At anyrate [*sic*], think it over, & ring me up in 20 minutes" (*DVW* 2:151).

But the constraint Woolf felt to praise "dear old Henry James" cannot wholly account for the unalloyed complimentary substance and tone of her first major *TLS* essay on James, her review of *The Middle Years*. Elegiac in mood, the review almost seems to be a public penance for the impertinence of Woolf's private repetition of Waterlow's account of James's last words. In place of the derisive anecdote ("'I wish to dictate a few faint and faded words—' after which he was silent and never spoke again"), we read, in the opening paragraph of the *TLS* piece,

> although we are aware that we shall hear his voice no more, there is no hint of exhaustion or of leave-taking; the tone is as rich and deliberate as if time were unending and matter infinite; what we have seems to be but the prelude to what we are to have, but a crumb, as he says, of a banquet now forever withheld. Some one speaking once incautiously in his presence of his "completed" works drew from him the emphatic assertion that never, never so long as he lived could there be any talk of completion; his work would end only with his life; and it seems in accord with this spirit that we should feel ourselves pausing at the end of a paragraph while in imagination the next great wave of the wonderful voice curves into fullness.

And the review concludes with what is almost a repudiation of Waterlow's report: "we can believe that if he could have chosen, his last words would have been like these, words of recollection and of love."[7] It is impossible to say whether Woolf's "like these" refers to James's words in *The Middle Years* or to her review, which might fairly be characterized as a work "of recollection and of love."

Woolf's discussion suggests one of the essential affinities between James's art and her own. For the poetry of Woolf's novels is above all reminiscential, a poetry of the past, and it is this that she sees as supreme in Henry James: "All great writers have, of course, an atmosphere in which they seem most at their ease and at their best. . . . For ourselves Henry James seems most entirely in his element, doing that is to say what everything favours his doing, when it is a question of recollection." Woolf's phrasing seems Jamesian here ("doing that is to say what everything favours his doing"), and she goes on to write sentences that might pass as brilliant imitations of Henry James's voice: for instance, "He comes to his task with an indescribable air of one so charged and laden with precious stuff that he hardly knows how to divest himself of it all—where to find space to set down this and that, how to resist altogether the claims of some other gleaming object in the background; appearing so busy, so unwieldy with ponderous treasure that his dexterity in disposing of it, his consummate knowledge of how best to place each fragment, afford us the greatest delight that literature has had to offer for many a year" (497). Woolf also touches on affinities between herself and Henry James when she writes that he "was not a person to accept laws or to make one of any circle in a sense which implies the blunting of the critical powers" (497) and when she remarks on "that solicitude for others, that immense desire to help which had its origin, one might guess, in the aloofness and loneliness of the artist's life" (498).

Immediately after applauding James for "the greatest delight that literature has had to offer for many a year," Woolf suggests the anxiety that his performance creates in her: "The mere sight is enough to make any one who has ever held a pen in his hand consider his art afresh in the light of this extraordinary example of it"

(497). She implies a sense of belatedness and decline, moreover, in her repeated comparisons between the world of James's youth and her own present. For instance, she writes that "the conditions of those days allowed a kind of conversation which, so the survivors always maintain, is an art unknown in what they are pleased to call our chaos," that "we read of little societies . . . meeting . . . to discuss the serious questions of the times, and we have the feeling that they could claim a more representative character than anything of the sort we can show now," that "undoubtedly the resources of the day—and how magnificent they were!—were better organized," that "the extravagant steps which they [such ladies as Mrs. Greville and George Eliot] would take to snare whatever grace or atmosphere they desired at the moment lend their lives in retrospect a glamour of adventure, aspiration, and triumph such as seems for good or for evil banished from our more conscious and much more critical day," and that "personality . . . seems to have been accorded a licence for the expression of itself for which we can find no parallel in the present day" (497–98). All in all, the celebratory pitch of the *Middle Years* review—which contains, incidentally, the highest praise Woolf would ever accord American literature in her statement that "to Americans, indeed, to Henry James and to Hawthorne, we owe the best relish of the past in our literature" (497)—cannot be accounted for merely by the pressure from *TLS* and its editor to praise "dear old Henry James." It is too deeply felt and too lovingly sustained for any such explanation. And it stands in remarkable contrast to the disparaging comments about James we have noticed in Woolf's correspondence of the preceding year.

Woolf's next major Jamesian essay is on Joseph Warren Beach's *The Method of Henry James;* her review appeared in *TLS* in late December 1918. In January of that year, she had praised James in her essay "Across the Border" (later reprinted as "The Supernatural in Fiction"): "If you wish to guess what our ancestors felt when they read *The Mysteries of Udolpho* you cannot do better than read *The Turn of the Screw.*" [8] In February 1918, she exclaimed in a letter to Sydney-Turner, "I am appalled at the number of things I can remember. Meredith, Henry James" (*LVW* 2:221). The following month, she noted in her diary her refusal to enlist as a devotee of Henry James: "He [Robert Trevelyan] wanted to know whether he could add my name to the list of devout Jacobeans. Percy Lubbock & Logan Smith play this very characteristic game, of exquisite interest of course to Bob. They've counted 20, & Bob was seriously exerting himself to find a 21st. But I refused—with some vehemence at first, thinking I was to be asked to subscribe to a memorial. Nothing so substantial; only an elderly cultivated game" (*DVW* 1 : 125 – 26). The student of influence will perhaps sigh with relief to record Woolf's refusal; had she happily signed on with Lubbock's hothouse clique of devout Jamesians, one might suspect her of a view of James too direct and ingenuous for the argument for a complex, ambivalent, and often repressed relation with the precursor that I am mounting in these chapters on Woolf and James. Nevertheless, Woolf did at one point subscribe to a homage to Henry James. In 1913, for James's seventieth birthday, an informal committee of his admirers took three hundred contributions of no more than £5 each with which a golden bowl was purchased for the Master, the balance going to Derwent Wood for a bust of James, while John Singer Sargent contributed without fee the portrait of Henry James that now hangs in the National Portrait Gallery in London. James repaid the donors with a printed letter of thanks, appending to it a list of their names. Later he arranged for them all to receive photographs of the Sargent portrait, signed by both him and the artist. Third-to-the-last on the alphabetical list of donors is Virginia Woolf. In August of 1918, then—just five months after refusing to join the Lubbock–Smith gang—Woolf lamented that she had found at Gordon Square (London) only one picture that she could bring to Asheham House; she wrote to Vanessa, "I'm in fearful straits, and have even had to unearth the Sargent portrait of Henry James" (*LVW* 2 : 265).[9] If this remark sounds derogatory, as though Woolf had been forced to dig up an old and not particularly appetizing bone, we must balance against it David Garnett's recollection of what Woolf did with that portrait. If the photo was something she had resurrected only because she was "in fearful straits," why did she place it where she did, keeping it before her when she worked the way Keats did Shakespeare's portrait?—"On her writing-table at Asheham," Garnett recalls, "she kept a framed and autographed photograph of Henry James."[10]

Working on her review of *The Method of Henry James,* Woolf noted in her diary, "it gives me distinct pleasure I own to formulate rapid views of Henry James & Mr Hergesheimer; chiefly because I slip in some ancient crank of mine" (*DVW* 1:224). Woolf's review has been slightly misquoted in one of the very best of the handful of discussions of the Woolf-James relation, by Jane Novak, who says that Woolf called herself "a fickle Jacobean," though in fact she only implies that she has at times belonged to a group she characterizes as "the fickle Jacobeans."[11] The review deserves attention as an extraordinary revelation of the young novelist's conflicted feelings about her American precursor; it is so loaded with ore for the present analysis that I will quote it at some length, beginning with the opening sentence:

> Henry James is much at present in the air—a portentous figure looming large and undefined in the consciousness of writers, to some an oppression, to others a [*sic*] obsession, but undeniably present to all. In either case, whether you suffer from the consciousness of Henry James or rejoice in it, you can scarcely do better than read what Mr. Beach has to say about him. He has seen we will not say the, but certainly a, figure in the carpet, which, considering the width of the fabric and the complexity of the pattern, is something of an achievement. . . . You will not come out top through reading Mr. Beach, but you will be made to enjoy thinking about Henry James and stimulated to frame theories to account for him; you may in the end find yourself with a pattern of your own.[12]

As in Woolf's memories of James from the first decade of the century, the Master is immense, monumental, "a portentous figure looming large." He is unavoidable; he afflicts writers, whether as an "oppression" or as an "obsession." One may "suffer from the consciousness of Henry James" or "rejoice in it," and the overall effect of the review is to make one feel that Woolf herself felt these two alternative responses to be inextricable in her own experience of James. One may "enjoy" thinking about James, but one must "be made to" do so, and the upshot of so doing is that "you may in the end find yourself with a pattern of your own." This last phrase ostensibly means that you may discover your own way of diagramming Henry James, but it also carries the latent suggestion that you may through study of James release your own creativity, create a pattern of your own just as Henry James wove the elusive figure in the carpet of his art.[13]

We must look to the second paragraph of the review for the "ancient crank" that Woolf relished being able to throw in as she formulated "rapid views of Henry James." Observing that she cannot "develop a fraction of the things which tempted us to amplify them as we read" *The Method of Henry James*, Woolf chooses instead to "brood for a moment upon the question in general," the question, that is, of Henry James:

> It is a commonplace to say that no other writer causes his readers to ask so many questions or has a following more sharply divided among themselves than Henry James. Mr. Beach is a Jacobean—that is to say he believes that in "The Wings of the Dove," "The Ambassadors," and "The Golden Bowl" Mr. James produced "the beautiful fruits" of a method which he had invented and perfected through a long series of failures and experiments. Other admirers cease to admire at or about the year 1889—the year of "The Tragic Muse." Both these sects can make out a good case for their beliefs, and are happy in their convictions. But more difficult to define and less enviable is the position of a third group, which cannot accommodate itself to either camp. The trouble with them is that they admire both periods, but with inexplicable lapses, almost unknown in the case of other writers, when from the extreme of admiration they turn to something like contempt. A sudden chill in an atmosphere of cordiality, a hint of callousness beneath the show of affection—by some such figures alone can they describe the insidious sensation which converts them from enthusiasts to outcasts. The worst of it is that they scarcely dare formulate their meaning, since any plain statement seems so grievously an over-statement. If you woke in the night and found yourself saying, "Henry James is vulgar—Henry James is a snob," you would annihilate these words, lest the very darkness should overhear them. In the light of day the utmost you can bring

yourself to murmur is that Henry James is an American. He had the American love of old furniture. Why these characteristics should at moments appear capable of such devastating effects is one of those puzzles that so often destroy the peace of mind of the fickle Jacobeans. His characters, so they say, are somehow tainted with the determination not to be vulgar; they are, as exiles tend to be, slightly parasitic; they have an enormous appetite for afternoon tea; their attitude not only to furniture but to life is more that of the appreciative collector than of the undoubting possessor.

Novak is right, of course, to suggest that Woolf counts herself among "the fickle Jacobeans." Woolf's image of one's waking at night and finding oneself saying "Henry James is vulgar" echoes her complaint to Strachey of 1915: "I read, and can't find anything but faintly tinged rose water, urbane and sleek, but vulgar" (*LVW* 2:67). In part, this passage reflects her sniffish attitude toward Americans who have assimilated to English life. Thus, her translation of the nighttime "Henry James is a snob" to the daylight murmur that "Henry James is an American" closely parallels observations she would make some seven years later, in an essay on American fiction:

> The more sensitive, or at least the more sophisticated, the Henry Jameses, the Hergesheimers, the Edith Whartons, decide in favour of England and pay the penalty by exaggerating the English culture, the traditional English good manners, and stressing too heavily or in the wrong places those social differences which, though the first to strike the foreigner, are by no means the most profound. What their work gains in refinement it loses in that perpetual distortion of values, that obsession with surface distinctions—the age of old houses, the glamour of great names—which makes it necessary to remember that Henry James was a foreigner if we are not to call him a snob.[14]

In other words, Woolf's "crank" is her objection to the James whose characters have, as she says in "The Method of Henry James," "an enormous appetite for afternoon tea"—precisely to the "tea-slop" Henry James who became a target, and a dodge, for James Joyce.

Doubtless Woolf is speaking hyperbolically in her description of the fickle Jacobeans, but the overstatement is nevertheless revealing. While finding much to admire in both the early and the late Henry James, the fickle Jacobeans find themselves subject to violent dislocation, to "the insidious sensation which converts them from enthusiasts to outcasts." The process is "inexplicable"; it has "devastating effects" that "destroy the peace of mind of the fickle Jacobeans." Apparently James is to them, as to Woolf's generalized "writers" of her opening paragraph, both an oppression and an obsession. The following, final paragraph of Woolf's review—the whole piece is just three paragraphs—heightens one's sense that what really discomfits Woolf is not James's nationality so much as the power of his art and of his example. For she puts her objections aside ("none of this seems of importance") to declare that James "was a great writer—a great artist. A priest of the art of writing in his lifetime, he is now among the saints to whom every writer, in particular every novelist, must do homage." Her review of *The Middle Years* had betrayed anxiety ("The mere sight is enough to make any one who has ever held a pen in his hand consider his art afresh"), and so does the peroration of "The Method of Henry James": "A glimpse of the possibilities which in his view gather round every story and stretch away into the distance beyond any sight save his own makes other people's achievements seem empty and childish."

We note that an element of compulsion attaches to Woolf's description of writers' responses to Henry James, not just in the "made to enjoy" of the first paragraph, but also in the "must do homage" of the last. At the same time, though Woolf expresses "inexplicable" repulsion from the snobby or "American" aspects of James, he exercises a strong attraction for her as well. Her closing comments cite his immense skill with words, so that "the limit of what can be expressed seems to be surpassed," making James "a source of perpetual wonder and delight." But the most important side of James for Woolf, what she saves for last, is his art of "weaving together . . . many themes into one theme, the making out of a design." Such a "weaving together" was a central concern for Woolf in her own art, and her words about Henry James might particularly be taken as descriptive of what she strives for in her novels at least from *Mrs. Dalloway* on. When she says that "the important side" of James "is suggested by the design which he made in order to explain his conception of 'The Awkward Age,'" and when she goes on to quote James's description, in the preface to that novel, of "'the neat figure of a circle consisting of a number of small rounds disposed at equal distance about a central object,'" she is very probably giving us the source or inspiration of the figure she drew of the structure of *To the Lighthouse:* "Two blocks joined by a corridor."[15]

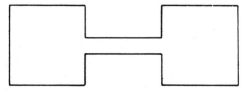

Finally, one notes Woolf's strong interest in James's theory of fiction. She refers in "The Method of Henry James" to James's "prefaces and sketches," remarking that "one had almost rather read what he meant to do than read what he actually did do." This interest is expressed also in a one-page manuscript of an unfinished review of two works by James, *Maud Evelyn* and *The Sacred Fount,* volumes 28 and 29 of *The Novels and Stories of Henry James* (Macmillan, 1921–23); there Woolf comments, "The significant thing about this edition is however that the famous prefaces are to be reprinted. So far as we know, this is the first time that they have been detached from the expensive New York edition & made available for readers with shallow purses. As they contain some of the most remarkable criticism of our time, this undoubtedly is the edition for ⟨lovers⟩ the Henry James student to possess."[16]

Three months later, Woolf reviewed *Within the Rim,* a posthumous collection of essays James wrote about the First World War. Though she begins by acknowledging that she approached the book with "tepid and formal respect" (not, to be sure, because it was by Henry James, but because "essays about the war contributed to albums and books with a charitable object even by the most distinguished of writers bear . . . such traces of perfunctory composition . . . that one is inclined . . . to leave them unread"), she quickly turns to praise of the volume, for "the process of reading these essays was a process of recantation." Of all Woolf's public pronouncements on James, this is perhaps the least mixed, the most unalloyed in its praise. For once, she does not dismiss James's celebration of England as a vulgar American excess—quite the contrary: "he had relished her [England] discriminatingly as only the alien, bred to different sounds and sights and circumstances, could relish others so distinct and so delightful in their distinctness." There is not the slightest hint of derision as Woolf hails James as the great apostle of high civilization: "But what he does in this little book . . . is . . . to present the best statement yet made of the largest point of view. He makes us understand what civilization meant to him and should mean to us." The review concludes, "If all our counsellors, we cannot help exclaiming, had spoken with that voice!" [17]

II

Early in 1920, Woolf was looking forward to reviewing Percy Lubbock's edition of *The Letters of Henry James,* unless (as we read in the last chapter) "someone else has done it for me during the influenza." At the same time, she was "stuck in the Ambassadors" (*LVW* 2:411). On April 2, she wrote to Vanessa, "I've been reading Henry James' letters till my brain rings and swings—do pictures affect you like that? He stayed in your hotel, by the way, and no doubt wore out some rich leather seat with his rotundity" (*LVW* 2:426).[18] Woolf associates not only disease ("the influenza") and immobility ("stuck in the Ambassadors") with James but also mental disequilibrium ("my brain rings and swings"). Woolf's extensive reading notes on the two volumes of James letters (twelve notebook pages of summary and comment plus several additional pages of quotations) suggest that she was very nearly overwhelmed by the revelation through James's letters of his dedication to his art and of his gargantuan energy. She notes, "everything gives way to work," "always thinks of everything from the view of work," and "'inexhaustible sensibility.'" She notes "the swing & rhythm & easy copious metaphors," she jots down the phrase "colossal old man," she remarks "the terrific sensitiveness," she observes "tremendous vitality really (don't lose sight of this—things tumbling into him all the time)," and she exclaims, "with what a gusto he lives!" [19] The review opens with images of being stunned. The experience of finishing one's reading of James's letters is likened to emerging from a cathedral with "the growl and boom of the organ still in the ears." [20] This auditory artillery assault of "the growl and boom" becomes, late in the review, "portentous and prodigious, . . . the voice of Henry James. There . . . we have exploded in our ears the report of his enormous, sustained, increasing, and overwhelming love of life." Overwhelming: "still dazed and well-nigh drowned," Woolf writes in the fourth sentence of the review, "our gesture at the finish is more one of exclamation than of interpretation." [20]

Woolf was led to protest in her diary that "the disease is my own, not caught from H. J., if thats any comfort" in response to the *Times* columnist who had accused her of falling, in this review, into some of "H. J.'s worse mannerisms" (*DVW* 2:29). The disease may have been her own; surely she aspired to make it so; but just as surely, it *was* caught from Henry James, and we can trace the course of the infection from Woolf's reading notes into the published review. Generally, of course, the syntax and the metaphoric profuseness of the prose of Woolf's review are Jamesian, as in the nearly parodic first sentence: "Who, on stepping from the cathedral dusk, the growl and boom of the organ still in the ears and the eyes still shaded to observe better whatever intricacy of carving or richness of marble may there be concealed, can breast the stir of the street and instantly and briskly sum up and deliver his impressions?" The vocabulary is Jamesian in detail, not just in particular key words, like *impression* here—in the reading notes, Woolf summarizes a James comment on Burne-Jones, that "B-J doesn't reach for impressions outside," and then adds "always impressions"— but also in the conceptions underlying the terms. For example, while Woolf sees that "all refers to his writing," she expresses disappointment that James does not very much discuss his art directly in the Lubbock volumes; James's life was a "long drawn process of adjustment and preparation . . . from first to last controlled and manipulated by a purpose which, as the years went by, only dealt more powerfully and completely with the treasures of a more complex sensibility. Yet, when we look to find the purpose expressed, to see the material in the act of transmutation, we are met by silence, we are waved blandly outside." How, in short, did James convert the life recorded in his letters into fiction? For the expression of her frustrated desire "to see the material in the act of transmutation," Woolf draws on James's words to H. G. Wells about the inadvisability of writing autobiographical fiction, taking *transmutation* from this passage, which she remarked in her reading notes as "good criticism of Wells": "There is, to my vision, no authentic, and no really interesting and no *beautiful*, report of things on the novelist's, the painter's part unless a particular detachment has operated, unless the great stewpot or crucible of the imagination, of the observant and recording and interpreting mind in short, has intervened and played its part—and this detachment, this chemical transmutation for the aesthetic, the representational, end is terribly wanting in autobiography brought, as the horrible phrase is, up to date." [21] Similarly, Woolf echoes James when she writes, "Nothing in the end has chilled or repressed him; everything has fed and filled him; the saturation is complete," for in her notes she took down James's words to his brother William, "The great thing is to be *saturated* with something—that is, in one way or another, with life; and I chose the form of my saturation." [22] The Jamesian *saturation* stayed in Woolf's critical vocabulary, surfacing later in Jamesian contexts, as in "Phases of Fiction," when, turning from the novelists she calls "The Psychologists" (including, prominently, Henry James) to "The Satirists and Fantastics," she writes, "The mind feels like a sponge saturated full with sympathy and understanding"; in the next paragraph of "Phases," incidentally, Woolf alludes to a famous passage in James's preface to *The Tragic Muse* when she says that "the loose, the baggy, shrivels up," echoing James's "but what do such large loose baggy monsters [*The Newcomes, Les Trois Mous-*

quetaires, and Tolstoy's *Peace and War (sic)*] . . . artistically *mean?*"[23]
When, for a final example, Woolf wants to describe the impersonality James aspired to share with his own creations, she can do
no better than to take a phrase, in quotation marks, that she had
copied into her reading notes from a comment by James about Walter Pater: James wanted, Woolf says in the *TLS* review, "to be 'the
mask without the face.'"

As we should by now expect, the review of *The Letters of Henry
James* includes an attack on James that is mounted and then, characteristically, retracted. Speaking of James's residence in Rye, Woolf
writes,

> One admits to a momentary malice. The seclusion is so deliberate;
> the exclusion so complete. . . . The voice that issued from the her
> mitage might well speak calmly, subtly, of exquisite emotions, and
> yet now and then we are warned by something exacting and even
> acid in its tone that the effects of the seclusion are not altogether be
> nign. "Yes, Ibsen is ugly, common, hard, prosaic, bottomlessly bour
> geois . . . [Woolf's elipsis]" "But, oh, yes, dear Louis ["Tess of the
> D'Urbervilles"] is vile. The pretence of 'sexuality' is only equalled by
> the absence of it, and the abomination of the language by the au
> thor's reputation for style."

And Woolf goes on to fault James's pronouncements on Meredith
and on Tolstoy and Dostoevsky as well.

The dramatic turn evidences Woolf's genuine appreciation, after
reading the Lubbock edition, not only of the heroism of Henry
James's life but also of one of the several major affinities between
herself and James that surface in this review, the commitment to artistic experiment.

> It is true that in order to keep these points at their sharpest [Woolf's
> citations of James's questionable judgments of Ibsen, Hardy, et al.]
> one has had to brush aside a mass of qualification and explanation
> which make each the apex of a formidable body of criticism. It is
> only for a moment that the seclusion seems cloistered, and the feel
> ings of an artist confounded with those of a dilettante.

Yet as that second flits across the mind . . . we realize what a catastrophe for all of us it would have been if the prolonged experiment, the struggle and the solitude of Henry James's life had ended in failure. Excuses could have been found both for him and for us. It is impossible, one might have said, for the artist not to compromise, or, if he persists in his allegiance, then, almost inevitably, he must live apart, for ever alien, slowly perishing in his isolation. . . . When, therefore . . . something yields, something is overcome, something dark and dense glows in splendour, it is as if the beacon flamed bright on the hilltop; as if . . . the crown of long deferred completion and culmination swung slowly into place. Not columns but pages . . . might be filled with comment and attempted analysis of this late and mighty flowering, this vindication, this crowded gathering together and welding into shape of all the separate strands, alien instincts, irreconcilable desires of the twofold nature. . . . here, by a prodigious effort of concentration, the field of human activity is brought into fresh focus, revealing new horizons, new landmarks, and new lights upon it of right and wrong.

In the reading notes, one can trace Woolf's growing appreciation of James's development; midway into volume two, she jotted down her observation that "the humour of the later letters seems much richer—also humanity." One also sees, in the passage just quoted at length, Woolf's recognition that James was an "alien" not merely because he was an American living in England but more essentially because he was a true artist ("the artist . . . must live apart, for ever alien"). Here was a point of contact between the two writers, for Woolf was an alien not only in her artistic vocation but also in being a woman, condemned to be an outsider by the patriarchal literary and educational establishments, as she so powerfully argues in *A Room of One's Own*. As a child of the establishment, and as someone with a divided sexual identity too (upon which she erected her doctrine of androgyny), Woolf also shares "the twofold nature" she ascribes to James as well as the aim of "welding into shape . . . all the separate strands."

There is one other point, earlier in the review, where I think that Woolf implicitly suggests her own identification with James. She speaks of James's "late maturity" in one paragraph and comments in the next, "When he wrote that [that London is "the best point of view in the world"] he was thirty-seven; a mature age; an age at which the native growing confidently in his own soil is already putting forth whatever flower fate ordains and natural conditions allow." Woolf herself was thirty-eight when she wrote her essay on *The Letters of Henry James,* just about the age at which she describes James in the context of his delayed maturity. We might observe that the trajectories of their careers up to early middle age are similar: James publishes his first novel, *Roderick Hudson,* in 1875, when he is thirty-two; Woolf publishes her first novel, *The Voyage Out,* in 1915, when she is thirty-three; James publishes his first masterpiece, *The Portrait of a Lady,* in 1881, when he is thirty-eight, and in 1920 Woolf's masterpieces still lie ahead—not for two more years, not till she is forty, will she evince in *Jacob's Room* something of the voice, style, and fictional strategies characteristic of the great works to come. Woolf may well have taken heart from the example of James, an outsider by nationality as she was by gender, coming late into his own as an artist and doing so with magnificent success.

At the same time, and indeed very probably because of the points of contact Woolf implicitly recognized between herself and Henry James, she is at pains to differentiate herself from him. Carol Dole astutely suggests that Woolf's desire to distinguish herself from James is expressed in the review of James's letters in her images of James's vitality, of his physical and mental health (Woolf calls James "Johnsonian in his sanity"), and of his giant's appetite: "For to be as subtle as Henry James," Woolf writes, concluding the penultimate paragraph of her review, "one must also be as robust; to enjoy his power of exquisite selection [more Jamesian diction, one notes, infecting Woolf's prose] one must have 'lived and loved and cursed and floundered and enjoyed and suffered,' and, with the appetite of a giant, have swallowed the whole." Dole comments, "The metaphor of the giant's appetite must, for a near anorexic, involve both repulsion and admiration, but certainly declares difference." Dole further suggests that Woolf's insistence in the review that James "never for a moment doubted the authenticity of his genius" is similarly a tactic of differentiation, asserting that "James—unlike herself—was largely unaffected by anxieties about the public reception of his work."[24] We find curious support for Dole's view in Woolf's reading notes, for in them she had in fact written, "doubt about his own achievement"; thus, her repeated assertion that James felt no doubt was deployed in direct contradiction of her own notation.

Woolf's review of *The Letters of Henry James* closes as worshipfully as it had begun. As she had fifteen years before (in her review of *The Golden Bowl*), she praises James for his beautiful phrasing, "each sentence, from the whole fling of his person to the last snap of his fingers, firmly fashioned and throwing out at its swiftest well nigh incredible felicities of phrase." But she praises him above all, in her final paragraph, for the impersonality he conferred on his work by putting upon it "the final seal" of "artistic form." What Woolf had said was most important about James in her piece on *The Method of Henry James* she repeats here in the *Letters* review in unmistakably Jamesian prose:

> Yet, if he shared with magnanimity, if he enjoyed hugely, there remained something incommunicable, something reserved, as if . . . it was not . . . into our hands that he placed his offerings. There they stand, the many books, products of "an inexhaustible sensibility," all with the final seal upon them of artistic form, which . . . sets apart the object thus consecrated and makes it no longer part of ourselves. In this impersonality the maker himself desired to share—"to take it," as he said, "wholly, exclusively with the pen (the style, the genius) and absolutely not at all with the person," to be "the mask without the face," the alien in our midst, the worker who when his work is done turns even from that and reserves his confidence for the solitary hour, like that at midnight when, alone on the threshold of creation, Henry James speaks aloud to himself "and the prospect clears and flushes, and my poor blest old genius pats me so admirably and lovingly on the back that I turn, I screw round, and bend my lips to passionately, in my gratitude, kiss its hands." So that is why, perhaps, as life swings and clangs, booms and reverberates, we have the sense of an altar of service, of sacrifice, to which, as we pass out, we bend the knee.

Woolf's next-to-last sentence, in which her prose ("alone on the threshold of creation, Henry James speaks aloud to himself") blends effortlessly with the prose of the Master, seems a compensation, wonderful and gorgeous in its own right, for the disease she unconvincingly denies having caught from him.

Two days after the publication of "The Letters of Henry James," Woolf observed in her diary that while writing it, "I was driven, as with shut eyes, eyes being indeed so intent upon Henry James as to see nothing else" (*DVW* 2:27). Six days after the publication of the review, she did in actuality what she had done in imagination, metaphorically, in its opening and closing: she went into a church to pay homage to Henry James, and implicitly qualified the homage in her report of the event: "I slipped out into Chelsea Church, & saw the tablet to H. J.—florid & cultivated if you like—spindly letters, & Jamesian phrases. Perhaps by Gosse" (*DVW* 2:30). The James praised on the plaque in Chelsea Old Church, we should note, is not the robust, dauntless experimenter and priest of art Woolf pictures in the *TLS* piece on the letters, but, in the language of the plaque, the "lover and interpreter of the fine amenities, of brave decisions and generous loyalties" (*DVW* 2:30 n. 10).

Earlier in the same diary entry, Woolf reported the attack in the *Times* (by Arthur Bingham Walkley) on her Jamesian mannerisms in "The Letters of Henry James." Woolf typically overresponded by doubting the value of all of her writing: "I delete the article from my mind with blushes, & see all my writing in the least becoming light." She goes on to accept Walkley's "true criticism" while asserting, as we have noted earlier, that "the disease is my own, not caught from H. J." The meditation that follows on writing for the elderly men of the literary establishment is worth quoting at length:

> I must see to it [the allegedly Jamesian "florid gush" in her writing] though. The Times atmosphere brings it out; for one thing I have to be formal there, especially in the case of H. J.; & so contrive an article rather like an elaborate design; which encourages ornament. Desmond, however, volunteered admiration. I wish one could make out some rule about praise & blame. I predict that I'm destined to have blame in any quantity. I strike the eye; & elderly gentlemen in

particular get annoyed. . . . Partly, its the "writing well" that sets people off—& always has done, I suppose. "Pretentious" they say; & then a woman writing well, & writing in the Times—that's the line of it. This slightly checks me from beginning *Jacob's room*. But I value blame. It spurs one, even from Walkley; who is (I've looked him out) 65, & a cheap little gossip, I'm glad to think, laughed at even by Desmond. But don't go forgetting that there's truth in it; more than a grain in the criticism that I'm damnably refined in The Times; refined & cordial: I don't think its easy to help it: since, before beginning the H. J. article, I took a vow I'd say what I thought, & say it in my own way. (*DVW* 2:29–30)

Judging by her reading notes, and by the conviction of the published review, I would argue that Woolf did say what she thought in "The Letters of Henry James" and that what really galled her was her not having said it "in my own way" sufficiently to have kept a Walkley, or anyone else, from branding her as Jamesian. This diary entry foregrounds, moreover, a recurrent feature of Woolf's relation to Henry James, that what she attacks in him is often some quality that she shares with him and that makes her vulnerable. When she charged Americans with being "so d——d refined for example Henry James" (in a letter to Ethel Smyth, March 23, 1931, *LVW* 6:529) she was very nearly repeating the criticism she accepted of her own work, "that I'm damnably refined in The Times." There is a similar irony, too, and a similar psychodynamic, in her display of her own anti-American snobbery whenever she attacks Henry James for being a snob. As Dole points out, it is doubtless not coincidental that the two last words in her essay "Am I a Snob?" are "Henry James." [25]

In the fall of 1920, Woolf recorded in her diary T. S. Eliot's comment that "a personal upheaval of some kind came after Prufrock, & turned him aside from his inclination—to develop in the manner of Henry James" (*DVW* 2:68). In April of the following year, midway through the composition of *Jacob's Room*, Woolf records a conversation with Lytton Strachey, in which they are discussing their "places," Strachey's among eminent biographers, Woolf's among novelists:

"I'm the 'ablest of living women novelists'" I said— So the British weekly says.

"You influence me" he said.

And he said he could always recognise my writing though I wrote so many different styles, "which is the result of hard work" I insisted. And then we discussed historians: Gibbon: a kind of Henry James, I volunteered. Oh dear no—not in the least he said.

"He has a point of view & sticks to it" I said. "And so do you. I wobble." (*DVW* 2:115)

Gibbon is "a kind of Henry James" because he maintains a consistent point of view. In defining herself in opposition to such a steady perspective, Woolf points to the fictional technique she was developing in *Jacob's Room*—about which more later, in our next chapter.

The following month, May 1921, in a review titled "Gothic Romance," Woolf wondered, "can we possibly say that Henry James was a Goth?"[26] In September, she wrote in her diary,

I have finished the Wings of the Dove, & make this comment. His [Henry James's] manipulations become so elaborate towards the end that instead of feeling the artist you merely feel the man who is posing the subject. And then I think he loses the power to feel the crisis. He becomes merely excessively ingenious. This, you seem to hear him saying, is the way to do it. Now just when you expect a crisis, the true artist evades it. Never do the thing, & it will be all the more impressive. Finally, after all this juggling & arranging of silk pocket handkerchiefs, one ceasees to have any feeling for the figure behind. Milly thus manipulated, disappears. He overreaches himself. And then one can never read it again. The mental grasp and stret[c]h are magnificent. Not a flabby or slack sentence, but much emasculated by this timidity or consciousness or whatever it is. Very highly American, I conjecture, in the determination to be highly bred, & the slight obtuseness as to what high breeding is. (*DVW* 2:136)

The month before, she had written about James in a letter to Roger Fry, one of the comparatively few letters that survive from a summer during which she spent nearly sixty days in bed, unable to write and afflicted by "headaches, sleeplessness, pains and frets" (editor's note, *LVW* 2:473): "I have been reading Henry James—the Wings of a Dove—for the first time. I have never read his great works; but merely pretended." Of course, one may argue about which are James's "great works," but even so Woolf's disclaimer here seems puzzling from one who had reviewed *The Golden Bowl* and who had already read *The Ambassadors, The American Scene*, and numerous other works by James. Perhaps she asserts that she has not read James's "great" works in order to establish that she has come as far as she has as a writer—"the ablest of living women novelists"—without the aid of the major Henry James. The rest of her comments to Fry are the usual mix of praise and blame: "Certainly this is very remarkable—I am very much impressed. At the same time I am vaguely annoyed by the feeling that—well, that I am in a museum. It is all deserted. . . . It is vast and silent and infinitely orderly and profoundly gloomy and every knob shines and so on. But—I am too feeble minded to finish" (*LVW* 2:478)

A year later, she wrote again about having read *The Wings of the Dove*, telling Ottoline Morrell, "I do admire poor old Henry, and actually read through the Wings of a Dove last summer, and thought it such an amazing acrobatic feat, partly of his, partly of mine, that I now look upon myself and Henry James as partners in merit. I made it all out. But I felt very ill for some time afterwards." Then Woolf added, "I am now reading Joyce, and my impression, after 200 out of 700 pages, is that the poor young man has only got the dregs of a mind compared even with George Meredith. I mean if you could weigh the meaning on Joyces page it would be about 10 times as light as on Henry James" (*LVW* 2:548). Although Woolf tells Ottoline Morrell in 1922 that she "felt very ill for some time afterwards," her diary entry of September 12, 1921 ("I have finished the Wings of the Dove"), coincides with her recovery from her summerlong illness and her return to work. Less than two months later, she would complete *Jacob's Room*. The discrepant facts of Woolf's recovery and of her report to Mrs. Morrell may perhaps be reconciled, however, if we consider the occasional solace James provided Woolf in times of malaise despite her associating him with disease—and perhaps even because of that association. For disease is part of the creative process for Woolf, just as it is in Harold Bloom's theory of influence. As she approached the end of *The Waves*, she wished that she might stay ill for two more weeks:"

> Once or twice I have felt that odd whirr of wings in the head which comes when I am ill so often—last year, for example, at this time I lay in bed constructing A Room of One's Own. . . . If I could stay in bed another fortnight . . . I believe I should see the whole of The Waves. . . . I believe these illnesses are in my case—how shall I express it—partly mystical. Something happens in my mind. It refuses to go on registering impressions. It shuts itself up. It becomes chrysalis. I lie quite torpid, often with acute physical pain—as last year; only discomfort this. Then suddenly something springs. (*DVW* 3:286–87)

The illness of reading *The Wings of the Dove*, then, was probably of this special, "mystical" sort, the dormant stage after which "suddenly somethings springs." *The Wings of the Dove* must have set going "that odd whirr of wings in the head."

The week after she finished *Jacob's Room*, Woolf mentioned her work on a new essay devoted to Henry James: "I am struggling with Henry James' ghost stories for The Times; have I not just laid them down in a mood of satiety?—" (*DVW* 2:142). James is triumphant in the review itself, though he comes in for some telling criticism along the way. Woolf condemns "The Great Good Place" as a failure in terms that recognize the essential realistic and dramatic genius of Henry James, for "beauty . . . must pass through ugliness or lie down with disorder before she can rise in her own person," and James "was much too fond of the world we know to create one that we do not know"; he was not a "visionary"—"his genius was dramatic, not lyric."[27] She judges James more successful in "The Friends of the Friends"; the tale produces "a strange emotion," finding "a weak spot" in the "armour" of our modern skepticism about the supernatural. Here Woolf makes a comment remarkably like that of A. R. Orage in the 1918 special Henry James number of *The Little Review* (about "how imperceptibly" James's "method of

dealing with real persons shades into his dealing with ghosts"[28]):
"Henry James has only to take the smallest of steps and he is over
the border. His characters with their extreme fineness of perception
are already half-way out of the body." I believe that James's use of
ghosts helped Woolf to create the ghostly persistence after death of
Jacob Flanders (in *Jacob's Room*) and of Mrs. Ramsay (in *To the
Lighthouse*)—more about this in the next chapter—for her remarks in "Henry James' Ghost Stories" show how well she understood the artistic and psychological dimensions, and uses, of the
supernatural in James. James's ghosts, she writes, "have their origin
within us. They are present whenever the significant overflows our
powers of expressing it; whenever the ordinary appears ringed by
the strange. The baffling things that are left over, the frightening
ones that persist—these are the emotions that he takes, embodies,
makes consoling and companionable." And in *The Turn of the
Screw,* where Henry James triumphs, making "us afraid of the
dark," we are afraid not of the apparitional Peter Quint but "of
something unnamed, of something, perhaps, in ourselves."

The essay on James's ghost stories also reiterates Woolf's sense of
James's vitality. Just when we think we have him "pinioned, tied
down, to all appearance lifeless, up he jumps and walks away." We
have forgotten, Woolf says, in our "wonder at his prodigious dexterity," "the genius, . . . the driving power which is so incalculable
and so essential" and which she sums up as James's "crude and
simple passion for telling stories." Although Woolf was allowed to
praise James by saying that his passion for narrative was "crude,"
she was forbidden to characterize anything in his art as *lewd,* as we
have mentioned earlier. Three days before publication of "Henry
James' Ghost Stories," Woolf recorded her capitulation to Richmond's censorship of the review. Having come "to the required conclusion in twelve minutes & a half," Woolf wondered "whether to
break off, with an explanation, or to pander, or to go on writing
against the current." She added that "poor Bruce [Richmond] . . . is
stern with me, not so much for disrespect to poor old Henry, but for
bringing blame on the Supplement" (*DVW* 2 : 151–52). We cannot
be sure, incidentally, where *lewd* would have appeared in the review,

but I conjecture that it was replaced by *obscene* when, pondering the meeting alone at night of "the live man and the dead woman" in "The Friends of the Friends" ("the spiritual and the carnal meeting together"), Woolf observes that the shock provided by the super-natural in the tale "is the queerest of shocks—tranquil, beautiful, like the closing of chords in harmony; and yet, somehow obscene."

The last of the six Jamesian essays Woolf published in *TLS* between 1917 and 1922 is "On Re-Reading Novels," ostensibly a review of new editions of Jane Austen, the Brontës, and George Meredith, but really Woolf's complex response to Percy Lubbock's codification of Henry James's novelistic precepts and practice in *The Craft of Fiction*. Woolf's reading notes are often detailed and extensive; for *The Craft of Fiction* they are unusually so, fourteen closely written pages of quotation and response to Lubbock's unfolding argument. Particularly in the first half of the notes, Woolf resists Lubbock's arguments, protesting, for example, against Lubbock's view that readers should treat the novel as an "object of art" and not "as a piece of the life around us": "Yes: but novels *are* life as well as art."[29] Woolf's chief disagreement with Lubbock, in the notes and in the published review, is that he elevates art over life and form over emotion. For Lubbock, form is the end; for Woolf form is the means to the end of expressing feeling. But the notes, and the review, make it clear that Woolf was very much impressed with Lubbock's work and that her initial resistance, while never relinquished, yielded a great deal of ground to her sense, as she read, that she was being instructed by Lubbock. Less than a quarter of the way through the volume, she writes, "This is all quite true, sound, & I daresay new." As she suggests in the review, her eyes were being opened to aspects of her own art she had not seen before: there she compares Lubbock's work to an x-ray that shows us for the first time the bones beneath the flesh: "It is surprising. It is even momentarily shocking. Our old familiar friend has vanished. But, after all, there is something satisfactory in bone—one can grasp it."[30] In the notes, with the shock of discovery, she exclaims, "what a queer mongrel art fiction is!"

Woolf follows Lubbock in placing James at the pinnacle of novelistic art, but she also suggests that one may legitimately attack James for the very qualities that place him there:

> Let us look not at each story separately, but at the method of story-telling . . . which runs through them all. Let us look at it in Richardson's hands, and watch it changing and developing as Thackeray applies it, and Dickens and Tolstoy and Meredith and Flaubert and the rest. Then let us see how in the end Henry James, endowed not with greater genius but with greater knowledge and craftsmanship, surmounts in "The Ambassadors" problems which baffled Richardson in "Clarissa." The view is difficult; the light is bad. At every angle some one rises to protest that novels are the outburst of spontaneous inspiration, and that Henry James lost as much by his devotion to art as he gained. We will not silence that protest, for it is the voice of an immediate joy in reading without which second readings would be impossible, for there would be no first. And yet the conclusion seems to us undeniable. Henry James achieved what Richardson attempted. "The only real *scholar* in the art" beats the amateurs. The late-comer improves upon the pioneers. More is implied than we can even attempt to state.

And Woolf goes on to describe James's triumph over the great novelists of the nineteenth-century with whom, earlier in the review, she had grouped him ("the masters—Tolstoy and Flaubert, and Dickens, and Henry James, and Meredith"): "The genius of Victorian fiction seems to be making its magnificent best of an essentially bad job. But it is never possible to say of Henry James that he is making the best of a bad job. In all the long stretch of 'The Wings of the Dove' and 'The Ambassadors' there is not the hint of a yawn, not a sign of condescension. The novel is his job. It is the appropriate form for what he has to say. It wins a beauty from that fact—a fine and noble beauty—which it has never worn before."

The holograph manuscript of this review intensifies both the positive and the negative elements of Woolf's view of James and also provides a heightened view of Woolf's sense of generational succession and rivalry. We find in the holograph many halting attempts to describe James's superiority. For example, Woolf writes that "the reader who has followed the progress of the theme as it passes from mind to mind through the century & a half in which it has been in existence will be forced to conclude that Henry James told his chapter of it more perfectly than any of his predecessors," then that "the last chapter . . . which Henry James told in the Ambassadors & the Wings of a Dove, was . . . the best in its telling of all," then that the same novels "pass the old boundaries, & suggest possibilities which the future must explore." [31] Even in these laudatory formulations, Woolf's resistance can be felt in her sense of compulsion—"will be *forced* to conclude," "*must* explore." In the manuscript, furthermore, Woolf initially expresses reservations about James in her own voice, not in that of an anonymous "some one" who "rises to protest." So she writes that "our feeling about Henry James is that he would have been a greater artist had he been less of a craftsman. . . . there is some obstacle in the way of finding it [the emotion] in the Wings of the Dove" and "we blame that very 'research into the theory of the art' which Mr. Lubbock advocates," for James "has sought a method at the expense of his emotions." There is perhaps some irony in Woolf's setting forth in this review what Harvena Richter rightly notes is the central precept of Woolf's own art of fiction—that "the 'book itself' is not the form which you see, but the emotion which you feel"—in opposition to Henry James, who eloquently argues in the Preface to *The Portrait of a Lady* (read, or, more probably, reread, by Woolf in 1934) that the "germs" of one's novels are the very "breath of life," that "the worth of a given subject" arises from its being "the result of some direct impression or perception of life," and that there is a "perfect dependence of the 'moral' sense of a work of art on the amount of felt life concerned in producing it." [32]

At the beginning of the published review, Woolf introduces the familial metaphor for literary succession. She notes that in reprinting Austen, the Brontës, and Meredith, her own generation of Georgians is "turning for solace and guidance not to their parents who are alive, but to their grandparents who are dead." (Literally, of course, Woolf's parents *are* dead, and the Victorians to whom she

pictures the contemporary reader turning—Meredith and Henry
James in particular—are of her parents' generation, indeed are of
their personal circle, and not of her grandparents'.) The incremen-
tal achievement across generations that she sketches in the review
("The late-comer [Henry James] improves upon the pioneers") is a
progression that allows us to speak "of infancy, of youth, and of
maturity." Implicit here is some anxiety that one may belong to a
generation past the mature prime of the art, condemned to look back
upon the "perfection" achieved by Henry James and by Flaubert
with a crippling, crippled, even senescent admiration, which is perhaps why Woolf defensively closes the review with a prevision of
new, vigorous development in the art of fiction: "Mr. Lubbock pru-
dently carries his survey no farther than the novels of Henry James.
But already the years have mounted up. We may expect the novel to
change and develop as it is explored by the most vigorous minds
of a very complex age. What have we not, indeed, to expect from
M. Proust alone?"—or from Virginia Woolf? In the holograph
draft, the richness and the burden of literary succession and inheri-
tance are intensified, for there, surveying the developing tradition,
"we feel like people admitted to watch an experiment which after
endless miscalculating finally succeeds in producing the perfect
product":

> & if we watch them at work we shall see that Tolstoy Flaubert & the
> others always take over some bequest from their forerunners, used it,
> explored it, & handed on to their successors in the art. We see, too,
> that the novelist tends to "shed his privileges." The direction of the
> art is towards strictness & economy. And yet the successors tend
> to "shed their privileges" with the object of giving their story the
> utmost effectiveness. And if Henry James brings the method to per-
> fection, & tells his chapter as well as it can be told, that is by "shed-
> ding his privileges."

If "perfection" and "health" may be equated, and if, as Harold
Bloom writes, "health is stasis"—for "if influence were health, who
could write a poem?"—then we can see why, in the draft, Woolf
first termed the protest against Henry James "a healthy one." It is

healthy to protest against the "health" of perfection, for to do so, paradoxically, is to resist the disease of influence, to fight, to engage with, the Jamesian "influenza," in an attempt to clear an imaginative space for one's own creative structures and strategies.[33]

There are at least twenty-five additional documents of the 1920s in which Woolf mentions Henry James. Since, however, I want to move on fairly quickly to the end of the decade, to another case—a far more extraordinary one than that of "On Re-Reading Novels"—of divergence between what Woolf drafted on James and what she published, I will make brief mention of just a few of them here, relegating the rest to a footnote at the end of this paragraph. Once again belying her denial that James's style infected her own, Woolf confided to her diary in late 1924, "No doubt Proust could say what I mean—that great writer whom I cannot read when I'm correcting, so persuasive is he. He makes it seem easy to write well; which only means that one is slipping along on borrowed skates. So Henry James gives one an unreal impetus; witness my writing after reading him" (*DVW* 2 : 322). In an essay published four days later, Woolf writes that Sir Walter Scott had "entirely ceased to influence others," that "the most impressionable beginner, whose pen oscillates if exposed within a mile of the influence of Stendahl, Flaubert, Henry James, or Checkov, can read the Waverley Novels one after another without altering an adjective."[34] I would stress that Henry James is the only one of these influential writers whose language is English—though one recalls, also, Woolf's similar thought about Mrs. Humphrey Ward (*DVW* 2 : 211)—and I would adduce in support of my argument that James was the writer whose work most troublesomely haunted Woolf a recollection offered by Quentin Bell: "my aunt did once say to me that she found no author more difficult to forget than James, that is to say that when she was writing she found that traces of his style remained with her when she had been reading him and this I think was quite a serious embarrassment."[35] Commenting on her meeting with Lord Ivor Churchill in 1926, she observes that he "by the bye, had read neither Henry James nor V. W." (*DVW* 3 : 68). Finally, in her review of E. M. Forster's *Aspects of the Novel*—titled "Is Fiction an Art?" for the

New York *Herald Tribune* but revised and reprinted a month later in the *Nation & Athenaeum* with the Jamesian title "The Art of Fiction"—Woolf defended James against what she called Forster's "notably harsh judgment" that James sacrifices life to form. "Why," she asks, "is the pleasure that we get from the pattern in *The Golden Bowl* less valuable than the emotion which Trollope gives us when he describes a lady drinking tea in a parsonage?" (*CE* 2:53). But two years later, as we shall see shortly, she sided with Forster on the same issue.[36]

III

"Phases of Fiction" is Virginia Woolf's longest critical essay and her most ambitious attempt to set forth a theory of fiction. It was first planned, in 1925, to be a book in a series, "Hogarth Lectures on Literature." Woolf struggled with it for years, set the project aside when she was drafting *To the Lighthouse,* gladly abandoned it for the ecstatic composition of *Orlando* in the last months of 1927, and pronounced it, when it was done and appearing in three installments in the *Bookman* in the spring of 1929, "my most hated book" (*LVW*, 4:55). Although Woolf was "never," according to Vijay Sharma, "pushed into criticism," she felt that she had been forced to write "Phases of Fiction," calling it "that bloody book which Dadie [George Rylands] and Leonard extort, drop by drop, from my breast" (*LVW* 3:428).[37] Similarly, in a diary entry, she called the just completed "Phases" "a book I hate; & was, as I think, wrongly pressed to undertake" (*DVW* 3:227). On the other hand, the day after she recorded having "just finished, very provisionally 'Phases of Fiction,'" in December 1928, she termed it "rather an interesting little book," though "I cannot get my mind down on to it, like a bird of prey firmly attached" (*DVW* 3:210, 211). Sometimes, in fact, the impetus for the book did seem to come from within, not from the coercive Rylands and Leonard: "I want," she wrote in May 1928, "to write some very closely reasoned criticism; book on fiction" (*DVW* 3:185), and eighteen months before that (February 5, 1927) she told Vita Sackville-West, "I've suddenly become absorbed in a book about reading novels, and can't stop making phrases" (*LVW* 3:325). Seven months later (August 22, 1927) she wrote to Vita that the book was "dull, dreary, long winded assinine" (*LVW* 3:412).

The radical fluctuations of Woolf's view of "Phases of Fiction" and the violence of her final feeling of hatred for the essay want explaining; so does its having been virtually ignored by commentators on Woolf.[38] For Woolf, the answer may lie in part in the scope of the essay. It may have been too ambitious. It was, after all, to be a book. And it therefore required sustained attention and a great deal of directed rereading of novels that interfered with Woolf's work on her own fiction and that did not consort well with her bent for letting curiosity and review assignments direct her reading; the broad-ranging anatomy of fiction she attempts in "Phases" really called for a lengthy and detailed program of study. She seems to me to betray some sense of the uncongeniality of the project when she notes, "It is a hand to mouth book. I scribble down whatever I can think of about Romance, Dickens &c. must hastily [?] gorge on Jane Austen tonight & dish up something tomorrow. All this criticism however may well be dislodged by the desire to write a story" (*DVW* 3:190). For the critics, perhaps the answer lies in the prolixity of the essay. Despite its division of the subject into categorical groupings of novelists ("The Truth-Tellers," "The Romantics," "The Character-mongers and Comedians," "The Psychologists," "The Satirists and Fantastics," and "The Poets"), it is a rambling, a loose and baggy, piece, one might say, compared to Woolf's briefer literary essays and reviews. And since Woolf says little in "Phases" that she does not say elsewhere as well, in shorter, tighter essays, why indeed should commentators have paid this one more heed, particularly in view of Woolf's condemnation of the piece?

Woolf's comments on Henry James in "Phases of Fiction" may seem to add little to what she has said about James before. Treating James with Dostoesvsky and Proust as one of "The Psychologists" and focusing on *What Maisie Knew*, Woolf sounds her by-now familiar, dissonant chord of praise and blame. Because in James we have "left every world"; because James turns "the visual sense" away from the external and material in order "to illumine the mind within" and consequently works with "intellectual imagery" "to make concrete a mental state"; because his method invites the reader into a process of analysis requiring "mental nimbleness and dexterity"; and because his mediated presentation of his heroine, Maisie, distances her from the reader; the pleasure we derive from James is "less direct" than what we get from Dickens, Eliot, and Austen. But that pleasure "has a fineness, a sweetness, which the more direct writers fail to give us," for "a thousand emotional veins and streaks are perceptible in this twilight or dawn which are lost in the full light of midday."[39] By freeing the reader from "the perpetual demand" "that we shall feel with his characters," James affords us a further pleasure when "we see the mind at work; we are amused by its power to make patterns; by its power to bring out relations . . . and disparities. . . . It is a pleasure somewhat akin, perhaps, to the pleasure of mathematics or the pleasure of music" ("Phases 2" 275–76).

Madeline Moore says that Woolf tells us in this description "how the good novelist frees the reader to be aware of the process of consciousness."[40] Yes: yet Woolf goes on immediately to make the same charge against which she had defended James in her review of *Aspects of the Novel,* that he sacrifices life and feeling to an abstract formalism: "through a feeling of timidity or prudery or through a lack of imaginative audacity, Henry James diminishes the interest and importance of his subject in order to bring about a symmetry which is dear to him. . . . We feel him there, as the suave showman, skilfully manipulating his characters; nipping, repressing; dexterously evading and ignoring, where a writer of greater depth or natural spirits would have taken the risk which his material imposes, let his sails blow full and so, perhaps, achieved symmetry and pattern, in themselves so delightful, all the same" ("Phases 2" 276). What this amounts to, a bit later on, is summed up marvelously in Woolf's observation that "Henry James himself, the American, ill at ease for all his magnificent urbanity in a strange civilization, was an obstacle never perfectly assimilated even by the juices of his own art." James blazes the trail for Proust: "But it is the measure of Henry

James's greatness that he has given us so definite a world, so distinct and peculiar a beauty that we cannot rest satisfied but want to experiment further with these extraordinary perceptions, to understand more and more, but to be free from the perpetual tutelage of this author's presence, his arrangements, his anxieties. To gratify this desire, naturally, we turn to the work of Proust" ("Phases 2" 276).

Woolf swerves back and forth through admiration and reservation. Though she includes James in a fictional school essential to her own endeavor as a novelist, that of "The Psychologists," she glories more in the other two authors she classifies with him, Proust and Dostoyevsky. James is the only writer in English whom Woolf places in this line. Of course, she had been ecstatic about Proust from her first encounter with *A la recherche du temps perdu*. For a reason that she voiced to herself, she could acknowledge Proust and yet defend herself against his influence, and Dostoyevsky's—for the same reason that James Joyce could comfortably avow high regard for Ibsen and Flaubert—because of their foreign language and traditions. "I wonder," she wrote in February 1923, "if this next lap [of her return to fiction] will be influenced by Proust? I think his French language, tradition, &c, prevents that: yet his command of every resource is so extravagant that one can hardly fail to profit, & must not flinch, through cowardice" (*DVW* 2:234).

Among several lengthy drafts of "Phases of Fiction," there are some half-dozen typescript pages with an extraordinary passage that does not correspond in any simple way to any part of the published essay, where the closest thing we find is the turn toward the end from synchronic anatomy to diachronic narrative. The distance we have traveled with Woolf in her survey of various types of fiction is at last presented in the published piece as unfolding in time: "But a shadow next falls upon that bright prospect [the "bright prospect" is Austen's reduction of the giants and dwarfs of romance to "perfectly proportioned and normal men and women," of "the chaotic world to English parsonage, shrubberies and lawns"], distorting the lovely harmony of its proportions. The shadow of our own minds has fallen upon it and gradually we have drawn within, and gone exploring with Henry James endless filaments of feeling and relationship in which men and women are enmeshed, and so we have been led on with Dostoyevsky to descend miles and miles into the deep and yeasty surges of the soul. At last Proust brings the light of an immensely civilized and saturated intelligence to bear upon this chaos and reveals the infinite range and complexity of human sensibility."[41] Again, James is featured as a transitional figure.

The passage I have just quoted, it appears, is the only vestige of the unpublished manuscript pages, of which I will give here nearly five in full, not only because they have never been printed and are central to my argument about Woolf and James but also because they contain one of Woolf's most revealing and insightful statements about the development of the novel and about changing modes of representation and because they have important implications for reading other essays by Woolf, notably "Mr. Bennett and Mrs. Brown." In addition, no one who has written about the Woolf-James relation seems to have known about Woolf's near-apotheosis of James in this manuscript passage.[42] In the quotation, angle brackets ⟨ ⟩ enclose Woolf's handwritten additions to the typescript and braces { } enclose her still legible deletions; I leave intact Woolf's typographical errors (without cluttering the text with *sics*) because they are sometimes ambiguous: is "floyts" *floats, flouts,* or something else?

> Again and again we say that it is the novel that does not suit these men of genius [Meredith and Hardy].
> What had happened, it may be, was something of this sort. Fiction we say, is closely attached to human charac and changes with the changes that take place in it. As the nineteenth cntury drew on the most gifted and most sensitive of its ⟨w⟩riters George Eliot, Meredith, Hardy, Henry James to some extent—were all ⟨a⟩ware of some new development in th⟨e⟩ human outlook. Was it that the old faiths had become transparent? Was it that the balance of thought and action had altered? Was it that contemplation had become more interesting than doing? Was it the influence of the Russian novelists ⟨becoming felt by⟩ {upon} the English? At any rate li[f]e no longer ended happily with a mariage or tragically with death ofn a battlefield. It was useless any longer to prtend that stories were interting, for what hap-

pens is not interesting; it is the reason ⟨or the unreason⟩ of what happens {or the unreason} that are interesting. Hence Hardy replaced the simple narrative of every day which trollo[p]e and jane aust n had followed at soeasy a pace with leaps and jumps of violent melodrama. These deaths and coincidences serve to symbolise the complete monstrosity of human life; for that is much more apparent to him than the reasonable order which life follws on the surface. And so too meredith distorts and crumples up the petty narrative of daily life and creates a bastard aristorcracy remot from vulgar habits and ⟨which⟩ {spouting a high strange tongue} and floyts the smooth progress of human events as high ahandedly as any dramatist. For so he can achieve poetry, intesnity, the arib arbitray heaping up of moments of passion. {Even while we adm ire their books we repeat} And feeling the strai, the distortion we say even while we admire their books, Meredith and Hardy are poets and not nov⟨e⟩lists; George Eliot was a thinker; she had not the specific powcr of the novelist.

But if we look more closely and compare these late nineteenth century hybrids with those whom we may call the classic novelists— Jane Austen, Trollope, Tolstoi—we shall come to see that the strain and discord are not the result of innovation—for theyc were all trying to express something new in the novel; but of compromise; ⟨—⟩ for None of them went far enough. The central figure they felt had changed; Jude the Obscure had feelings and needs that h were unknown to his predesccors; but they kept him and his like tethered to a world of convention which had not changed. The strain and the discord are the result of that conflict. The character wanted to ponder to loiter, to think to reason; often to wait lost in the analysis of his own sensations. But the novel decreed that ne must get up and go into dinner; that he must fall in love; his love a firas [affairs] must engross his attention; there must be a marriage or a catstrophe on the la t page.

And one might argue, what we have just said about the classic novels proves that this was indeed a necessity. The novel has a certain nature, a certain character. It requires a particular orinetation - some special poise and balance between the inner and the outer— in order that it shall produce its finest effects. At least the novel was brought to perfection by writers who obeyed the law that there should be a certain balance between thought and action, a certain time , a certain gradual development of character . . Destroy what it is con eneint to call a convention, and you destroy the novel; as these unsatisfactory books — Th e Beauchamps Careers, the Jude the Obscures amply testify. In support of this criticism, one might point to t the fact that Hardy himself ceased to write fiction and turned to poetry; and that Meredith also gave the first place in his affections ⟨illegible handwritten interpolation⟩ to his poetry.

But just as we are about to conclude that the novel was wrecked about 1900 (if a date is any help to us) ⟨about 1900⟩ and that nothing more can be expected of it, we rememberr Henry james. Surely in those later difficult books some amalgamation, some orientation has been discovered. He had not Hardys poetic genius; he had not Merediths intellectual vitality—that may be; but his novels are satisfactory and complete in a way that theirs are not. In the Wings of a Dove or The Ambassadors there is no violent disruption as in the others; Milly has dominated her world and brought it into harmony with herself as certainly as Moll Flanders or Clarissa Harlow dominated and harmonised their worlds. These huge tight-stuffed rather airless b ooks of henry james are in truth the bridge upon whch we cross from th classic novel which is perfect of its kind to that other form   f literature which if names have any importance shoul someday be christened anew—the modern novel, the novel of the twentieth century. For though the new orientation which henry james brought bout was limited—it serves we feel only to express one type of mind, one type of character—he showed that it was possible to bring about a new relation without any compromise. And therefore his books have ammagnificent unity, are in harmony throughout. Thog we may criticise what he is doing, we never feel that he is being forced to do it against his will. He has the same mastery {in} ⟨over⟩ his world that Tolstoi has {in} ⟨over⟩ his.

It remained for a greater writer, {inhe} ⟨who {iner inher} inherited much that James had discovered with too great effort to pass on to a much greater triumph. It was left to Proust to bring into relation between the covers of one vast novel the modern character and the modern world.[43]

In some respects this is the most superlative praise Woolf ever bestowed on Henry James. It makes him the supreme pioneer of the modern. It compares him to Tolstoy, whom Woolf calls, both in the drafts and in the published essay, "the greatest of novelists" ("Phases 2" 271). Here Woolf attributes to James, moreover, an achievement that she grants him nowhere else, the discovery of a new mode of fiction that was perfectly accommodated to the momentous changes in human character that Woolf dates here at the turn of the century. Hardy could not make the transition, and Meredith and George Eliot could not. Henry James did, and that is why his major-phase novels are "in truth the bridge upon whch we cross" to "the modern novel, the novel of the twentieth century."

Why did Woolf suppress this passage? The pages from which it is drawn seem to be the only ones surviving from what I conjecture might have been a very differently framed version of "Phases of Fiction" (and probably a quite long one, since these pages are numbered from 87 through 91). The suppressed pages have some points of resonance with the published sections on "The Psychologists" and "The Poets," as well as with the brief published passage in which the shadow of our own minds falls on the "bright prospect" and we go exploring the dark corridors of consciousness with Henry James. But the unpublished pages are distinctive in their historical orientation, in their insistence on chronology and even on dating ("about 1900"). We know that Woolf struggled with the form of her essay; she even drafted part of a fictionalized version of it, "Notes of a Day's Walk." In that version, as we noted in the preceding chapter, she wrote, "an interesting book might be written upon influence how some writers are far more infectious than others. They [*sic*] young can hardly read ~~Meredith~~ Henry James or Mere[d]ith without copying them." If there was a version of "Phases" that was chronological in its organization, then Woolf may have abandoned it precisely because the historical dimension would have brought her anxiety of influence too close to the surface and also because, more specifically, Henry James played too prominent a role in the development thus highlighted. If, moreover, Woolf did abandon a version of the essay that cut too close to the bone of her anxiety about the influence of powerful predecessors and about her own place in the history of fiction, then her feelings about having flinched from such an investigation may help to account for the violent dislike she came to feel toward the essay in the taxonomic form she at last resorted to for it.

Finally, the suppressed pages from "Phases of Fiction" cast an interesting light on passages in other essays by Woolf, including ones where James is conspicuously absent. For instance, these pages present an interesting contrast with the description of James in "On Re-Reading Novels"; in the Lubbock review, James is the culmination and the perfection of the history of the novel, whereas in the unpublished "Phases" pages he is transitional, "the bridge" to the modern, not an end point in a line of development but a junction between two distinct modes of art and of consciousness. Woolf's famous essay "Mr. Bennett and Mrs. Brown" glaringly omits any mention of Henry James, as many readers must have noticed.[44] Why? Why does Woolf say there that the year of the change in human character so momentous for fiction was 1910, not 1900? Why does she state that "the men and women who began writing novels in 1910 . . . had this great difficulty to face—that there was no English novelist living from whom they could learn their business" and that "the most prominent and successful novelists in the year 1910 were, I suppose, Mr. Wells, Mr. Bennett, and Mr. Galsworthy" when she knew perfectly well that in 1910 Henry James was the most prominent living author of novels in English (if he was not, strictly speaking, an English novelist)?[45] Even without the unpublished pages of "Phases," one might have suggested that Woolf left James out of "Mr. Bennett and Mrs. Brown" as a repression symptomatic of the anxiety of influence she felt about him, and that she set the change in character in 1910 because all of James's great novels had been published by then. The pages Woolf chose to keep out of "Phases of Fiction" allow us to make the same suggestion about "Mr. Bennett and Mrs. Brown" much more emphatically. The date of the change might have been set in 1900, as Woolf sets it in the "Phases" manuscript, but then she would have had to give James his due, as she does in the unpublished pages. The 1910 date, moreover, not only is offered in a context that ignores James, but it also puts the novels of James's major phase on the premodern side of the divide. In 1924, the original date of "Mr. Bennett and Mrs. Brown," the attraction of setting the mark at 1910 may have been enhanced by that year's importance as the transition from the Edwardian to the Georgian era and as the date of Roger Fry's first Postimpressionist exhibit. But in the late twenties, as the "Phases" manuscript makes clear, Woolf saw that to acknowledge Henry James as the bridge to the modern, one had to set back the momentous year by a decade. Having uncovered the "Phases" manuscript, we can read James's absence in "Mr. Bennett and Mrs. Brown" as intensifying his presence there, the way Mrs. Newsome's absence in James's *The Ambassadors* intensifies her presence for Strether.

One final note about "Phases of Fiction" apropos of *The Ambassadors*. During her composition of "Phases," Woolf published "The Narrow Bridge of Art," an important essay that articulates a rationale for the experiments she would undertake in *The Waves*. The novel of the future that Woolf projects in "The Narrow Bridge of Art" will "give not only or mainly people's relations to each other and their activities together, as the novel has hitherto done, but it will give the relation of the mind to general ideas and its soliloquy in solitude." The novel that is mainly of "people's relations to each other" Woolf assigns in the same paragraph to the province of "the psychological novelist." We might surmise that she has James in mind, though she does not name him in this essay, by virtue of her having made James, in the section of "Phases" on "The Psychologists," the only writer in English. This surmise becomes a near certainty when we hear Woolf's echo of James in her declaration of weariness with the psychologists: "The psychological novelist has been too prone to limit psychology to the psychology of personal intercourse; we long sometimes to escape from the incessant, the remorseless analysis of falling into love and falling out of love, of what Tom feels for Judith and Judith does or does not altogether feel for Tom. We long for some more impersonal relationship. We long for ideas, for dreams, for imaginations, for poetry."[46] Woolf's "remorseless analysis" is a clear echo of a phrase that echoes again and again in a dialogue early in *The Ambassadors*:

"And you should hear," she [Miss Gostrey] added, "the ease *I* take—and I above all intend to take—with Mr. Waymarsh."

Strether thought. "About *me?* Ah that's no equivalent. The equivalent would be Waymarsh's himself serving me up—his remorseless analysis of me. And he'll never do that"—he was sadly clear. "He'll never remorselessly analyse me." He quite held her with the authority of this. "He'll never say a word to you about me."

She took it in; she did it justice; yet after an instant her reason, her restless irony, disposed of it. "Of course he won't. For what do you take people, that they're able to say words about anything, able remorselessly to analyse?"[47]

In other words, "Phases of Fiction" can help us to see that an important covert subtext of "The Narrow Bridge of Art" is that Woolf offers an early formulation of her project for *The Waves,* giving the mind's "soliloquy in solitude," in sharp contradistinction to the interpersonal world of Henry James's fiction.

To close this chapter, I want to give a few of Woolf's most important comments on James after "Phases of Fiction" (saving the rest for the footnote at the end of the chapter) so that we can move on quickly to consideration of the ways in which her fiction inscribes, as it develops, her responses to Henry James. In 1933, in Siena, Woolf made one of her finest observations about Henry James:

Yes I am reading—skipping—the Sacred Fount—about the most inappropriate of all books for this din—sitting by the open window, looking across heads & heads & heads—all Siena parading in gray & pink & the cars hooting. How finely run along those involuted threads? I don't—thats the answer. I let 'em break. I only mark that the sign of a masterly writer is his power to break his mould callously. None of H. J.'s timid imitators have the vigour, once they've spun their sentence, to smash it. He has some native juice—figure; has driven his spoon deep into some stew of his own—some swarming mixture. That—his vitality—his vernacular—his pounce & grip & swing always spring fresh upon me, if at the same time I ask how could anyone, outside an orchis in a greenhouse, fabricate such an orchid's dream! Oh these Edwardian ladies with pale hair, these

tailored "my dear men"! Yet compared to that vulgar old brute
Creevey—L. is here bitten by a flea—H. J. is muscular, lean. (*DVW*
4 : 157)

Woolf balances her recognition of James's vital "pounce & grip &
swing" with the effete image of the novelist as hothouse flower. It is
the same old ambivalence, but what strikes me as sharper here than
anything we have seen before is Woolf's recognition of James's masterly experimental power "to break his mould carelessly." Woolf's
description here of James's "stew of his own," moreover, may well
arise from her recollection of his description (in a letter to H. G.
Wells of which we have already taken note) of "the great stewpot or
crucible of the imagination."[48] The following year, Woolf linked
James's modernity to his having "of course receded further and further from the spoken word" (meaning that he used dialogue less
and less, not that he became any less "vernacular" than what she
had observed in *The Sacred Fount*); James "finally I think only used
dialogue when he wanted a very high light" (*LVW* 5 : 335).

In 1935 she wrote twice to Stephen Spender about his newly published book *The Destructive Element,* a study of modern literature
and culture that centers on Henry James. Spender emphasizes the
moral and political dimensions of James's achievement, for "James
was a very great artist if only because the suffering of his characters
was not born of self-pity; it was an intuition, and it was true. His
artistic creations have a kind of awareness which is deeper than his
own consciousness; they knew what the years were all the while
meaning. And we, in these later times, are inundated by the meaning. It is the business of certain writers not to escape it."[49] Woolf
praised Spender for the James discussion, calling it "very hard and
genuine. . . . I suspect you are quite right about his development,
and it puts him in a new light," but "the last part of the book, about
the living writers and Lawrence, seems to me more doubtful," no
doubt in part because Spender mentions Woolf only twice, once in a
clearly belittling way (*LVW* 5 : 407).[50] In any case, Woolf wrote to
Spender early in the summer; before the season was over, she gave a

title, *The Years,* to the novel she had been working on for nearly three years (see *DVW* 4:338). I believe that Woolf probably took the title from Spender's description of James's creations, who "knew what the years were all the while *meaning.*" She herself was writing at a time of crisis: the day before the diary entry in which she first mentions *The Years* as a title, she wrote, in reference to Mussolini's territorial designs on Abyssinia, "The most critical day since Aug 4th 1914. So the papers say" (*DVW* 4:337). As a reviewer of Lubbock's edition of Henry James's letters, moreover, Woolf would have been able to recognize Spender's "they knew what the years were all the while *meaning*" as an allusion to what Henry James wrote in a letter bearing the watershed date August 4, 1914: "The plunge of civilization into this abyss of blood and darkness . . . is a thing that so gives away the whole long age during which we have supposed the world to be, with whatever abatement, gradually bettering, that to have to take it all now for what the treacherous years were all the while really making for and *meaning* is too tragic for any words."[51]

We have already mentioned, in the previous chapter, Woolf's 1939 comparison of James and Dickens in which James seems to come off better but to which Woolf appends, "these are influenza musings" (*DVW* 5:215), and also the passage in "The Leaning Tower" in which Woolf moves from the germ-of-genius/influenza analogy to the progression from Scott to James as exemplifying the mysteries of influence and finally to a family-romance trope for literary succession. In "The Leaning Tower" (originally a paper read in May 1940 to the Workers' Educational Association, Brighton), James is presented as the culmination, for writers of Woolf's generation, of the "great tradition": "Put a page of their writing under the magnifying-glass and you will see, far away in the distance, the Greeks, the Romans; coming nearer, the Elizabethans; coming nearer still, Dryden, Swift, Voltaire, Jane Austen, Dickens, Henry James" (*CE* 2:170). In a diary entry about her work on this paper, she noted of the next literary generation, "the leaning tower" generation of 1925–39, "They haven't explored, like H. James, the individual; they haven't deepened; theyve cut the outline sharper." And just before these sentences, she observed, "they have demolished the romance of 'genius' of the great man, by diminishing themselves" (*DVW* 5:267). And now we are at last ready to turn in the next chapter to the stratagems Woolf used in her fiction to keep from being diminished or demolished herself by the genius of Henry James.[52]

Chapter Five

A Stew of One's Own:
Virginia Woolf's Fiction and
the Burden of Henry James

I

"The transition from the old to the new," writes Harvena Richter, "from a stable world dealing with absolutes to one committed to the present moment of feeling, was visualized by Virginia Woolf as 'the narrow bridge of art' across which the writer must pass, re-nouncing old methods and taking with him very few of his former tools."[1] But as we have discovered in the suppressed manuscript pages of "Phases of Fiction," the late novels of "henry james are in truth the bridge," and even in the essay "The Narrow Bridge of Art" Woolf's unnamed antagonist is Henry James, the acme of the "remorseless analysis" of the older psychological novel that Woolf hoped she would supersede with a new form of fiction.

Woolf was bent on originality from the beginning to the end of her career. Responding in 1909 to Clive Bell's critique of an early draft of *The Voyage Out* (then titled *Melymbrosia*) Woolf made *difference* from other writers the aim and rationale of her art. Bell had told her, "I think you should be careful not to wonder how some other novelist would have written your book,—as if he could have written it!"[2] Woolf replied, "I admit the justice of your hint that sometimes I have had an inkling of the way the book might be written by other people. It is very difficult to fight against it; as diffi-cult as to ignore the opinion of one's probable readers—I think I gather courage as I go on. The only possible reason for writing down all this, is that it represents roughly a view of one's own. My boldness terrifies me" (*LVW* 1:383). A similar declaration in December 1940, within three months of her death, makes clear how Woolf's drive for differentiation is powered by her anxious awareness of other writers and also how that drive is impelled by her consciousness of gender: "I actually opened Matthew Arnold & copied these lines [*from 'Thyrsis'*]. While doing so, the idea came to me that why I dislike, & like, so many things idiosyncratically now, is because of my growing detachment from the hierarchy, the patriarchy. When Desmond praises East Coker [T. S. Eliot's poem had been published in the spring], & I am jealous, I walk over the marsh saying, I am I; & must follow that furrow, not copy another. That is the only justification for my writing & living" (*DVW* 5 : 347). What she most admired in Henry James in 1933, as we have seen, is that he had "driven his spoon deep into some stew of his own" (*DVW* 4 : 157).

Louise DeSalvo suggests that the 1909 phrase "a view of one's own" reflects the impression Forster's *A Room with a View* had made on Woolf. "Mostly," says Phyllis Rose of *The Voyage Out*, "she was trying to write like Conrad, to some extent like E. M. Forster."[3] But though there are some parallels between Forster's chronicle of Lucy Honeychurch and Woolf's of Rachel Vinrace, and though Conrad's influence marks the intense, occasionally purple descriptions of sea, jungle, and tropical river in *The Voyage Out*, the influence above all others against which Woolf was finding it very difficult to fight as she drafted and redrafted her first novel was that of Henry James. Given that the novel was undertaken some time— we are not sure precisely when—after her 1905 judgment that "there is no living novelist whose standard is higher [than Henry James's], or whose achievement is so consistently great," some time, furthermore, between her expectation of 1907 that, when "old and famous," she would "discourse like Henry James" and her recollection of 1909 that she had said that her "view of life was that of a Henry James novel," we should not be surprised to find throughout *The Voyage Out* traces of James and of Woolf's resistance to him.

There are passages in *The Voyage Out* that seem Jamesian in style, tone, and subject matter. For example, the satiric description of Rachel Vinrace's education resembles the description of Isabel

Archer's education in *The Portrait of a Lady,* though Woolf's account is colored by a barely submerged bitterness and rage that one does not find in Henry James. Of Rachel, Woolf writes, "there was no subject in the world which she knew accurately. Her mind was in the state of an intelligent man's in the beginning of the reign of Queen Elizabeth; she would believe practically anything she was told, invent reasons for anything she said." Rachel's "one definite gift," her musical ability, is "surrounded by dreams and ideas of the most extravagant and foolish description" (*VO* 34). Of Isabel Archer, James writes, "her errors and delusions were frequently such as a biographer interested in preserving the dignity of his subject must shrink from specifying. Her thoughts were a tangle of vague outlines which had never been corrected by the judgement of people speaking with authority. In matters of opinion she had had her own way, and it had led her into a thousand ridiculous zigzags" (*PL2* 1 : 67).[4] Similarly, Woolf's narrator is given to generalizing epigrams reminiscent of those delivered by James's narrators during his middle period. For instance, Woolf's narrator observes that "the preliminary discomforts and harshness, which generally make the first days of a sea voyage so cheerless and trying to the temper, being somehow lived through, the succeeding days passed pleasantly enough" (*VO* 31); at another point the narrator comments, "Whether the flimsiness of foreign sheets [newspapers] and the coarseness of their type is any proof of frivolity and ignorance, there is no doubt that English people scarcely consider news read there as news" (*VO* 112). Narratorial stance and tone in these examples are similar to James's in *The Portrait of a Lady;* they recall the opening sentence of that novel, "Under certain circumstances there are few hours in life more agreeable than the hour dedicated to the ceremony known as afternoon tea" (*PL2* 1 : 1) and sentences such as this: "It is the good fortune of a man who for the greater part of a lifetime has abstained without effort from making himself disagreeable to his friends, that when the need comes for such a course it is not discredited by irritating associations" (*PL2* 1 : 146).

But such local parallels are less to the point than the broad structural and thematic resonances between Virginia's Woolf's first novel

and a considerable body of fiction by Henry James. Like many of
James's novels and tales, *The Voyage Out* is a quest for experience
involving a transatlantic voyage. Woolf's Rachel Vinrace is typical
of the protagonists of James's fictions in this mode—a youthful in-
nocent who will, in James's words about Isabel Archer, "affront
[her] destiny" (*PL2* 1:xiii). Like many of James's young women,
Rachel has been orphaned; her mother is dead, and her father is
emotionally and intellectually remote on the rare occasions when
he is not absent. Also like many of James's young women, Rachel
consequently comes under the tutelage of an older woman; her relation with Helen Ambrose recalls many similar configurations in
James's fiction—for example, Olive Chancellor and Verena Tarrant
in *The Bostonians* (especially in the undercurrent of sexual feeling
between Helen and Rachel); Mrs. Touchett and Isabel, or Madame
Merle and Isabel, in *The Portrait of a Lady;* and Susan Stringham
and Milly Theale in *The Wings of the Dove*. Like Henry James in
The Awkward Age and *What Maisie Knew*, Woolf is engaged in
The Voyage Out with the problems created by a patriarchal order
committed to the imprisoning protection of young, unmarried
women. They must not be unchaperoned. They must not walk out
alone. Above all, they must be protected from any knowledge that
would disturb their virginal purity, ideally a blankness. In *The Voyage Out*, as in *The Awkward Age*, these problems surface in recurrent discussions of recommended reading for young women. The
"modern books, books in shiny yellow covers" that Rachel Vinrace
reads in preference to her Aunt Helen's recommendations of "DeFoe,
Maupassant, or some spacious chronicle of family life" (*VO* 124)
recall the "French novel in blue paper" that Nanda Brookenham
reads in James's *The Awkward Age*, confirming to the fastidious
Vanderbank that she has been too exposed, too unprotected, to be
his bride.[5] Rachel's books are at any rate potentially subversive of
the values embodied in chronicles of family life, suggesting "harsh
wranglings and disputes about facts which had no such importance," in Mrs. Ambrose's view, "as the moderns claimed for them"
(*VO* 124).

The deepest thematic resonances between Woolf's first novel and the world of James's fiction have to do with marriage and with the connection both authors make between love and death. As Phyllis Rose comments, *The Voyage Out* "endorses marriage, intimacy, but its emotional message, its hidden message, is the primacy of the self."[6] Rose's comment might easily be applied to *The Portrait of a Lady,* among other works by James. Marriage in James is almost always unsatisfactory because it is almost always a trap for the free spirit, the "very mill of the conventional" in which Isabel Archer is ground (*PL2* 2:415). James himself chose never to marry. Women were among his closest friends, but he did not want them sexually. And his belief that marriage could be detrimental to an artist is expressed often in his work, most famously in "The Lesson of the Master" and in "The Author of 'Beltraffio.'" Again and again, moreover, the eligible women in his fiction do not marry. Claire de Cintré retreats into the Carmelite convent in *The American.* Catherine Sloper rejects the tarnished suitor on whom she had once set her heart in *Washington Square.* Fleda Vetch renounces Owen Gereth in *The Spoils of Poynton.* And Nanda Brookenham will retire at the end of *The Awkward Age* to an asexual relation with her protector, Mr. Longdon, who belongs to her grandmother's generation.

Virginia Woolf's complex ambivalence about marriage was acted out in her companionable but apparently asexual union with Leonard Woolf and was expressed in a variety of ways throughout her essays and her fiction, especially, as Alex Zwerdling suggests in his helpful recent book on Woolf, in *To the Lighthouse.* Although Woolf's heroine in *The Voyage Out* becomes engaged, she dies as if by her own volition in order to evade the marriage. Phyllis Rose says, "Rachel's illness inevitably seems connected with her engagement to Terence—she withdraws into herself as she always does when threatened." And Madeline Moore observes, "Her capitulation to illness then is the delirious expression of her chosen suicide."[7] In Henry James's *The American,* our sympathies are enlisted on behalf of Newman's courtship of Claire de Cintré, but her living death, in a convent where the nuns' "only human utterance" is a "dirge over their buried affections," may be read as James's assertion that Claire is better off thus immured than she would have been as an object of conspicuous consumption for Christopher Newman, who wants, to perfect his accumulation of capital, "a lovely being perched on the pile." [8] In *The Voyage Out*, we are moved by the loss Terence Hewet suffers and by his anguished expression of that loss—"'Rachel! Rachel!' he shrieked, trying to rush back to her" (*VO* 354)—but Woolf's intense, brilliant representation of Rachel's desire to escape Terence, culminating in her death, may be read as the novelist's assertion that the self is better off not violated by the contingency of another person inevitable in marriage as well as by the system of patriarchal power inscribed in the institution despite the egalitarian intentions of the engaged couple: "All sights were something of an effort, but the sight of Terence was the greatest effort, because he forced her to join mind to body in the desire to remember something. She did not wish to remember; it troubled her when people tried to disturb her loneliness; she wished to be alone. She wished for nothing else in the world" (*VO* 347).

The dark relation between love and death is central to *The Voyage Out;* as de Rougemont makes clear, love/death is a recurrent configuration of Western literature. What is particularly important for the present argument is the strikingly similar forms of the love/death themes in Woolf and James. [9] Woolf would have found variations on the theme throughout Henry James's oeuvre, from his earliest tales (e.g., "The Story of a Year," "A Most Extraordinary Case," and "A Passionate Pilgrim") to his latest (e.g., "The Altar of the Dead"), and from his apprentice novels (e.g., *Roderick Hudson*) through his first indisputably great novels (e.g., *The Portrait of a Lady* [see Joseph Wiesenfarth's argument that the great love scene in the novel is the deathbed dialogue between Ralph Touchett and Isabel]), to his late elegaic masterpiece *The Wings of the Dove*. [10] "Daisy Miller," James's most famous tale of love and death (first published by Woolf's father in the *Cornhill Magazine*), is particularly apt for comparison with *The Voyage Out*. [11] Daisy and Rachel are both young female naïfs. During sojourns abroad where the unfamiliar forces each of them through a hermeneutic process of understanding herself and the world, Daisy and Rachel choose to succumb to disease rather than to submit to the inevitable burden of experience.[12] Each elects a *Liebestod* of her own.

In addition, Daisy and Rachel are both trapped in a social system that bristles with defenses against what the barely repressed imagination of society takes to be the beastial carnality of human beings. The system of chaperonage that Daisy is ostracized for violating is based not only on the belief that young women are sacred objects to be protected from offense but also on the beliefs that they should not be subject to "undue temptation" and that any male given the chance will take advantage of an unguarded young woman.[13] It is a scandal that Daisy walks the streets of Rome with Giovanelli; the implication that she verges on being a streetwalker is barely submerged among her accusers in James's tale. Frederick Newberry, in fact, has argued that James revised the tale for the New York Edition so as to suggest to the reader that when Mrs. Costello calls Daisy a "horror," Winterbourne misunderstands her, hearing "whore" instead.[14] In *The Voyage Out*, Rachel asks Helen Ambrose to tell her, "'what are those women in Piccadilly.' 'In Piccadilly? They are prostitutes,' said Helen. 'It *is* terrifying—it *is* disgusting,' Rachel asserted" (*VO* 81). Then, after this disturbing information has sunk in for a few minutes, Rachel bursts out, "'So that's why I can't walk alone!'" (*VO* 82). One way of explaining Rachel's opting out of life in the end is that she sees no middle ground between the horror attached to walking alone and the loss of independent selfhood entailed in marriage.

Woolf resists James in a variety of ways in *The Voyage Out*. She begins by reversing James's transatlantic direction. She takes her heroine from the Old World to the New, not, as James takes most of his protagonists, from the New to the Old. The exotic South American setting of *The Voyage Out* is in many ways extraneous to the important concerns of the novel. If Rachel Vinrace encountered the Cambridge graduates Hirst and Hewet in an English or European setting, one would see more readily that Woolf is operating on Henry James's turf. That she did not want to seem to do so may account for her use of the superficial structure of Conrad's *Heart of Darkness*—especially apparent in her introducing Rachel aboard the *Euphrosyne* in the Thames estuary and in her making the voyage up the tropical river the climax and the fatal turning-point of Rachel's life. Another reversal of James is in the character of her heroine. For despite the many similarities between Rachel Vinrace and Henry James's young women, particularly his American girls such as Daisy Miller and Isabel Archer, there is one striking difference: James's heroines are utterly (often unjustifiably) confident of themselves and of their own selfhood. They might all declare, with Isabel Archer, "I don't know whether I succeed in expressing myself, but I know that nothing else expresses me" (*PL2* 1:288), whereas poor Rachel is barely beyond William Blake's Thel in her grasp of a nascent, shadowy selfhood. Rachel can only stammer, to Helen Ambrose, "I can be m-m-myself . . . in spite of you, in spite of the Dalloways, and Mr. Pepper, and Father, and my Aunts, in spite of these?" (*VO* 84).[15] On this point, Woolf's portrayal of her heroine seems almost deliberately antithetical to James's.

Woolf also resisted James by letting point of view in her novel jump from character to character in a most un-Jamesian way, not just from paragraph to paragraph but even from sentence to sentence within paragraphs, as in the following leap from Rachel's viewpoint to Terence Hewet's: "'A man,' she repeated, and a curious sense of possession coming over her, it struck her that she might now touch him; she put out her hand and lightly touched his cheek. His fingers followed where hers had been, and the touch of his hand upon his face brought back the overpowering sense of unreality" (*VO* 282). This treatment of point of view recalls her remark to Strachey that Gibbon was "a kind of Henry James" because "he has a point of view & sticks to it" whereas "I wobble" (*DVW* 2:115). Commenting on the remark to Strachey, Virginia Blain writes, "Her 'wobbling' is her ability to undermine the very idea of any centralized moral standpoint, any authoritarian idea of 'omniscience,' by a strategy of continual modulation of tone of voice."[16] More to the point, in my view, is her wobbling from character to character for narrative viewpoint.

Another aspect of *The Voyage Out* that marks Woolf's resistance to James is his absence from the considerable list one might compile

of authors discussed in the bookish talk to which Woolf's characters are given. As we noticed in the last chapter, James was a great
fad among the Cambridge men in Woolf's circle throughout the
years during which she was writing *The Voyage Out*. But the Cambridge men Hirst and Hewet never mention Henry James. Even so,
of the many writers named in the novel, the three most prominently
mentioned are Milton, Jane Austen, and Gibbon—and, as we know,
Woolf associated two of these three, Austen and Gibbon, with Henry
James (for the Austen-James connection, see ch. 4, n. 36). In the as-
piring novelist Hewet, moreover, Woolf created the first of a number
of writers in her fiction who can be linked to Henry James as well as
to herself. Hewet as a writer resembles Woolf in many ways. He
reads "a novel which some one else had written, a process which he
found essential to the composition of his own" (*VO* 295–96), recalling Woolf's strenuous effort to fight against wondering "how
some other novelist would have written" *The Voyage Out*. Hewet
tells Rachel that his aim as an author is "'to write a novel about
Silence, . . . the things people don't say'" (*VO* 216). Phyllis Rose
observes that his aspiration "has frequently been taken as identical
to Woolf's own." [17] But it might as easily be taken as a reformula-
tion of Woolf's 1905 description of *The Golden Bowl:* "The trag-
edy . . . is acted in dumb show. . . . Mr James has a singular power
of intimating what four separate people are thinking and showing
us the silent conflict of their thought without making his character
speak and act." She continued to associate silence with James, remarking in 1921 of *The Turn of the Screw,* "Perhaps it is the silence
that first impresses us." [18] In dying in order to escape marriage to
Hewet, Rachel is escaping a Jamesian character, one whose parallel
with Henry James is nowhere clearer than in the imaginary speech
against marriage Hewet makes to his fiancée: "'I loathe marriage,
I hate its smugness, its safety, its compromise, and the thought of
you interfering in my work, hindering me'" (*VO* 243–44). Hewet
speaks here as though he were a disciple of Henry St. George in
James's "The Lesson of the Master."

In the opening pages of Woolf's second novel, *Night and Day,*
Woolf introduces another novelist, one who resembles Henry James

far more closely than Hewet. When Ralph Denham, the male romantic lead in Woolf's comedy of manners, enters the Hilbery
house on the second page of the novel, "Mr. Fortescue, the eminent
novelist," has just "reached the middle of a very long sentence,"
which he "kept . . . suspended while the newcomer sat down" (*ND*
10). Recalling Woolf's penultimate diary entry—"I mark Henry
James's sentence. Observe perpetually"—Fortescue studies the
heroine of Woolf's novel, Katharine Hilbery, "Observing her for a
moment or two, as novelists are inclined to observe." Then, "lying
back in his chair, with his opaque contemplative eyes fixed on the
ceiling, and the tips of his fingers pressed together," he delivers a
considerable disquisition elaborating Katharine's observation that
"'I should think there would be no one to talk to in Manchester'"
(*ND* 11). Fortescue does not merely talk; resuming conversation, he
builds "up another rounded structure of words" (*ND* 12). After the
fourth page of the novel, Mr. Fortescue, "a considerable celebrity"
(*ND* 11), does not appear again, though Katharine's mother speaks
of him toward the end of the opening chapter: "'The truth is, dear
Mr. Fortescue has almost tired me out. He is so eloquent and so
witty, so searching and so profound that, after half an hour or so, I
feel inclined to turn out all the lights. But perhaps he'd be more
wonderful than ever in the dark'" (*ND* 21). The idea that Fortescue
might be "more wonderful than ever in the dark" is a forecast of
Woolf's memory in "A Sketch of the Past" that James's talk "made
the drawing room seem rich and dusky" (*MB2* 158). Finally, I am
not the only reader who has identified Mr. Fortescue with Henry
James. Paula Smith links the description of Fortescue discoursing
while "lying back in his chair" with Leonard Woolf's anecdote
about Henry James's leaning back as he discoursed during Virginia
Woolf's childhood at Hyde Park Gate:

> I was amused to see that during tea, as he [Henry James, in 1912]
> talked, he gradually tilted back his chair until it was balanced on the
> two back legs, he maintaining equilibrium by just holding on to the
> edge of the table. Now the Stephens had told me that when they were
> children and Henry James came to tea, or some other meal, which he

often did, he had a habit of doing this when he talked. As the long sentences untwined themselves, the chair would tilt slowly backwards and all the children's eyes were fixed on it, fearing and hoping that at last it would overbalance backwards and deposit Henry James on the floor. Time after time he would just recover himself, but then indeed at last it one day happened; the chair went over and the novelist was on the floor, undismayed, unhurt, and after a moment completing his sentence.[19]

Fortescue's long sentences and the aura of performance surrounding his utterances suggest strongly that he is a figure of Henry James, and so does Mrs. Hilbery's epithet "dear Mr. Fortescue," for Bruce Richmond had called James "dear" in deploring Woolf's use of the word *lewd* in "Henry James' Ghost Stories," and Woolf had echoed that appellation ten years afterward in the notes for her speech of January 21, 1931—"Dear old Henry James—he must be praised" (see ch. 4, n. 5, and related text). Finally, when Mrs. Hilbery asks, "'what *is* the present?'" she answers her own question: "'Half of it's the past, and the better half, too, I should say,' she added, turning to Mr. Fortescue" (*ND* 14), for who could better appreciate her observation than Henry James/Fortescue, famous for his "sense of the past" (the phrase echoed in the title of his posthumous novel of 1917)? Had Woolf herself not recognized, in 1917, that "the mellow light which swims over the past . . . seems to have been his [James's] natural atmosphere and his most abiding mood" and that "to Henry James . . . we owe the best relish of the past in our literature"?[20]

Why does Woolf introduce Fortescue in chapter one only to drop him entirely thereafter? It would appear that Woolf has given "the eminent novelist" of *Night and Day* a rather Jamesian characteronym—like, for instance, James's Christopher Newman and Adam Verver—for what *Fortescue* suggests is that Woolf has taken *strong cues* for her second novel from Henry James. James/Fortescue is introduced as a talisman and palimpsest of what Woolf saw—but would not openly acknowledge—as her inescapable literary lineage. Thus Fortescue presides over what David Garnett has recognized as the distinctively Jamesian opening chapters of *Night and Day*.[21] Fortescue appears, furthermore, just as we are introduced to the intense anxiety Woolf's heroine Katharine Hilbery feels about her own literary lineage, an anxiety that closely parallels Woolf's feeling of belonging to a generation of epigones in the shadow of such giant predecessors as George Meredith and Henry James. We recall that in "A Sketch of the Past" Woolf follows her description of James's making "the drawing room seem rich and dusky" with the statement that "I cannot remember ever to have felt greatness since I was a child" (*MB2* 158). Katharine Hilbery is the grandchild of a great poet, Richard Alardyce. Gazing on her grandmother's portrait in chapter one, Katharine dreams of being "the companion of those giant men, of their own lineage, at any rate, and the insignificant present moment was put to shame" (*ND* 16). "Isn't it difficult to live up to your ancestors?" Ralph Denham asks Katharine, and she replies, "I dare say I shouldn't try to write poetry" (*ND* 17). In chapter two, we read that "Katharine had her moments of despondency. The glorious past, in which men and women grew to unexampled size, intruded too much upon the present, and dwarfed it too consistently, to be altogether encouraging to one forced to make her experiment in living when the great age was dead" (*ND* 39). Doubtless Woolf satirizes and criticizes, in these opening chapters and throughout *Night and Day*, the ancestor worship to which the Hilberys submit themselves; Mrs. Hilbery's mawkish literary idolatry in particular is often exposed as silly. But satire and criticism of a fictional equivalent to Woolf's own anxiety about being too much in thrall to the powerful predecessor figured in Fortescue are her main defensive strategies against that anxiety. Because the book was a sustained experiment in the tradition of the novel of manners, *Night and Day* allowed Woolf to essay the conventional forms and formulae of the genre and at the same time to put them behind her. This twofold enterprise guaranteed that the treatment of tradition in *Night and Day*, like Woolf's inveterate treatment of Henry James, would be ambivalent through and through.

When Woolf pokes fun, at the outset of *Night and Day,* at the small room the Hilberys keep as a "religious temple" housing the "relics" of Richard Alardyce (*ND* 15), she implicitly attacks those who make a fetish of literary mastery, doing so in a way that recalls what John Carlos Rowe has recently shown to be Henry James's demolition of fetishized mastery in *The Aspern Papers*.[22] Yet Woolf's emulation of the masters of the novel of manners—and most of all of Henry James—is the most salient aspect of the novel. This emulation led Katherine Mansfield to charge, in Woolf's paraphrase, that Woolf was "a decorous elderly dullard . . . ; Jane Austen up to date" (*DVW* 1:314). Yet, as David Daiches points out, the social comedy reminiscent of Austen in *Night and Day* is after all of considerably less interest to Woolf than the process of introspection, especially in Katharine, who affords Woolf recurrent opportunities to express what Daiches calls "that characteristic interest in a state of mind which is at once emotional and speculative." Daiches also notes that when Woolf was writing *Night and Day* she still felt "that the more intelligent she makes the character the more communicable such states of consciousness in the character can be made."[23] In these respects, Woolf's second novel is far more Jamesian than Austenian; as an introspective young woman of emphasized intelligence, Katharine is a daughter of Isabel Archer and only a granddaughter of Austen's Emma.[24]

The Jamesian traces are so pervasive in *Night and Day* that I can only mention a few of them here. They range from small details to large structural designs. For example, the novel opens with echoes of the names of the principal characters introduced in the first chapter of James's *The Portrait of a Lady,* Katharine's uncle Sir Richard Warburton (*ND* 16) recalling James's Lord Warburton, and her father's protégé (and her future husband) Ralph Denham recalling James's Ralph Touchett, Isabel Archer's cousin. Another character, introduced later, is Katharine's cousin Henry, who, far more closely than Ralph Denham, resembles Henry James's Ralph Touchett, not merely in his cousinly relation to the heroine but also, more particularly, in his stance toward life in general—his "gentle, honest eyes were rather skeptical than glowing" and "he gave the impression that he had not yet found the cause which suited his temperament" (*ND* 197, 198)—and in his deep solicitude for his cousin: "Promise me, Katharine," he says "that if I can ever help you, you will let me" (*ND* 201). He is not named Henry for nothing.

Yet another Jamesian character, the suffragette Mary Datchet (who, with some adjustment for the transposition from London to Boston, would be at home in the world of Miss Birdseye and Dr. Prance in James's *The Bostonians*), may be said to exemplify the way in which James's characteristic vocabulary and themes operate in *Night and Day:* we might note, for instance, Woolf's ascription to Mary of a "moral sense" (*ND* 183), a term practically patented by Henry James and one, moreover, that Woolf included in her reading notes on *The Golden Bowl*.[25] Realizing that Ralph Denham will not love her for herself, Mary Datchet takes the customary course of the Jamesian protagonist (from Claire de Cintré and Christopher Newman, through Fleda Vetch, to Merton Densher and Lambert Strether): she renounces, for though she cannot "take an easy pleasure in the relief of renunciation," she has in fact "renounced everything that made life happy, easy, splendid, individual" (*ND* 261). Later, Katharine weeps "the tears of some profound emotion, happiness, grief, renunciation . . . and Cassandra, bending her head and receiving the tears upon her cheek, accepted them in silence as the consecration of her love" (*ND* 403–4). Mary's feeling "that faith, faith in an illusion, perhaps, but, at any rate, faith in something, was of all gifts the most to be envied" and her emphatic addition that "an illusion it was, no doubt" (*ND* 258) recall Lambert Strether's declaration in *The Ambassadors* that "one has the illusion of freedom; therefore don't be, like me, without the memory of that illusion."[26] Earlier in the novel, another passage seems related to the same famous speech by Strether: "It's life that matters, nothing but life—the process of discovering, the everlasting and perpetual process, . . . not the discovery itself" (*ND* 135), says Katharine to herself, and her words recall Strether's exhortation to Little Bilham, "Live all you can; it's a mistake not to. It doesn't so much matter what you do in particular, so long as you have your life."[27]

The shifting but always balanced relations among the characters in *Night and Day* are reminiscent of the balanced relations in

James's novels, and indeed Katharine's interest in "tracing out the lines of some symmetrical pattern, some arrangement of life" (*ND* 314) among the principals in the novel is very much like Maggie Verver's interest in analyzing and restoring the equilibrium of relations among the members of the Verver clan. Ralph Denham images his closeness to Katharine and William Rodney's exclusion in terms that seem to be drawn from Maggie's image of her closeness to Prince Amerigo and of Charlotte Stant's exclusion. In Woolf's novel, "Denham felt himself very secure; he saw Rodney as one of the lost birds . . . ; one of the flying bodies of which the air was full. But he and Katharine were alone together, aloft, splendid, and luminous with a twofold radiance" (*ND* 398). In James's novel, "They [Maggie and Amerigo] were together thus, he and she, close, close together—whereas Charlotte, though rising there radiantly before her, was really off in some darkness of space that would steep her in solitude and harass her with care." [28] The occasion of Ralph's image of his closeness to Katharine is a walk with Rodney in chapter twenty-eight, an episode designedly parallel to his earlier walk with Rodney in chapter five. This technique of duplication of incidents in *Night and Day*—and one might cite numerous other examples, most notably, perhaps, the recurrent scenes before the portrait of Richard Alardyce—is also highly Jamesian. Woolf would have found numerous examples of such duplicated episodes in *The Golden Bowl*, episodes such as Maggie Verver's early and late talks with her father in the garden at Fawns. The alternation throughout *Night and Day* between scenes of dialogue among characters and passages of solitary introspection and analysis follows the pattern of Henry James's characteristic alternation of picture and scene, as in, for instance, the passage from chapter twenty-seven to chapter twenty-eight or as in the transitions within chapter twenty-eight itself from Ralph's meditation (*ND* 384–86) to his encounter with Mary Datchet (*ND* 387–92) to his interior monologue during a walk through the streets of London (*ND* 392–96) to the conversation he has with Rodney at the end of the chapter (*ND* 396–99).

As Phyllis Rose remarks, "Critics have reached remarkable unanimity about the place *Night and Day* occupies in Virginia Woolf's career—it is her attempt to prove herself the master of the classical tradition of the English novel, to create solid characters and place them in realized settings, to have them speak to one another in credible dialogue and to advance the plot through dramatic scenes."[29] Since the great master of the classical tradition of the novel in Woolf's own time was Henry James, it is not surprising to find that James stirs behind the arras, as it were, throughout Woolf's novel. If we were to apply Harold Bloom's revisionary ratios to the Woolf/James relation, we might say that *clinamen* as well as *tessera*—misprision as well as completion and antithesis—is enacted in *The Voyage Out* and that *Night and Day* is the scene of *kenosis,* or repetition and discontinuity. In Bloom's "pragmatic formula" for *kenosis,* "Where the precursor was, there the ephebe shall be, but by the discontinuous mode of emptying the precursor of *his* divinity, while appearing to empty himself of his own."[30] Thus, in the most important of Katharine Hilbery's moments before the portrait of "the young man who was her grandfather" (*ND* 319), the poet Richard Alardyce, Katharine thinks that "doubts, questionings, and despondencies . . . would be more welcome to him than homage," for "the dead asked neither flowers nor regrets, but a share in the life which they had given her, the life which they had lived" (*ND* 320).

Night and Day embodies a strategy of emptying Henry James of his divinity—or, we might say, rather, of his mastery or authority—by Woolf's appearing to relinquish her own. Thus Woolf implicates James "in the life which [he] had given her." In this light, *Night and Day* may be seen as correlative with the more openly antitraditional experiments in fiction Woolf was making in the late teens and early twenties in her short fiction (in, that is, *The Mark on the Wall* [1917], *Kew Gardens* [1919], and *Monday or Tuesday* [1921]). A few months before the publication of *Night and Day,* moreover, Woolf issued an important attack on the traditional novel. The occasion was a *TLS* essay titled "Modern Novels." In a rehearsal of "Mr. Bennett and Mrs. Brown," Woolf took aim at the "materialist" novelists Wells, Galsworthy, and above all Arnold Bennett. These writers, while representing the world with meticulous detail and while observing the conventions of well-formed fiction, create works in which "life escapes," for they fail to capture the life of consciousness, the spiritual, "that innermost flame which flashes its myriad messages through the brain." [31] Woolf does not mention Henry James in this essay, but her revision of a key passage when she prepared it a few years later for republication as "Modern Fiction" in *The Common Reader* (1925) suggests that in this essay, too, as in the slightly later "Narrow Bridge of Art," James stirs in the background. In the *TLS* version, she wrote,

> It is not possible that . . . if one were free and could set down what one chose, there would be no plot, little probability, and a vague general confusion in which the clear-cut features of the tragic, the comic, the passionate, and the lyrical were dissolved beyond the possibility of separate recognition? The mind, exposed to the ordinary course of life, receives upon its surface a myriad impressions—trivial, fantastic, evanescent, or engraved with the sharpness of steel. From all sides they come, an incessant shower of innumerable atoms, composing in their sum what we might venture to call life itself; and to figure further as the semi-transparent envelope, or luminous halo, surrounding us from the beginning of consciousness to the end. Is it not perhaps the chief task of the novelist to convey this incessantly varying spirit? [32]

In *The Common Reader,* this passage became,

> The mind receives a myriad of impressions—trivial, fantastic, evanescent, or engraved with the sharpness of steel. From all sides they come, an incessant shower of innumerable atoms; and as they fall, as they shape themselves into the life of Monday or Tuesday, the accent falls differently from of old; the moment of importance came not here but there; so that, if a writer were a free man and not a slave, if he could write what he chose, not what he must, if he could base his work upon his own feeling and not upon convention, there would be no plot, no comedy, no tragedy, no love interest or catastrophe in the accepted style, and *perhaps not a single button sewn on as the Bond Street tailors would have it. Life is not a series of gig lamps symmetrically arranged;* life is a luminous halo, a semi-transparent envelope

surrounding us from the beginning of consciousness to the end. Is it not the task of the novelist to convey this varying, this unknown and uncircumscribed spirit?[33]

James is concealed, I think, in the lines I have italicized here. "Life is not a series of gig lamps symmetrically arranged" is an about-face for Woolf, a repudiation of what she had hailed in 1918 as the "important side of James," the "making out of a design," exemplified in her review of *The Method of Henry James* by her quotation of James's Preface to *The Awkward Age:* there she quotes James's description of the plan for that novel as "the neat figure of a circle consisting of a number of small rounds disposed at equal distance about a central object. The central object was my situation, my subject in itself . . . and the small rounds represented so many distinct lamps."[34] The Jamesian reference of "Bond Street" is less certain, but given the clear covert allusion to James in Woolf's "lamps symmetrically arranged" one may well suspect that she has in mind the opening paragraph of *The Golden Bowl,* in which the impeccably outfitted Prince Amerigo has "strayed simply enough into Bond Street"; indeed, Woolf's reading notes on *The Golden Bowl* open with the notation, "Chap. 1: Roman Prince in Bond Street."[35]

Certainly, in any case, we can only read Woolf's next novel, *Jacob's Room,* as an intentional departure from the Jamesian world of *Night and Day.* Everything in *Jacob's Room* that belongs to the material solidity and formal coherence of the traditional novel is decentered. Woolf has systematically created a work in which there is indeed "no plot, little probability, and a vague general confusion in which the clear-cut features of the tragic, the comic, the passionate, and the lyrical [are] dissolved beyond the possibility of separate recognition." A pastiche of fragments, *Jacob's Room* teases the reader with the mystery of Jacob Flanders: he moves through the lives of many observers, some of whom love him—his mother, his girlfriends, his Cambridge classmates, including characters whose names have a distinctly Jamesian resonance (e.g., Bonamy, the good friend, and Sandra Wentworth Williams, whose maiden name recalls the Wentworth family of James's *The Europeans*)—but he never achieves any solidity. We do not know him. He is more absence than presence. Even before he dies, he is a ghost. Quite imperceptibly, he becomes a phantom, haunting those who knew him after his death (a Great War battlefield death, though we are not told so—must infer it from circumstantial evidence), hauntingly present at last to Bonamy and his mother in the creaking of his chair in the room to which he will never return.

Jacob's Room may be accounted a political novel, a chronicle of how the patriarchy educates young men such as Jacob, educates them exquisitely, exclusively, lavishly—yet futilely, too, because theirs is an education for death. But because Woolf is so bent on formal experimentation in this novel, on wobbling in point of view from character to character as she moves from fragment to fragment of the "narrative," and on developing an impersonal narrative voice the salient feature of which is its eschewal of its own authority, this may be one of the oddest, least tendentious of all political novels. It was written at a time when she was preoccupied with Henry James: during the fourteen-month period of Woolf's composition of *Jacob's Room* (September 1920–November 1921), she read (as we may recall from the preceding chapters) *The Ambassadors, The Wings of the Dove,* and Lubbock's *The Letters of Henry James;* she wrote her essay on James's ghost stories (published the month after she finished *Jacob's Room*); she reviewed the letters; and she protested against the charge that she sounded like James in that review: "the disease is my own, not caught from H.J." *Jacob's Room* rebels against the symmetrical gig-lamp design of the well-made Jamesian novel and against the solid materiality of the Jamesian world (a trait she had attacked in her 1905 review of *The Golden Bowl*, where James's description of a balustrade—"fine iron-work, eighteenth-century English"—was offered as an instance of "detail which, perpetually insisted on, fatigues"). But *Jacob's Room* is aligned with another side of James that I believe Woolf drew on without being able to acknowledge her indebtedness, the side of James that makes him, in many recent studies, a key transitional figure in the development of fiction from a metaphysics of presence to a metaphysics of absence, the James who purposely left his protagonists *"en l'air"* since he knew, as he wrote in his notebooks nearly two years before Virginia Woolf's birth, "the *whole* of anything is never told," and the James whose characters, as Woolf recognized in "Henry James' Ghost Stories," "are already half-way out of the body."[36] Jacob Flanders is emphatically such a character, and one might conjecture that the most passionately artistic/political statement of *Jacob's Room*, formulated by the Virginia Woolf who poignantly appreciated, in her review of *Within the Rim*, what the Great War had meant to Henry James, is that what went smash on the battlefields of Flanders was the whole Jacobite sense of life and civilization, so that Jacob's room and the space of the Jamesian novel are alike emptied out—emptied and haunted. The final, plangent image in Woolf's novel, when Jacob's mother "held out a pair of Jacob's old shoes" ("What am I to do with these, Mr. Bonamy?" she asks), might then be read as Woolf's question, "How am I to fill the shoes of Henry James?"—to which *Jacob's Room* itself is a bold, experimental answer. For Henry James was always "Jacobean" for Virginia Woolf, as in her reference to "the fickle Jacobites," and of course the title *Jacob's Room* bears directly on the argument I have been sketching out here: she wanted a room of her own, and envied Jacob *his*.

In her next novel, *Mrs. Dalloway*, Woolf at once extends and consolidates her rebellion against the conventions of traditional fiction and, paradoxically, expands the Jamesian and political dimensions of her art. Formally, Woolf might seem to wobble as much in *Mrs. Dalloway* as in *Jacob's Room*, making violation of the Jamesian principle of consistency of point of view the very principle of her own artistic form. But *Mrs. Dalloway* surpasses *Jacob's Room* in part because Woolf establishes a clear emotional rhythm in the later novel between internal and external world, between elation and despair, between the divine madness of creativity and the demonic madness of psychological disintegration, between the sealing off of feeling and the intense expression of feeling. If *Jacob's Room* may be thought of as a political novel, *Mrs. Dalloway* is even more deeply enmeshed in criticism of the social order, with the public dimensions of the fiction emphasized by their alternation with and impingement on Woolf's depiction of the world of private sensation.[37] From the opening pages of *Mrs. Dalloway*, when "a male hand" draws the blind over the window of a limousine that bears the Prince of Wales, maybe, or the Prime Minister, but that carries in any case "the voice of authority," Woolf attacks the coercive rigidity of masculine authority in all realms: personal, artistic, and political (*MD* 19–20). Seeking to demolish the claims to authority of such figures of patriarchal despotism as Sir William Bradshaw, Dr. Holmes, and the Prime Minister, Woolf simultaneously subverts the "masculine" formal authority, the solid compositional blocks, of a Henry James.

But, as in *Jacob's Room*, Woolf seems in *Mrs. Dalloway* to be in touch in some subterranean way with the antipatriarchal side of Henry James, the side of James that, as we see more and more in recent criticism, was bent on deconstructing his own claims, and the claims of his art, to be definitive, authoritative, masterful. Some dozen years ago, writing in the vanguard of a by-now well-established strain of feminist commentary on Woolf, Phyllis Rose argued that Woolf's formal experiments are typical of the modernist distrust of "strong authority" and that "authority, the rigid imposition of form upon matter," is associated with "masculinity."[38] More recently, Carol Gilligan has provided a new way in which we might think of the ethical and thematic, as well as formal, affinity between James and Woolf. In her brilliant study *In a Different Voice*, Gilligan differentiates between a "male" morality of a priori rights and ideals and a "female" "morality of responsibility" that disturbs men and often draws their fire because of its "contextual relativism." "Women's moral weakness," Gilligan argues, "is thus inseparable from women's moral strength," for "sensitivity to the needs of others and the assumption of responsibility for taking care lead women to attend to voices other than their own and to include in their judgment other points of view." As Gilligan observes, "the different voice I describe is characterized not by gender but theme" and "its association with women is an empirical observation" not intended to "represent a generalization about either sex." There is an "interplay of these voices within each sex," and I would suggest that there is an interplay in both Henry James and Virginia Woolf of the "male" and "female" perspectives Gilligan delineates and that, furthermore, this interplay is a salient aspect of the androgyny of James and Woolf alike.[39]

Both male and female critics, for instance, have attacked Henry James's valorization of Maggie Verver in *The Golden Bowl* because her "assumption of responsibility for taking care" and the "contextual relativism" that characterizes her behavior violate rigid "male" prescriptions about honesty and straightforward dealing with others. Maggie may be judged much more generously than such critics allow if she is taken as an exemplar of Gilligan's "different voice." In *Mrs. Dalloway,* the thematic accompaniment of what Rose would have us see as, in effect, the antimasculine form of the novel is Clarissa Dalloway's contextual morality of care, exemplified above all in her intense empathy with Septimus Warren Smith and in her distaste for what she sees in herself and in others as rigid, cold, hard, and unyielding. Thus she stands in the end, for all her own shortcomings and ambivalences, in opposition to the inflexible, hidebound morality of Sir William Bradshaw and Dr. Holmes, who police society in the name of abstract, coercive principles of "Proportion" and "Conversion." The close parallel between the Woolfian and Jamesian perspectives may be seen even more clearly, however, in *To the Lighthouse.* Recall, for a moment, the critical chapter in *The Golden Bowl* (book five, chapter two) in which Maggie lies to Charlotte by assuring her, with a Judas-like kiss, that she has never thought that Charlotte has wronged her. Maggie does so after reflecting that the scene of her life is one that "she might people, by the press of her spring, either with serenities and dignities and decencies, or with terrors and shames and ruins." [40] Numerous commentators excoriate Maggie for her lie to Charlotte.[41] But here is Mrs. Ramsay, inwardly raging against her husband's insistence on the facing of facts and against his implied accusation that she "in effect, told lies": "To pursue truth with such astonishing lack of consideration for other people's feelings, to rend the thin veils of civilisation so wantonly, so brutally, was to her so horrible an outrage of human decency that, without replying, dazed and blinded, she bent her head as if to let the pelt of jagged hail, the drench of dirty water, bespatter her unrebuked. There was nothing to be said" (*TL* 51). What Henry James endorses in Maggie Verver and Woolf in Mrs. Ramsey is precisely the contextual morality of care anatomized by Gilligan.

To return to *Mrs. Dalloway,* I would suggest that the James novel with which Woolf's first masterpiece might most fruitfully be paired is *The Ambassadors.*[42] I am thinking in particular of the age of the principal characters (Strether is fifty-five, Clarissa Dalloway and her peers—Peter Walsh, Richard Dalloway, Hugh Whitbread, and Sally Seton—are all in their mid-fifties); of the thematics of both novels, which confront a rigid morality (in James the provincial, straitlaced morality of the "New England conscience" of Woollett, Massachusetts; in Woolf the authoritarian, repressive morality of the British upper class) with the protagonists' deepening sense of its inadequacy to the richness, variety, and responsibilities of life; of the protagonists' inability finally to make a clean break with their antecedents, so that Strether returns to Woollett " 'in order to be right' " and Clarissa Dalloway returns from her epiphanic moment of identification with Septimus Warren Smith to her compromised, if radiant, role as "the perfect hostess"; and of the susceptibility of both novels to being read as unusual variations on the bildungsroman, as bildungsromans of middle age, if you will, in which mature protagonists escape the narcissism that typifies the usual youthful heroes of the genre.[43]

There are a number of fleeting Jamesian traces in *Mrs. Dalloway* that suggest the precursor's pressure on Woolf. For instance, in Regent's Park, Mrs. Dempster observes of Maisie Johnson, "That girl . . . don't know a thing yet" (*MD* 39), which may be read as an answer to the question implicit in James's title *What Maisie Knew.* But I would place far greater emphasis on the clear threads tying *Mrs. Dalloway* to *The Ambassadors.* Clarissa's commitment to life recalls Strether's "Live all you can" exhortation: "What she liked was simply life. 'That's what I do it for,' she said, speaking aloud, to life" (*MD* 183–84). Strether's initial walk through Paris streets to the Luxembourg Gardens, and Peter Walsh's walk through London streets to Regent's Park, are strikingly similar in their rejuvenating effects on these middle-aged gentlemen. Here, indeed, Woolf's language closely echoes James's. Here is James:

> It was the difference, the difference of being just where he was and *as* he was, that formed the escape—this difference was so much greater than he had dreamed it would be; and what he finally sat there turning over was the strange logic of his finding himself so free. He felt it in a manner his duty to think out his state, to approve the process, and when he came in fact to trace the steps and add up the items they sufficiently accounted for the sum. He had never expected—that was the truth of it—again to find himself young, and all the years and other things it had taken to make him so were exactly his present arithmetic.[44]

And here is Woolf:

> And down his mind went flat as a marsh, and three great emotions bowled over him; understanding; a vast philanthropy; and finally, as if the result of the others, an irrepressible, exquisite delight; as if inside his brain by another hand strings were pulled, shutters moved, and he, having nothing to do with it, yet stood at the opening of endless avenues, down which if he chose he might wander. He had not felt so young for years.
>
> He had escaped! was utterly free—as happens in the downfall of habit when the mind, like an unguarded flame, bows and bends and seems about to blow from its holding. I haven't felt so young for years! thought Peter, escaping. (*MD* 78)

Woolf repeats James's key words, *escape, free, young*. Finally, the last line of *Mrs. Dalloway* seems unmistakably to echo the close of *The Ambassadors*. James's novel concludes with, " 'Then there we are!' said Strether";[45] Woolf's, with "It is Clarissa, he said. For there she was" (*MD* 296). James's *there* is abstract. Woolf's *there* is actual. But the effect in each case is to close the novel on a note of irresolution, of suspension, conveying the sense the authors share, in James's words, that "the *whole* of anything is never told."[46]

II

Of all of Woolf's novels, *To the Lighthouse*, her next performance, is the most Jamesian in its assurance, harmony, and balanced design; at the same time, *To the Lighthouse* expresses Woolf's rising anxiety about literary influence. In this novel, the concern with influence is intimately tied in with Woolf's fictionalized but avowedly autobiographical study in family relations. The influence anxiety, moreover, seems no less easy to exorcise than the ghosts of her parents, which the novelist came to believe she had laid to rest in the process of composing the novel—of course, she had not done so, as witness her later history, notably, for example, her composition of *Moments of Being*. If, as Paula Smith suggests, Woolf's express concern with design while she was composing *Mrs. Dalloway* was Jamesian, her conception of the three-part structure of *To the Lighthouse* was even more so.[47] As I have suggested, Woolf's diagram of the novel seems inspired by Henry James's geometrical figures for his novels, by, for instance, the design of *The Awkward Age* that Woolf cited as an emblem of James's importance in her review of *The Method of Henry James*. That the novel she produced was less symmetrical than she had planned, with a narrow corridor connecting, not equal units, but a large block with a smaller one—as Alex Zwerdling points out—makes her procedure all the more Jamesian, since such unplanned foreshortening repeatedly befell Henry James, as he laments in the Preface to *The Wings of the Dove*.[48]

We have just taken note, in the parallel between Maggie Verver and Mrs. Ramsay, of one of the principal Jamesian elements in this novel—and, indeed, throughout Woolf's fiction: the gendered operation of a relativistic morality of care, feminine and antipatriarchal in its bearings. Considering the parallel with Henry James, one is not surprised to find Mrs. Ramsay, the embodiment of this contextual morality, apprehensive that she is thereby subject to the very charge that numerous commentators have brought against Maggie Verver: "Wishing to dominate, wishing to interfere, making people do what she wished—that was the charge against her" (*TL* 88). Maggie, describing her policy of keeping Charlotte Stant and Prince Amerigo in the dark about her own knowledge of their adultery, says, "And that's how I make them do what I like!" a declaration that leads Fanny Assingham to call Maggie "terrible," establishing the keynote for much (to my mind misguided) commentary on the novel.[49] If, moreover, Mrs. Ramsay is a Jamesian character, Lily Brisco, whose quest for a transcendent moment of vision achieved through art is a simulacrum of Virginia Woolf's quest, is a Jamesian artist, particularly in her effort to gather the disconnected and disparate into a unified whole: "If only she could put them [Mr. Ramsay's disconnected words "Alone" and "Perished"] together, she felt, write them out in some sentence, then she would have got at the truth of things" (*TL* 219). Lily's desire to "compose" an otherwise inchoate field of observation and to do so as an act of love is thoroughly in the spirit of the Henry James who wrote that "you can only take what groups together" and that "really, universally, relations stop nowhere, and the exquisite problem of the artist is eternally but to draw, by a geometry of his own, the circle within which they shall happily *appear* to do so." [50] "Love," Lily reflects, "had a thousand shapes. There might be lovers whose gift it was to choose out the elements of things and place them together and so, giving them a wholeness not theirs in life, make of some scene, or meeting of people (all now gone and separate), one of those globed compacted things over which thought lingers, and love plays" (*TL* 286). Lily's imagination, like Lambert Strether's, and like Henry James's, is inveterately dialectical, though it works less toward synthesis than toward balance, "that razor edge of balance between two opposite forces" (*TL* 287), as Lily puts it to herself. Other Jamesian elements in *To the Lighthouse* include the tropes with which the characters conceive of each other (e.g., "and James, as he stood stiff between her knees [Mrs. Ramsay's], felt her rise in a rosy-flowered fruit tree laid with leaves and dancing boughs into which the beak of brass, the arid scimitar of his father the egotistical man, plunged and smote" [*TL* 60]), the ghostly appearance to Lily Briscoe of Mrs. Ramsay (*TL* 300), and, in general, the interiorization of the action in the novel.[51]

One of the recurrent, characteristic moments of internalized drama in James's fiction occurs when a central character meditates on something observed in the physical disposition or attitude of another character or characters—when Isabel Archer, in *The Portrait of a Lady,* for example, reflects on the meaning of the colloquy she has glimpsed between Madame Merle and Osmond and seizes upon the image of Osmond seated while Madame Merle stands as a revelation of their intimacy, or when Strether, in *The Ambassadors,* intuits in his sighting of Madame de Vionnet and Chad together on the river the sexual nature of their relation, seeing in the boating couple, even before he has identified them as known to him, "that they were expert, familiar, frequent." [52] Such moments of voyeuristic intuition in James may be attributed in part to the nature of the novel of manners, which predicates a world in which nuances of physical disposition and gesture may be the outward signs of moral relations and of networks of social power. At the same time, these moments may in part be laid, in many instances, to the distance dividing the celibate, homoerotic Henry James from the world of heterosexual relations into which such epiphanic glimpses are generally directed. The famous Max Beerbohm drawing of Henry James puzzling over two pairs of shoes, a man's and a woman's, set outside a bedroom door in a country-house corridor emblematizes Jamesian voyeurism. Virginia Woolf, I believe, exhibits a similar voyeurism, and for similar reasons: because, that is, of the generic demands of the novel of manners and because of a deeply personal disengagement from heterosexual relations. We recall the numerous scenes of peering into windows in Woolf's earlier fiction: Rachel Vinrace and Helen Ambrose, for example, peeping through the hotel windows in *The Voyage Out,* and Ralph Denham's gazing protractedly from the street into the Hilbery's windows in *Night and Day.* Part 1 of *To the Lighthouse,* titled "The Window," is a culmination of this motif: Mrs. Ramsay looks out on various characters through the window where she is reading to James, and they look in at her. In *To the Lighthouse,* furthermore, characters are constantly sizing each other up from afar, and constantly drawing conclusions from their observations. Mrs. Ramsay, inveterate matchmaker, engineer of the Paul Rayley–Minta Doyle engagement, watches two distant walkers: "Ah, but was that not Lily Briscoe strolling along with William Bankes? She focussed her short-sighted eyes upon the backs of a retreating couple. Yes, indeed it was. Did that not mean that they would marry? Yes, it must! What an admirable idea! They must marry!" (*TL* 108–9).

Admirable as is her idea—admirable as is Mrs. Ramsay in many respects—her shortsightedness here is not just ocular, but oracular, too. The future that she foresees, that Bankes and Briscoe "would marry," does not come to pass. Mrs. Ramsay's misprision here might be read as an implicit send-up or deconstruction of the many scenes of observation and intuition in Henry James's fiction. For though there are scarcely any overt signs of struggle against the Jamesian influence in *To the Lighthouse*—it is, as I have already remarked, a novel Jamesian in its assurance and in other respects as well—the anxiety of influence generally is a central theme of *To the Lighthouse*. This concern is focused on the figure of Mr. Ramsay, and in a scrawled marginal note in her holograph manuscript of the novel Woolf in fact attaches the term *anxiety* to him: the note reads, "anxiety about his own books & his own fame." [53] In the published novel, Mr. Ramsay's desperate insecurity about his reputation and his need for constant reassurance about his professional standing are frequently expressed and dramatized. In one passage, for example, we read that "he would always be worrying about his own books—will they be read, are they good, why aren't they better, what do people think of me," and Mrs. Ramsay wonders "if they had guessed at dinner why he suddenly became irritable when they talked about fame and books lasting" (*TL* 177). The novel arraigns Mr. Ramsay for his self-centered, consumingly self-important obsession with his books and his fame, and Charles Tansley, his student, is targeted in the same way, particularly when we are told that Tansley's dissertation is about "the influence of something upon somebody" (*TL* 22) and, alternatively, about "the influence of somebody upon something" (*TL* 156).

Since Leslie Stephen suffered from the same obsessive concern with comparative failure as an intellectual that Woolf depicts in his fictional embodiment, Mr. Ramsay, one might think that this aspect of the character is purely mimetic. In fact, however, it is clearly both mimetic and expressive of Woolf's own anxieties about literary influence, anxieties that surface obsessively in her essays, diaries, and letters, as we saw in the preceding chapter, and that are tellingly sounded at an even higher pitch in her next novel, *Orlando,* where there is no question of holding the mirror up to Leslie Stephen. To write a novel in which one attempts to come to terms with one's parents, as Woolf did in *To the Lighthouse,* is of course to attempt to come to terms with oneself. Woolf's lampoon of the anxiety about influence and reputation of the "writer father" with whom she, as a writer, identified is a projection of her own anxieties of influence and reputation, tied up here with what Gilbert and Gubar term the anxiety of authorship, which is depicted in Lily Briscoe's recalling years afterwards how Charles Tansley had whispered in her ear, "Women can't paint, women can't write" (*TL* 75, 237, 238).[54]

Mr. Ramsay is also, to be sure, the tyrant father, just as Mrs. Ramsay, no less forcefully though less conspicuously, is the tyrant mother, but there are great positive values invested in the couple as well, for Woolf's ambivalence, her love/hate for her parents and for these characters—for Julia Stephen/Mrs. Ramsay, the angel in the house whom she was compelled to kill to be a writer, and for Leslie Stephen/Mr. Ramsay, the tyrant father/writer father whose continued life would have spelled the death of the writer in Woolf—runs very deep throughout this novel and may be said to account in no small measure for its richness and complexity. The climactic moment in part one, balancing the climax of Lily's vision in part three, is Mrs. Ramsay's silent communication of her love for her husband (*TL* 185–86), which follows their communion while they are reading—she Shakespeare's sonnets, he Sir Walter Scott: "They had nothing to say, but something seemed, nevertheless, to go from him to her. It was the life, it was the power of it" (*TL* 179). In turn, this communion while reading comes fast on the heels of the passage, already cited, in which we are told that Mr. Ramsay "would always be worrying about his own books" (*TL* 177), so that when Mr. Ramsay thinks, "Well, let them improve upon that" (*TL* 180), as he finishes a chapter of Scott, one may recall Woolf's clear implication—in "The Leaning Tower" passage linking influenza, literary influence, and family history—that Henry James had indeed improved upon Scott: "Read a page of Scott; then of Henry James; try to work out the influences that have transformed the one page into the other. . . . Books descend from books as families descend from families" (CE 2:163).[55] Thus, in the midst of this most Jamesian of Woolf's mature novels (and here I am excepting the immature and overtly Jamesian *Night and Day*), in one of the key passages in which Woolf seems to project her own anxiety of influence onto the character of Mr. Ramsay, the covert presence and pressure of Henry James may be detected.

And this conjunction of Mr. Ramsay and Henry James should not be surprising given the association in Woolf's mind that we posited two chapters back between Leslie Stephen and Henry James, and given her transference to the literary relation with James of the ambivalences that characterized her deepest feelings about her father. What is surprising, however, is to find traces of the concealed literary father, Henry James, in the child of the fictionalized literal father, Mr. Ramsay—to find these traces, to be precise, in James Ramsay. Foremost among these traces is the child's name, which echoes the novelist's. Like Henry James, moreover, James Ramsay is supersensitive: a "bundle of sensitiveness (none of her children was as sensitive as he was)" (*TL* 66). Most curiously, James Ramsay is characterized late in the novel as "James the lawgiver, with the tablets of eternal wisdom laid open on his knee" (*TL* 251). It is not easy to understand this epithet, "James the lawgiver," in terms restricted to *To the Lighthouse* and to Woolf's characterization of James Ramsay in the novel; but if one is prepared to entertain a submerged correlation of James Ramsay and Henry James, then one finds one's clue in Henry James's status as the giver of the laws of representation, codified by his disciples Beach and Lubbock in books that Woolf had reviewed, and at once emulated and resisted by Woolf in this novel.

The resistance, the underground battle against the Jamesian laws, is expressed here above all by the strategy of inverting James's priority, making him not a powerful precursor but one's own creation, making him not an elder but a child, not a forefather but, symbolically at least, a sibling at most, and finally by assigning to him the role of ambivalent rebel against the law of the father—the role that Woolf herself is playing against the law of the literary father, Henry James/Leslie Stephen. Indeed, James's oedipal rage against his father, detailed throughout the novel (see *TL* 10 and 57–58 for early examples), is expressed in terms, and climaxes in a passage, strikingly reminiscent of Woolf's early description of Henry James on the street in Rye. We recall Woolf's response to James's marking her as a writer, a response aggravated perhaps, if only unconsciously, by the patrilineal emphasis James gives her literary identity:

> "My dear Virginia, they tell me—they tell me—they tell me—that you—as indeed being your fathers daughter nay your grandfathers grandchild—the descendant I may say of a century—of a century—of quill pens and ink—ink—ink pots, yes, yes, yes, they tell me—ahm m m—that you, that you, that you *write* in short." This went on in the public street, while we all waited, as farmers wait for the hen to lay an egg—do they?—nervous, polite, and now on this foot now on that. I felt like a condemned person, who sees the knife drop and stick and drop again. Never did any woman hate "writing" as much as I do. But when I am old and famous I shall discourse like Henry James. (*LVW* 1:306)

The first time that James thinks of killing his father, on the second page of *To the Lighthouse*, Mr. Ramsay stands "lean as a knife, narrow as the blade of one" (*TL* 10). And, in the last episode of the novel, when James again feels murderous, we read that "it was not him, that old man reading, whom he wanted to kill, but it was the thing that descended on him—without his knowing it perhaps: that fierce sudden black-winged harpy, with its talons and its beak all cold and hard, that struck and struck at you (he could feel the beak on his bare legs, where it had struck when he was a child) and then made off, and there he was again, an old man, very sad, reading his book" (*TL* 273–74). James Ramsay sees his father, as Virginia Woolf saw Henry James, as a knife. Woolf saw Henry James's knife "drop and stick and drop again," and James Ramsay feels his father's assaults as a similar repetitive plunging down, as the beak that "struck and struck at you."[56] And both James Ramsay and Virginia Woolf transform the figures of the old men, Mr. Ramsay and Henry James respectively, into female birds, James making his father into a harpy (a foul mythological creature, part bird and part woman) and Woolf making Henry James into a hen. Finally, the attitudes of both young persons, James Ramsay en route to the lighthouse and Virginia Woolf in Rye, are deeply ambivalent, for James hungers above all for the praise of the father against whom he would rebel (for the illustrative detail on this point, see *TL* 306), while Woolf anticipates that she will at last "discourse like Henry James." I would argue, indeed, that it is only in the light of this concealed, complex, and intricate correspondence between the two Jameses—and thus between the James Ramsay/Mr. Ramsay relation and the Virginia Woolf/Henry James relation—that we can read the full significance of the nearly simultaneous events that close the novel, the reaching of the lighthouse by "James and lawgiver," who steers the boat and the novel to its climax, and the drawing by Lily Briscoe, the Woolfian artist, of a final line in the center of her painting, which she is only able to do a moment after she realizes that the boat has reached its goal.

This hitherto unrecognized subtext in *To the Lighthouse,* in which the vessel of patriarchal authority essentially enables the triumph of Lily Briscoe's artistic vision, may help to explain the rising pitch of the influence-tormented music of Woolf's next novel, *Orlando*. For though *Orlando* is often read—and rightly read, to be sure—as a love letter to Vita Sackville-West, as extended parody and mock-biography, and, withal, as the zestful jeu d'espirit that Woolf herself felt it to be as she was composing the book, it is a novel with a dark subtext that, in the nineteenth-century section, almost threatens to overwhelm the lighter, playful, generally predominant elements of the book.[57] While Woolf wrote in her diary that she had "abandoned myself to the pure delight of this farce" and that "it is all a joke; & yet gay and quick reading I think; a writers holiday," she also noted that "it has to be half laughing, half serious," and, right after calling it "a writers holiday," she wrote,

"I feel more & more sure that I will never write a novel again" (*DVW* 3:162, 168, 177). What led her to this last, gloomy (and happily unfulfilled) prevision was, I believe, the deep sense expressed throughout *Orlando* of the oppressive weight of the literary past, of the difficulty of resisting it and of forging for oneself a differentiated literary identity.

Woolf's hero/heroine Orlando is a writer with an acute sense of the intertextuality of her productions; indeed, she is in possession of virtually all of the salient aspects of Harold Bloom's theory of literary influence. "Was not writing poetry," she thinks, "a secret transaction, a voice answering a voice?" (*OR* 292). Orlando, moreover, envisions the Other with whom one conducts such a transaction as an opponent, concluding her meditation on Victorian literature with the reflection that "when anybody comes to a conclusion it is as if they had tossed the ball over the net and must wait for the unseen antagonist to return it to them" (*OR* 262). All of the metaphors of disease and infection that Woolf deploys in her discussions of influence (as we saw in the preceding chapters) are available to Orlando. Orlando is "afflicted with a love of literature," an "infection" or "disease" borne by a "germ," and writing is "that other scourge" that follows easily "once the disease of reading has laid hold upon the system" (*OR* 69–71). Genius is a "disease" "now stamped out in the British Isles" (*OR* 188). When Nick Greene—who in his Renaissance embodiment had expressed a stifling sense of the greatness of the literature of the past, wishing to imitate Cicero's "style so that you couldn't tell the difference between us" (*OR* 84)— appears before Orlando much later as "the most influential critic of the Victorian age" (*OR* 249), he makes her feel that "one must always, always write like somebody else," and thereupon "the tears formed themselves in her eyes" (*OR* 257).

The acute influence anxiety expressed throughout this novel is not overtly connected with Henry James, for *Orlando* displays few of the obvious Jamesian elements evident in *To the Lighthouse* (for instance, the formal balance, distorted by foreshortening, of that novel). The insistently oppositional descriptions of Orlando early in the novel are, to be sure, like nothing so much as the descriptions of the title character of James's early tale "Benvolio," for Orlando is "a welter of opposites" (*OR* 23), his mind working at one point "in violent see-saws from life to death" (*OR* 44). *Orlando* seems, in addition, to contain several allusions to *The Wings of the Dove*. For example, Orlando is "launched without delay, and with some splash and foam at that, upon the waters of London society," and we read shortly thereafter that "society is everything and society is nothing" (*OR* 174, 176), observations that echo Lord Mark's account of London society in book four of James's novel: "He explained . . . that there was no such thing to-day in London as saying where any one was. Every one was everywhere—nobody was anywhere. . . . was there anything but . . . the vague billows of some great greasy sea in mid-Channel?"[58] The most notable allusion in *Orlando* to *The Wings of the Dove* occurs in connection with the trope of the disease of writing: "He would give every penny he has (such is the malignity of the germ) to write one little book and become famous; yet all the gold in Peru will not buy him the treasure of a well-turned line. So he falls into consumption and sickness, blows his brains out, turns his face to the wall" (*OR* 75). This echo of James's famous, frequently reiterated biblical pronouncement in *The Wings of the Dove* that Milly Theale has "turned her face to the wall" makes Henry James covertly present in a key passage in *Orlando* that develops the writing-disease-germ trope so often linked to James in Woolf's essays, letters, and diaries.[59] I would also recall at this juncture a point noted earlier, the connection Leon Edel has drawn between the description in *Orlando* of the eyes of Shakespeare, the ideal, androgynous artist, and Woolf's early description of the eyes of Henry James (see chapter 3, n. 4, and related text). Finally, the most precise (though also covert) connection between Henry James and the pervasive anxiety of influence expressed in *Orlando* is encoded in these lines: "She had formed here in solitude after her affair with Greene, or tried to form . . . a spirit capable of resistance. 'I will write,' she had said, 'what I enjoy writing'; and so had scratched out twenty-six volumes" (*OR* 160). The capacity for "resistance" that Orlando does not fully develop—the phrase "or tried to form" strongly implies that her effort is at most only partially successful—leads her to "scratch out" the exact number of volumes in the New York Edition of Henry James.[60] To become her own author, to write what she enjoyed writing, Orlando, like Virginia Woolf, had to muster resistance to the Jamesian oeuvre, seeking, in effect, to murder James symbolically by scratching out the twenty-six volumes of his collected works!

This desire to efface James may be seen as underlying Woolf's most radical departure from the traditional art of fiction, a departure she made in her next novel, *The Waves*. Her most overtly Jamesian novel had been *Night and Day*. Even though her famous debate with the Wells-Bennett-Galsworthy school of materialist, realistic fiction (notably in "Mr. Bennett and Mrs. Brown") might be considered an implicit defense of James's novels of consciousness as well as an explicit defense of her own fictional theory and practice, Woolf thought of *Night and Day* as a "novel of fact," and, looking back in 1932, as she got under way on *The Partigers* (later to become *The Years*), she described herself as having abstained since *Night and Day* "from the novel of fact all these years" (*DVW* 4:129). One may aptly describe Woolf's development as a novelist from *Jacob's Room* through *The Waves* as a trajectory climbing away from the "novel of fact" and reaching its apogee in *The Waves*—with Woolf being drawn back thereafter by the strong gravitation of historical actuality from a poetic and symbolic rendering of experience to the more conventionally realistic and material fictional worlds of *The Years* and *Between the Acts*.

As Phyllis Rose suggests, Woolf wanted to make *The Waves* "a frontal assault on the nature of the novel."[61] And, as I observed in the last chapter and recalled in the opening of this chapter as well, in her essay "The Narrow Bridge of Art" Woolf formulated her project for *The Waves* in opposition to the psychological novel of Henry James. She would "give the relation of the mind to general ideas and its soliloquy in solitude" rather than the Jamesian "remorseless analysis" of personal relations. The result, in my view (and with all due respect to readers who avidly defend *The Waves*) is a failed novel, an experiment ruined by its remorseless, relentless, self-conscious insistence on being poetic. Yet it is a magnificent failure. And despite its being driven by a sort of anti-Jamesian motive force, which suggests that the pressure of Henry James is always there, if only as the "unseen antagonist" (*OR* 262) on the other side of the net, *The Waves* shows that for Woolf James's presence, too, remained inescapable.

For James may be detected in *The Waves* in the central one of its six mystically interfused characters, in Bernard, who, as has been often noted (recently, for instance, by Sandra Gilbert and Susan Gubar), is the figure of the novelist, a clear surrogate for Virginia Woolf herself.[62] Bernard has many characteristics that Woolf associated with Henry James, including, for example, an irrepressible predilection for metaphor and the habit of observing perpetually.[63] These might, however, be characteristics of many literary artists. What ties Bernard to James more specifically is Neville's repeated image of Bernard's "twiddling a bit of string" whenever his storytelling falters (see *WV* 41 and 54). This image, I would suggest, is drawn verbatim from H. G. Wells's famous (or infamous) account of the failure of James's fiction: "The thing his novel is *about* is always there. It is like a church lit but without a congregation to distract you, with every light and line focused on the high altar. And on the altar, very reverently placed, intensely there, is a dead kitten, an egg-shell, a bit of string."[64]

That the "bit of string" emblematizes Woolf's anxiety about Henry James, via her recall of Wells's attempted demolition of the Master, seems to me to be made convincing by two points. First, the image is initially Neville's of Bernard, and Neville and Bernard are constantly accusing each other of being subsumed in someone else's influence. Thus, Neville thinks of Bernard, "Once you were Tolstoi's young man; now you are Byron's young man; perhaps you will be Meredith's young man. . . . I am one person—myself" (*WV* 93–94), and Bernard imagines Neville alone in his room thus: "Then he stretches his hand for his copy-book—a neat volume bound in mottled paper—and writes feverishly long lines of poetry, in the manner of whomever he admires most at the moment" (*WV* 97). Second, later in the novel, remembering Bernard's words when they were children, Susan transforms the Wellsian image of Henry

James's/Bernard's "bit of string" into Henry James's own famous image for romance as a literary mode: "I jumped up," Susan recalls, "and ran after the words that trailed like the dangling string from an air ball, up and up, from branch to branch escaping. Then like a cracked bowl the fixity of my morning broke" (*WV* 209).[65] James's image, his "air ball," appears in the Preface to *The American*: "The balloon of experience is in fact of course tied to the earth, and under that necessity we swing, thanks to a rope of remarkable length, in the more or less commodious car of the imagination; but it is by the rope we know where we are, and from the moment that cable is cut we are at large and unrelated. . . . The art of the romancer is, 'for the fun of it,' insidiously to cut the cable."[66] Not only does Susan imagine herself chasing the "cut cable," "the dangling string" of Bernard's discourse drawn up and away by an escaping balloon, but she immediately follows this image with another recollection of a famous James image, for her "cracked bowl" echoes the famous cracked vessel of *The Golden Bowl*.[67] Bernard himself, the most privileged of the six characters in *The Waves*, particularly by virtue of his long soliloquy that closes the novel (and that sums up with as much authority as can be imagined in the fictional world of this novel, which takes a stance toward language and meaning that challenges all authority)—Bernard himself echoes the Jamesian balloon when he thinks, "Who is to foretell the flight of a word? It is a balloon that sails over tree-tops" (*WV* 127–28).

   That Virginia Woolf should have had to make the figure of the novelist in *The Waves* a male, and that she should, moreover, have had to embed in that character a concealed but unmistakable identity with the very writer in opposition to whom she was trying to forge a new kind of fictional art in this novel—an art that might now be seen in retrospect as Woolf's closest approach to *l'écriture féminine*—these tensions, ironies, contradictions, or what you will, seem somehow sad, bespeaking an underlying desperation in Woolf about the possibilities of her art, about the autonomy of her writerly imagination, and about female literary authority. In *The Waves*, the figure of woman writing—"The lady sits between the two long windows, writing"—appears only in the imaginary childhood realm of

"Elvedon," "an unknown," perilous, irrecoverable, and mournful land: "'I see the lady writing. I see the gardeners sweeping,' said Susan. 'If we died here, nobody would bury us'" (*WV* 16). If Woolf is in some sense Bernard (she is, of course, invested in the other characters in *The Waves* as well, notably Rhonda), if Bernard is Henry James, and if Woolf's effort in *The Waves* is precisely to be not-James, then what we have uncovered in the foregoing analysis is a formula for literary self-destruction that perhaps presages Woolf's own death. We should recall that the suicide in *The Waves*, Rhoda, is consumed with the terror of an uncertain personal identity; as Madeline Moore notes, Rhoda "seeks her identity by imitation." The agony that drives Rhoda to take her own life may be understood as parallel to the agony of Woolf's buried but enduring struggle with Henry James for literary identity.[68]

For both of Woolf's last two novels, *The Years* and *Between the Acts*, are in some sense capitulations to the strong predecessor. *The Years*, as we have noted in passing, was seen by Woolf as a return to "the novel of fact" that she had last attempted in her most overtly Jamesian novel, *Night and Day*. We know, moreover, as we have also noted, that Henry James was in Woolf's thoughts, as an antagonist of sorts, when she embarked on the essays that were at one time to form an integral part of the Ur-form of *The Years*, *The Partigers*. I would suggest, moreover, that insofar as this often— especially initially—brilliant novel fails (as I believe, on the whole, it does), its major shortcomings may be read as effects of resistance to the Jamesian influence, and here I am thinking particularly of two points: first, Woolf's decision not to establish a single character as preeminent, when what the book really wants to give it thematic and emotional unity is something like a Jamesian "central intelligence," and, second, her decision not to "go behind" (in Henry James's phrase) the action she presents, an aspect of the novel that Phyllis Rose terms "a tight-lipped refusal to elaborate."[69] Woolf perhaps acknowledges as much when, late in *The Years*, she has Sara tell North, "You only catch half the lesson of the Teacher, the Master," a comment that I would read as Woolf's own judgment on her relation to the author of "The Lesson of the Master."[70] As I suggested in the preceding chapter, it is likely that Woolf's title for this novel had a Jamesian origin, and certainly Eleanor's sense that what has come into view is "the end of everything we cared for" is consonant with James's anguished, elegaic letter of August 4, 1914 and also with these words written by James six days later to the novelist Rhoda Broughton: "You and I, the ornaments of our generation, should have been spared this wreck of our belief that through the long years we had seen civilization grow and the worst become impossible. The tide that bore us along was then all the while moving to *this* as its grand Niagara—yet what a blessing we didn't know it. It seems to me to *undo* everything, everything that was ours, in the most horrible retroactive way." [71]

When Woolf returns in her final novel, *Between the Acts,* from the sprawling form of *The Waves* and *The Years* to a more classical, more Jamesian, unity of place and time, we may say that she incurs the devastation of what Harold Bloom calls the *apophrades,* the return of the dead. For *Between the Acts*—completed shortly before Woolf's death in 1941 and published later that year—is Woolf's "country-house" novel, and in its close intrigue, in the repressed adulterine potential of Isa's relation to her husband and to Mr. Haines, in the riddle that the pageant becomes for its audience, and in the focus not on an individual but on a group, a social system, Woolf's final fiction may be read as a literary reincarnation of elements in *The Golden Bowl* and, especially, of James's country-house novel, *The Sacred Fount,* which, as we know, made Woolf feel that its "masterly" author had "driven his spoon deep into some stew of his own." James's "vitality" came upon Woolf as an assault, practically the leap of a beast, for "his pounce & grip & swing always spring fresh upon me" (*DVW* 4:157). James's narrator in *The Sacred Fount* ends with the sense that he has failed to corroborate his vision of human relations and their meaning. Woolf, I suggest, feels that she has failed in relation to Henry James, and her consciousness of having failed is represented in Miss La Trobe's sense of having failed to convey her vision to the audience of the pageant, which parallels the failure of the *Sacred Fount* narrator, not to mention Henry James's own notorious failure to win an audience for his plays. I believe, moreover, that Woolf took from *The Sacred Fount* the bird imagery that from the outset of *Between the Acts* represents the basis of life and passion in an elemental and savage nature. On the first page of Woolf's novel, we read that "a bird chuckled outside. . . . It was a daylight bird, chuckling over the substance and succulence of the day, over worms, snails, grit," and Miss La Trobe's pronouncement of her failure is followed by a memorable avian enactment of the primitive, frightening current of instinct on which life surges forward:

> "A failure," she groaned, and stopped to put away the records.
> Then suddenly the starlings attacked the tree behind which she had hidden. In one flock they pelted it like so many winged stones. The whole tree hummed with the whizz they made, as if each bird plucked a wire. A whizz, a buzz rose from the bird-buzzing, bird-vibrant, bird-blackened tree. The tree became a rhapsody, a quivering cacophony, a whizz and vibrant rapture, branches, leaves, birds syllabling discordantly life, life, life, without measure, without stop devouring the tree.[72]

In the context of Miss La Trobe's failure and of Isa's passion—an elemental, animal passion channeled into the conjugal, animal copulation forecast ten pages later, on the last page of the novel: "Alone, enmity was bared; also love. Before they slept, they must fight; after they had fought, they would embrace"—the resonance between Woolf's imagery and James's is striking. When the *Sacred Fount* narrator speaks with May Server, overhead "the passage of a flight of rooks made a clamour," May's "grimace" "fluttered like a bird with a broken wing," and the narrator sees "as I had never seen before what consuming passion can make of the marked mortal on whom, with fixed beak and claws, it has settled as on a prey. . . . Voided and scraped of everything, her shell was merely crushable."[73]

Is it any wonder that Woolf's comments to friends about Henry James became, in the 1930s, more acerbic—even, we might say, more desperate? Stephen Spender recalls that when he first met the Woolfs (close to the time that Virginia Woolf was reading *The Sacred Fount*), they described Henry James to him as a "frozen-up monster." Elizabeth Bowen, who met Woolf in 1932, recalls that "she foresaw him [Henry James] as a danger to me" and that Woolf "had rather a horror of Henry James as an influence."[74] With *Between the Acts*, I surmise that Woolf felt, and felt no doubt unjustly—for this novel is surely her most successful since *Mrs. Dalloway* and *To the Lighthouse*—that she herself had been overwhelmed with the horror of the Jamesian influence. Miss La Trobe, Woolf's final portrait of the artist as a woman, succumbs to a desperation that, according to Lyndall Gordon, "signals Virginia Woolf's own." And, Gordon adds, Woolf "complained of having lost, as never before, the urge to write."[75] Thus, in her third-to-last diary entry (February 26, 1941), Woolf moves from the notation "finished Pointz Hall, the Pageant: the Play—finally Between the Acts this morning" to "but shall I ever write again one of those sentences that gives me intense pleasure?" (*DVW* 5:356–57). This is followed, in her penultimate diary entry (March 8, 1941), by remarks on James that we have mentioned earlier: "I mark Henry James's sentence: Observe perpetually. Observe the oncome of age. Observe greed. Observe my own despondency" (*DVW* 5:357–58). James's sentence is the exhortation "Observe perpetually," but we may also read that what James sentences Woolf to is "my own despondency." The same Jamesian stance must have been on her mind in one of her last letters, addressed to one of Henry James's old friends, the actress Elizabeth Robins: "But I remember a saying of Henry James—all experiences are of use to a writer. I think he was talking about a nervous breakdown" (March 13, 1941, *LVW* 6:478). Here is the climactic Woolfian association between Henry James and disease, this time not with the influenza with which she was recurrently afflicted but with the at last more deadly mental distress to which she was to succumb just two weeks after the letter to Robins, when she took her own life on March 28, 1941. By virtue of both positive and negative example, by virtue of his roles as a model whom she would emulate and as a strong precursor against whom she would struggle for differentiation, Henry James played a powerful part in the self-creation of Virginia Woolf, and a part in her self-destruction as well—doing so, moreover, not only in his own person but also as one who functioned for Woolf as representative of the forces by which she felt herself to have been formed, coerced, and violated, as a leading symptom of the seemingly inescapable ills of the patriarchy. In the end we may say that Woolf triumphed, for we value the work that she left, her achievement as one of the greatest novelists and most powerful essayists in English, precisely because she was driven to make hers a unique voice, a special vision, indisputably Woolfian, inalienably not-James.

❧

Conclusion

Given the consensus that has emerged in much feminist discourse that gender makes a radical difference in one's response to tradition and authority, what are we to make of the similarities in the responses of James Joyce and Virginia Woolf to Henry James? For the similarities are very striking. As I have read these influence relations, both Joyce and Woolf learned a great deal from Henry James, emulated him, and sought to keep their relation to James out of sight. Both Joyce and Woolf developed through imitation of James and resistance to him. Both were ambivalent in their pronouncements upon James, Joyce damning James for his "tea-slop" but praising his art in *The Portrait of a Lady* and Woolf making us feel again and again that she was one of the "fickle Jacobeans." Both defensively figured James in similar ways, as effete and even as female (Joyce, for example, in having Bloom confuse Beaufoy/James with Mrs. Purefoy, and Woolf in picturing James as a hen about to lay an egg). Both sought in their fiction to reverse James's priority. Both Joyce and Woolf, moreover, develop metaphors associated with the problem of influence that are astonishingly consonant with the metaphors and analogies that develop Harold Bloom's theory of influence—tropes of paternity and origin, of biological destiny, of generational rivalry and the Freudian family romance, and of disease. In their relations with Henry James, Joyce and Woolf demonstrate how suggestive and helpful the Bloomian model can be for considering the question of influence in the modern novel.

There are, to be sure, striking differences as well. Woolf's pronouncements on James were numerous, as we have seen, whereas Joyce spoke seldom of James in his early years and practically never thereafter. Joyce seems successful, and notably unanxious, in concealing and resolving his "oedipal" attachment to James, whereas Woolf, as I have argued, feels herself to be less successful (though she succeeds no less than Joyce in achieving an art that is uniquely, distinctively hers). Joyce conquers whatever threat James may have presented to him, in part by dint of the weapons of ridicule and laughter, in part by departing more and more radically from James's psychological realism. Woolf, too, pokes fun at Henry James, sometimes deliciously so, but more often than not with almost simultaneous notations of the toll James takes on her—like the statement that "I felt very ill for some time afterwards" with which she ends her droll report of having read *The Wings of the Dove*—and her novels after *The Waves* hauntedly retraverse the terrain of the Jamesian novel.

Reviewing such differences, then, one might suppose that gender is a major determinant. One might propose, for example, that Joyce more completely covers up and resolves the influence relation just as boys resolve their Oedipus complexes more completely than girls.[1] Since one knows from *A Room of One's Own* and *Three Guineas*— and from numerous other biographical sources—that Woolf acutely analyzed the oppressive literary, social, political, and economic effects of what she called "the patriarchy," it is not surprising to find that rage underlies her response to a powerful, oppressive male precursor. From this perspective, moreover, my analysis of the Woolf-James relation suggests how much Woolf herself was a victim of the networks of patriarchal power and authority she analyzed in those generative texts of modern feminism. One may readily conclude that her response to Henry James was gendered from the start, as Christine Froula suggests in proposing that Woolf's first review of James turned against the male Master criticism that Woolf had shortly before seen leveled at female novelists in general.[2]

Nevertheless, generalized conjectures about the role of gender in influence relations, however plausible, must remain only conjectures, at least until we have a much larger sample of female and male writers and precursors than I have examined in *Covert Relations*. One should bear in mind, moreover, that usefully illuminating as they often are, the metaphors and analogies for influence employed by Bloom, Gilbert and Gubar, Joyce, and Woolf are only metaphors and analogies. Literary traditions are not families. Precursors are not fathers or mothers, nor are those who come after them their sons and daughters. All of these metaphors may be powerful aids to thinking about influence relations, but they also have serious limitations, particularly if they are held as anything more than figurative and provisional. Insofar as they become embedded in consciousness, they can indeed victimize people, wrongly persuading us, for instance, that originality and authority are male prerogatives, and promoting the anxiety of authorship that Virginia Woolf herself experienced.

To minimize and mitigate these dangers, one might prefer to move away from gender-inflected models of influence, such as Bloom's oedipal model, and to attempt descriptions that are more gender-neutral, emphasizing that both women and men have a strong motive to deny influence in order to establish their own originality. As I suggested in the Introduction to this book, Bloom's fixation on the "anxiety" of influence may be most useful in pointing to wider and deeper meanings, perhaps to a mythic, tribal process entailing both veneration and destruction of the master or chieftain, or to a process that need not be marked by anxiety whereby artists consume the towering innovators in order to create anew. In addition, as Janice Doane and Devon Hodges have recently argued, both Bloom and Gilbert and Gubar insist on "integrity and [sexual] difference." [3] Bloom sees the drama of literary influence played out in the intergenerational warfare of fathers and sons; conceding that the largely male tradition may be seen as operating in Bloomian terms, Gilbert and Gubar develop the notion of female anxiety of authorship and look forward to the discovery of a female tradition. Without gainsaying that one of the important projects of feminist criticism has been the disclosure of much neglected, ignored, and suppressed writing by women, I believe that the relation of women (and men) to female precursors may be as entangled and ambivalent as the relation of men (and women) to male precursors. To pursue the family metaphor of so much influence study, as Gilbert and Gubar do, would certainly be to discover that mothers may disable as well as enable; for, in correcting the antifemale biases of Freud's reading of psychological development, commentators such as Melanie Klein, Helene Deutsch, and Nancy Chodorow have shown that the mother-daughter relation is as fraught with tension and buried violence as that of fathers and sons, that the daughter may alternate, for example, between total rejection of the mother and complete identification with her. Entrance into the "mother country" cannot guarantee freedom from such conflict.

Doane and Hodges emphasize throughout their argument (and, notably, in their Introduction) that concepts of maleness and femaleness are culturally produced, provisional, and constantly changing. James Joyce and Virginia Woolf recognized that sexual identity is not fixed, and both saw the ideal artist as androgynous. Joyce creates in Leopold Bloom the most celebrated protagonist of modernist literature, and Bloom is "the new womanly man"; everywhere in her work—through, for example, the jeu d'espirit of *Orlando* and the complex network of entwined identities in *The Waves*—Woolf looks to a vantage point above and beyond the special interests and privileges of either sex. Following their lead, students of literary influence may profit by looking beyond insistence on sexual difference to a recognition of the fluidity of sexual identity and therefore of the shifting ground that men and women have in common.

Notes

Introduction

1. For perhaps the strongest feminist attack to date on Bloom, see Janice Doane and Devon Hodges, *Nostalgia and Sexual Difference*, 81–93. Doane and Hodges offer a critique not only of Bloom but also of feminist critics who have modified Bloom's theory and built upon it, notably Sandra Gilbert and Susan Gubar, commentators who see the Bloomian "anxiety of influence" complicated in female writers by what they term an "anxiety of authorship" and who propose that both anxieties may be vanquished by the discovery of a "mother country," a female line of continuity and tradition; see their *The Madwoman in the Attic*, esp. chs. 1 and 2. Gilbert and Gubar, according to Doane and Hodges, present a feminist mirror image of Bloom's theory, and both positions are flawed, in Doane and Hodges' view, by "a tenacious insistence upon integrity and [sexual] difference" that "can only be tentatively maintained" (92).

2. Leon Edel, "How I Came to Henry James," 161–62; see also his *The Modern Psychological Novel*.

3. See, especially, Paul B. Armstrong, *The Challenge of Bewilderment;* Charles Caramello, "Reading Gertrude Stein Reading Henry James"; Kenneth Graham, *Indirections of the Novel;* Sergio Perosa, *Henry James and the Experimental Novel;* John Carlos Rowe, *The Theoretical Dimensions of Henry James;* Tzvetan Todorov, *The Poetics of Prose*, esp. chs. 10 and 11; and Allon White, *The Uses of Obscurity*.

Chapter One

1. Stanislaus Joyce, *My Brother's Keeper*, 105–6.

2. The following note appears in Don Gifford and Robert J. Seidman, *Notes for Joyce:* "Mr Philip Beaufoy, Playgoers' Club, London—a real person who did contribute (terrible?) stories to *Titbits* in the 1890s. The joke resides in the contrast between Beaufoy's literary stature and his name, which means literally 'good faith,' together with his fashionable London address. The story attributed to him here is fictional" (59). On the same page, noting Joyce's schoolboy tale, the annotators remark, "this particular

story appears to have been Joyce's private joke at the expense of his own adolescence." Stanislaus Joyce also points to the existence of a real Philip Beaufoy in *My Brother's Keeper,* 106.

3. Henry James, *The Wings of the Dove* (1902), 173, 183.

4. Henry James, "Notes for The Ivory Tower," 287.

5. Ezra Pound, *Pound/Joyce,* 33.

6. Ezra Pound, "The Notes to 'The Ivory Tower,'" *Little Review* 5, no. 4 (August 1918): 62–63 and 5, no. 5 (Sept. 1918), 52.

7. If the vocabulary of *Ulysses* were randomly distributed throughout the text, then the probability of such links occurring between randomly selected passages of the same length (as those in "Calypso," "The Wandering Rocks," and "Circe") would be one in several million.

8. James Joyce, *Ulysses: "Telemachus," "Nestor," "Proteus," "Calypso," "Lotus Eaters," and "Hades," a Facsimile of Page Proofs for Episodes 1–6,* 232 [date stamp] and 235.

9. James Joyce, *Ulysses: "Wandering Rocks" and "Sirens," a Facsimile of Page Proofs for Episodes 10 and 11,* 151 [date stamp] and 153.

10. James Joyce, *Ulysses: "Circe" and "Eumaeus," a Facsimile of Placards for Episodes 15–16,* 33 [date stamp] and 35.

11. Quoted in Leon Edel, *The Life of Henry James* (Harmondsworth: Penguin, 1977), 2:691, 505.

12. See, for example, "masterstroke" in Henry James, "Mrs. Medwin," in *The Better Sort,* 141.

13. Stanislaus Joyce, *My Brother's Keeper,* 105.

14. Henry James, *The Princess Casamassima,* 542.

15. James Joyce to Stanislaus Joyce, January 13, 1905 (*LJJ* 2:76).

16. James, "Notes for The Ivory Tower," 306, 313, 318, 322. Wouldn't Joyce, incidentally, have found a savor bitter yet piquant in the following remark by James in these notes: "I should like to stick Rosanna at the beautiful Dublin [in Lenox, Mass.], if it weren't for the grotesque anomaly of the name" (346)?

17. This allusion seems to have escaped the notice of annotators Gifford and Seidman, of Weldon Thornton (*Allusions in Ulysses*), and also of William M. Schutte in his *Joyce and Shakespeare.*

18. Richard Ellmann, Introduction to Stanislaus Joyce, *My Brother's Keeper,* 19.

19. The confidants are Mr. and Mrs. B. D. Hayes of New York City. In *Ulysses* a "colonel Hayes" is mentioned (*U* 479), and Gifford and Seidman inform us (*Notes for Joyce*, 425) that the reference is to Baxter Hayes, chief inspector for police for an Irish railway. That there are characters named B. Hayes in "The Birthplace" and in *Ulysses* seems to me, however, to be sheer coincidence (of the sort peculiarly generated by Joyce's work).

20. Richard Ellmann in *LJJ* 2:203. Much earlier in the same letter Joyce prescribes a "kick in the arse" for Henry James for his "tea-slop about" Italy (*LJJ* 2:207).

21. See John Sullivan, *G. K. Chesterton*, 134. Chesterton's Shakespeare essays (the second one in two parts) were printed in January, September, and October 1904 in *Good Words*, a weekly then published in London (where, in October 1904, Joyce and Nora stopped briefly en route to the Continent).

22. Another, less likely identity of "G. R." among Joyce's Dublin associates is George Roberts.

23. Unless, following a widespread publishers' practice, the publishers put the volume with James's Introduction to *The Tempest*, dated 1907, on sale in the fall of 1906.

24. Henry James, Introduction to *The Tempest*, xv, xvii–xviii, xix, xxvii, xxix, xxxi.

25. Ibid., xxxi. For the date of Joyce's original working out of the Shakespeare theory set forth by Dedalus in *Ulysses*, see *JJ* 155.

26. Joyce's style manuals, both of which entirely omit American writers, were George Saintsbury's *History of English Prose Rhythm* and W. Peacock's anthology *English Prose*. See *JJ* 475, and J. S. Atherton, "The Oxen of the Sun," 315.

27. Fredric Jameson tentatively suggests that James may be detected in "Eumaeus": "Indeed," Jameson writes, "I am tempted to say, judging from the sentence structure, the elaborate periphrases, the use of occasional foreign expressions as well as cautiously isolated 'colloquial' ones, that this chapter really constitutes Joyce's attempt at a parody or pastiche of a writer he had no particular sympathy or respect for, namely Henry James. (If so, it is not a very good pastiche. . . ." See Jameson, "*Ulysses* in History," 138–39.

28. Ellmann relates the following anecdote about Joyce and Gilbert Seldes: "Joyce was ill at ease and walked up and down with suppressed excitement. Finally he stopped and said, 'Mr. Seldes, I know that the *Dial* is not an eleemosynary institution—' Then he smiled delightfully, 'Oh dear, this is rather like a sentence by Henry James, isn't it? Let's start again'" (*JJ* 525).

Chapter Two

1. Hugh Kenner, *The Pound Era*, 20.

2. Stanislaus Joyce, *My Brother's Keeper*, 238.

3. C. P. Curran, *James Joyce Remembered*, 30, 52.

4. Mary Colum and Padraic Colum, *Our Friend James Joyce*, 149–50: "He spoke of Henry James, remarking that it was evident that he had influenced Proust. He praised *Portrait of a Lady*, dwelling with much delight on the presentation of Isabel Archer."

5. *The Dublin Diary of Stanislaus Joyce*, 86.

6. James Joyce to Stanislaus Joyce, November 19 and December 3, 1904, January 12, March 15, and April 4, 1905, *LJJ* 2:71, 72, 76, 85, 87.

7. Stanislaus Joyce, *My Brother's Keeper*, 94; *LJJ* 2:85–86.

8. See ch. 1, n. 28; ch. 2, n. 4; and, for the Henry James allusions in *Finnegans Wake*, Adeline Glasheen's *Third Census of Finnegans Wake*, 38–39, 100, 141, 297.

9. Curran, *James Joyce Remembered*, 52.

10. Harry Levin, *James Joyce*, 49–50.

11. *The Complete Notebooks of Henry James*, 13.

12. In the Mangan essay, Joyce wrote of the constant tension between two literary schools, the classic and the romantic, remarking that the conflict between them is the condition for achievement and that the fusion of the two is a proper object for the artist to strive to attain. See *The Critical Essays of James Joyce*, 74–75. As early as 1890, the Viennese critic Hermann Bahr had identified such a synthesis as the task of modern literature (in *Zur Kritik der Moderne* [Zurich, 1890]), and Malcolm Bradbury and James McFarlane, who cite Bahr, seem substantially to agree in their helpful essay "The Name and Nature of Modernism" in *Modernism: 1890–1930*, 43, 48.

13. Homer Obed Brown, *James Joyce's Early Fiction*, 7–8; Fogel, *Henry James and the Structure of the Romantic Imagination*, esp. pp. 1–8.

14. *The Dublin Diary of Stanislaus Joyce*, 92–93. Also in Stanislaus's diary, James Joyce would have read that "Henry James is the most refined and most modern writer in modern English Literature" (89) and that "a certain asexuality is over Henry James's men and women" (91). An insight akin to Stanislaus's in this last remark may underlie Joyce's having Beaufoy say that "the love passages" in his novels "are beneath [not *above*] suspicion" (*U* 374).

15. James Joyce, "The Dead," in *Dubliners*, 278, 274.

16. James Joyce to Stanislaus Joyce, c. September 24, 1905, *LJJ* 2:111.

17. Only one other commentator seems to have noticed the possible relation between these two stories. See Joan Zlotnick, "Influence or Coincidence."

18. Joyce, "The Dead," 277.

19. See, in *LJJ* 2, Joyce's letters of January 19, 1905, and of December 3 and 7, 1906; in addition to saying that Stanislaus has "no special affinity" for Henry James, Joyce writes derisively to his brother about "your prosy old friend H. J." and "your friend H. J." By 1906, when these letters were written, Stanislaus had severely qualified his admiration of Henry James (see *The Dublin Diary of Stanislaus Joyce*, 101).

20. A. R. Orage. "Henry James and the Ghostly," 43.

21. James Joyce, "Eveline," in *Dubliners*, 48.

22. Kenner, *The Pound Era*, 38.

23. Zack Bowen, "Epiphanies, Stephen's Diary, and the Narrative Perspective of *A Portrait of the Artist as a Young Man*."

24. For an extended discussion of the water imagery in *The Wings of the Dove*, see ch. 2, "The Sea-Change in *The Wings of the Dove*," in my *Henry James and the Structure of the Romantic Imagination*, esp. pp. 70–82.

25. James Joyce, *A Portrait of the Artist as a Young Man*, 238, 199.

26. Harold Bloom, *A Map of Misreading*, 17.

27. Kenner, *The Pound Era*, 3, 7, 15, 16, 18. Eliot's remark, quoted by Kenner (18), was first published in January 1918 in *The Egoist*.

28. James Joyce to Harriet Shaw Weaver, July 20, 1919, *LJJ* 1:129.

29. *Concise Oxford Dictionary*, 6th edition (1976), p. 675.

30. For further information on the Eton suit and morning dress, see C. Willett Cunnington, *A Dictionary of English Costume*, 74, and C. Willett Cunnington and Phillis Cunnington, *Handbook of English Costume in the Nineteenth Century*, 311, 315, 316.

31. Herbert Gorman, *James Joyce*, 45.

32. See, on this last point, Harold Bloom, *Poetry and Repression*, 2.

33. Henry James, "Honoré de Balzac, 1902," 90. For the fullest exposition of Adeline Tintner's view of Henry James's "rewriting" of great authors of the past, see her *The Book World of Henry James*, and, for a brilliant opposing view of James as subject to influence anxiety, John Carlos Rowe's *The Theoretical Dimensions of Henry James*.

34. Ezra Pound, *Pound/Joyce*, 44. See also Pound's letter to Joyce of January 17 and 19, 1914, in *Pound/Joyce*, 24, and Pound's essay "Mr. James Joyce and the Modern Stage," 123.

35. Arthur Power, *Conversations with James Joyce*, 44–47.

Chapter 3

1. Quoted by Leon Edel in *Henry James Letters: 1895–1916*, 504 n. 1. A year and a half later, James wrote again, this time to Woolf's aunt, Anne Thackeray Ritchie, of "the promise of Virginia's printed wit" (504).

2. *Henry James Letters: 1895–1916*, 437.

3. Quentin Bell, *Virginia Woolf*, 1:122.

4. Leon Edel points out this parallel in his helpful, detailed discussion of the Stephens' relations with Henry James in *Henry James, the Master: 1901–1916*, vol. 5 of *The Life of Henry James* (Philadelphia and New York: J. B. Lippincott, 1972), 393.

5. Virginia Woolf, "A Sketch of the Past," in *Moments of Being* (1976), 83.

6. Ibid., 136.

7. Phyllis Rose, *Woman of Letters*, 260–61.

8. Carol Dole, "Oppression, Obsession: Virginia Woolf and Henry James," seminar paper, Cornell University, 1982. I am grateful to Ms. Dole for permission to quote from the manuscript of this essay, a revision of which has been published in the *Southern Review*, n.s. 24 (1988): 253–71.

9. See Jane Marcus, *Virginia Woolf and the Languages of Patriarchy*, esp. ch. 4, "Liberty, Sorority, Misogyny."

10. Virginia R. Hyman, "Reflections in the Looking-Glass: Leslie Stephen and Virginia Woolf," 204.

11. See Lyndall Gordon, *Virginia Woolf*, esp. chs. 1 and 2, and Vanessa Bell, *Notes on Virginia's Childhood*.

12. Ellen Bayuk Rosenman, *The Invisible Presence*, 4.

13. Gordon, *Virginia Woolf*, 15; Hyman, "Reflections in the Looking-Glass," 216.

14. Leonard Woolf, *Sowing*, 198–99.

15. Virginia Woolf, "Sara Coleridge," in *The Death of the Moth and Other Essays*, 111.

16. Holograph manuscript, "Sara Coleridge," University of Sussex, Monk's House Papers B.5.

17. Virginia Woolf, "The Man at the Gate," in *The Death of the Moth*, 106. Leonard Woolf's dating of the composition of the essay is in his footnote on p. 104.

18. Typescript, "The Man at the Gate," University of Sussex, Monk's House Papers B.5.

19. Virginia Woolf, "The Man at the Gate," in *The Death of the Moth*, 106–7.

20. Louise A. DeSalvo gives a summary of the works Woolf mentions reading and hearing read (by her father) in the 1897 diary in "1897: Virginia Woolf at Fifteen," 88–91. The 1897 diary itself is in the Berg Collection of the New York Public Library.

21. B. J. Kirkpatrick, *A Bibliography of Virginia Woolf*, 135; S. P. Rosenbaum, "Three Unknown Early Essays by Virginia Woolf," 1–4.

22. Woolf's notes are titled "The Golden Bowl," University of Sussex, Monk's House Papers B.1a.

23. Virginia Woolf, "Mr. Henry James's Latest Novel," 339. Quotations from this review in the text that follows are also on this page.

24. Virginia Woolf, "The Method of Henry James," 655.

25. Rosenbaum, "Three Unknown Early Essays of Virginia Woolf," 2.

26. Henry James, *English Hours*, 195–96. All citations of Virginia Woolf's review of *English Hours*, titled "Portraits of Place," are to Rosenbaum, "Three Unknown Early Essays of Virginia Woolf," 3–4.

27. Paula Vene Smith, "The Library and the Tea Table: Virginia Woolf and the Fiction of Henry James," Ph.D. dissertation, Cornell University, 1987. I am grateful to Ms. Smith for sharing with me her work on James and Woolf.

28. Leonard Woolf, *Sowing*, 120.

29. For Leonard Woolf's account of the rage for James at Cambridge, see *Sowing*, 119–29.

30. Leonard Woolf to Lytton Strachey, July 23, 1905, quoted in Quentin Bell, *Virginia Woolf*, 1 : 177.

31. Harold Bloom, *The Anxiety of Influence*, 94–95.

32. For a recent feminist attack on Bloom's patriarchal stance (and on some of the responses of other feminist critics to Bloom), see Janice Doane and Devon Hodges, *Nostalgia and Sexual Difference*, 81–93.

33. Typescript, "Notes of a Days Walk," University of Sussex, Monk's House Papers B.7.

34. Quentin Bell, *Virginia Woolf*, 1:37–38; Stephen Trombley, *"All that Summer She was Mad": Virginia Woolf and Her Doctors*, 9; Leon Edel, "The Madness of Virginia Woolf," 194.

35. Richard Collier, *The Plague of the Spanish Lady: The Influenza Pandemic of 1918–1919*; W. I. B. Beveridge, *Influenza: the Last Great Plague: An Unfinished Story of Discovery*, 30–33; and see also A. A. Hoehling, *The Great Epidemic*.

36. Virginia Woolf, "The Leaning Tower," *CE* 2:162–63. Woolf read the essay to the Workers' Educational Association in May 1940. Later in the piece, James is again the endpoint of a literary tradition. Speaking of the writers up to 1914, for whom "the model, human life" was a constant, Woolf says, "Put a page of their writing under the magnifying-glass and you will see, far away in the distance, the Greeks, the Romans; coming nearer, the Elizabethans; coming nearer still, Dryden, Swift, Voltaire, Jane Austen, Dickens, Henry James" (*CE* 2:169–70).

37. Harold Bloom, Introduction to *Modern Critical Views: Virginia Woolf*, 2. This introduction is reproduced verbatim as section 2 of the Introduction to *British Modernist Fiction: 1920–1945*, ed. Bloom, 6–11.

38. Virginia Woolf, "The Leaning Tower," *CE* 2:169.

39. Virginia Woolf, "Women and Fiction," *CE* 2:146.

40. Virginia Woolf, "How It Strikes a Contemporary," *CE* 2:154, 158.

41. Virginia Woolf, *A Room of One's Own*, 79.

42. Virginia Woolf, "Speech before the London/National Society for Women's Service, January 21, 1931," in *The Pargiters: The Novel-Essay Portion of* The Years, xxix, xxxi.

43. Quentin Bell, *Virginia Woolf*, 1:57.

44. Dole, "Oppression, Obsession."

Chapter Four

1. See G. A. Holleyman, *Catalogue of Books from the Library of Leonard and Virginia Woolf*. *The Aspern Papers* is a 1926 reprint. *The Sacred Fount* was published before 1915, but the volume is dated, in Virginia Woolf's hand, 1923, and we know from her diary that she did not read it until ten years after that date.

2. Holleyman, *Catalogue of Books*, Introduction, 1.

3. See Paula Vene Smith, "The Library and the Tea Table."

4. Virginia Woolf, "Speech before the London/National Society for Women's Service, January 21, 1931," xxxi.

5. Virginia Woolf, "Speech [Manuscript Notes]," in *The Partigers*, 163.

6. The concept of "anxiety of authorship" was developed by Sandra Gilbert and Susan Gubar to describe the fear of the female writer that she cannot create because she is female and because of the ways in which Western culture has connected textuality and sexuality, assigning potency, generative power, and authority to the male, and, to the female, the role of the blank page on which the male inscribes himself—with an accompanying taboo against the self-articulation of the blank page. See Sandra Gilbert and Susan Gubar, *The Madwoman in the Attic*, chs. 1 and 2, esp. pp. 48–53.

7. Virginia Woolf, "The Old Order," 497, 498. Further page citations will be given in the text.

8. Virginia Woolf, "Across the Border," 55.

9. For an account of the seventieth-birthday tribute to James, see Leon Edel, *Henry James, the Master: 1901–1916*, vol. 5 of *The Life of Henry James* (Philadelphia: J. B. Lippincott, 1972), 483–89. Edel reprints James's letter of thanks to the three hundred donors, along with the list of their names, in *Henry James Letters: 1895–1916*, vol. 4 of *Henry James Letters*, 664–68. Since Virginia Woolf was one of the donors, James would have given the photograph of the Sargent portrait to her and not, surely, as Nigel Nicolson reports in a footnote (*LVW* 2:265), to Leslie Stephen, who had been dead since 1904.

10. David Garnett, *Great Friends*, 125. Garnett observes, "If, as Angelica suggested, she Virginia [*sic*] were a racehorse, I should expect to find Laurence Sterne and Henry James in her pedigree. The opening chapters of *Night and Day* have a distinct flavour of James. Later on, though the texture of her writing is quite unlike that of Henry James, there is the same kind of sensitive analysis characteristic of the novels of James's middle period" (124).

11. Jane Novak, *The Razor Edge of Balance*, 28.

12. Virginia Woolf, "The Method of Henry James," 655. Quotations from this review in the text that follows are also on this page.

13. Woolf's allusion to James's tale "The Figure in the Carpet" suggests that it should perhaps be added to the list of works she had read by Henry James.

14. Virginia Woolf, "American Fiction," 3.

15. Manuscript notes for *To the Lighthouse*, Berg Collection, New York Public Library.

16. Holograph manuscript, review of *Maud Evelyn* and *The Sacred Fount,* Berg Collection, New York Public Library.

17. Virginia Woolf, "Within the Rim," 163.

18. Here again Woolf refers to James's size. Both Carol Dole and Paula Smith suggest that Woolf's fascination with James's imposing physical presence and her mention in the review of James's letters of his gusto and appetite can be related to her eating disorders and to the near-emaciation those disorders caused. See Paula Vene Smith, "The Library and the Tea Table," and Carol Dole, "Oppression, Obsession."

19. Virginia Woolf, holograph reading notes, "Henry James. Letters," University of Sussex, Monk's House Papers B.2.

20. Virginia Woolf, "The Letters of Henry James," 217–18. Quotations from this review in the text that follows are also on these pages.

21. Henry James, *The Letters of Henry James,* ed. Percy Lubbock, 2:181–82.

22. Ibid., 1:142. Woolf's notes in the Berg Collection read, "The great thing to be saturated with something. I chose the form of my saturation. Strange sense of life being a thing one can deliberately try—outside oneself—."

23. Virginia Woolf, "Phases of Fiction" (1929), in *CE* 2:89; Henry James, "Preface to *The Tragic Muse,*" in *The Art of the Novel,* 84.

24. Dole, "Oppression, Obsession."

25. Dole writes, "Her admission there [in "Am I a Snob?"] that 'I want coronets; but they must be old coronets; coronets that carry land with them and country houses' is disquietingly reminiscent of her discussion of James's obsession with 'the age of old houses, the glamour of great names.' . . . One begins to suspect that Woolf's irritation at some of James's qualities is grounded in the recognition that she shares them." I do not think, however, that Woolf is always so witting as Dole's word *recognition* implies. I do not see her quite at the stage of saying to herself, "I attack James's snobbery because I am afraid that I myself am a snob." James, I conjecture, gets into "Am I a Snob?" because of an *unconscious* connection Woolf makes along these lines.

26. Virginia Woolf, "Gothic Romance," 288.

27. Virginia Woolf, "Henry James' Ghost Stories," 849. All quotations from this review in the text that follows are on pp. 849–50 of the number of *TLS* in which it appeared.

28. Orage, "Henry James and the Ghostly," 43.

29. Virginia Woolf, holograph reading notes on Percy Lubbock, *The Craft of Fiction,* Berg Collection, New York Public Library.

30. Virginia Woolf, "On Re-Reading Novels," 466. All quotations from this review in the text that follows are on pp. 465–66 of the number of *TLS* in which it appeared.

31. Virginia Woolf, holograph draft of "On Re-Reading Novels," Berg Collection, New York Public Library. All quotations from Woolf's draft that follow in text are from this manuscript.

32. Harvena Richter, *Virginia Woolf: The Inward Voyage,* 30; James, *The Art of the Novel,* 43, 45. For Woolf's reading of James's Preface to *The Portrait of a Lady,* see *DVW* 4:241. Woolf may have read James's Preface earlier, either in the New York Edition (1907–9) or in the early twenties in the collected Macmillan edition of James's works, which she praised in her unpublished review for reprinting "the famous prefaces" (see n. 16, this chapter, and related text).

33. Harold Bloom, *The Anxiety of Influence,* 95.

34. Virginia Woolf, "The Antiquary," 293.

35. Quentin Bell, letter to the author, October 18, 1989. Professor Bell goes on to say, "She found the same thing with Mrs. Humphrey Ward but that was not a serious embarrassment."

36. Other references to James during the 1920s may be found in *LVW* 2:601; *LVW* 3:78, 89, 111; *LVW* 6:506 (letter of November 7, 1924)— three of the items in volumes 3 and 6 of *LVW* concern the Woolfs' publication of *Henry James at Work,* by Theodora Bosanquet, James's last secretary—*LVW* 4:32, 54; *DVW* 3:67, 94–95, 137, 214, 227; "Mr. Conrad: A Conversation," 681–82; "Jane Austen at Sixty," 434 ("She would have been the forerunner of Henry James and of Proust"); "The Patron and the Crocus," 46; "Joseph Conrad," 493; "American Fiction," 1–3; "The Russian Point of View"; "Thomas Hardy's Novels," 33 ("Some [novelists], like Henry James and Flaubert, are able not merely to make the best use of the spoil their gifts bring in, but control their genius in the act of creation; they are aware of all the possibilities of every situation, and are never taken by surprise"); and "On Not Knowing French," 348.

37. Vijay Sharma, *Virginia Woolf as Literary Critic,* 111. Sharma, incidentally, is mistaken in attributing to Woolf a remark actually by Lytton Strachey: "I've seen Henry James twice since I came and was immensely impressed. I do not mean only seen with the eye—I wish I knew him." See Sharma, p. 26, and *Virginia Woolf and Lytton Strachey,* 27.

38. Among critics of Woolf, only Mark Goldman pays significant attention to "Phases of Fiction." See his *The Reader's Art: Virginia Woolf as Literary Critic,* passim. Elsewhere, I do not find any discussion of this essay per se. Sharma mentions it by name once and quotes it in passing four or five times. Jane Novak quotes it several times in *The Razor Edge of Balance.* Lyndall Gordon quotes the essay three times in *Virginia Woolf,* Har-

vena Richter quotes it twice in *Virginia Woolf,* and so does Maria DiBattista in *Virginia Woolf's Major Novels.* It is mentioned once by Makiko Minow-Pinkney in *Virginia Woolf and the Problem of the Subject,* by Ellen Bayuk Rosenman in *The Invisible Presence,* by Madeline Moore in *The Short Season between Two Silences,* and by Mark Hussey in *The Singing of the Real World.* In a number of the very best books on Woolf, there is no trace of the existence of "Phases of Fiction," including, among others, Jean Guiget, *Virginia Woolf and Her Works;* Joan Bennett, *Virginia Woolf;* Alice van Buren Kelley, *The Novels of Virginia Woolf;* Avrom Fleishman, *Virginia Woolf;* Jean O. Love, *Virginia Woolf;* Phyllis Rose, *Woman of Letters;* Lucio P. Ruotolo, *The Interrupted Moment;* Alex Zwerdling, *Virginia Woolf and the Real World;* and Jane Marcus, *Virginia Woolf and the Languages of Patriarchy.*

39. Virginia Woolf, "Phases of Fiction," part 2. Parenthetic citations of "Phases 2" in the text that follows are to this installment of the serialization of the essay.

40. Madeline Moore, "Nature and Community: A Study of Cyclical Reality in *The Waves,*" 225.

41. "Virginia Woolf, "Phases of Fiction," part 3, 409–10.

42. Aside from commentators cited earlier (Quentin Bell, Carol Dole, Leon Edel, Jane Novak, Vijay Sharma, and Paula Smith), the most important discussions of the James-Woolf relation are Ethel Cornwell, *The Still Point,* 161–63; Diane Levine Cousineau, "Henry James and Virginia Woolf"; Mary Virginia Gibson, "Event and Consciousness in Certain Novels of Henry James and Virginia Woolf"; Mark Goldman, *The Reader's Art,* 36–39; Gerald Hoag, "Henry James and the Criticism of Virginia Woolf"; Vivien Jones, *James as Critic,* 194–98; Ellen Douglass Leyburn, "Virginia Woolf's Judgment of Henry James"; Judith Ryan, "The Vanishing Subject"; Sheldon Sacks, "Novelists as Storytellers"; J. Oates Smith, "The Art of Relationship"; Carol Simpson Stern, "Parties as Reflectors of the Feminine Sensibility"; Marianna Torgovnick, *The Visual Arts, Pictorialism, and the Novel;* "Panel Discussion 2," in *Virginia Woolf,* ed. Eric Warner; René Wellek, "Virginia Woolf as Critic"; and Hana Wirth-Nesher, "Limits of Fiction."

43. Typescript, "Phases of Fiction," University of Sussex, Monk's House Papers B.6.

44. Leyburn notes this omission in her essay "Virginia Woolf's Judgment of Henry James."

45. Virginia Woolf, "Character in Fiction," 417–18. This essay has come to be known as "Mr. Bennett and Mrs. Brown," the title under which it was reprinted (a title borrowed, incidentally, from a much shorter review Woolf published in 1923).

46. Virginia Woolf, "The Narrow Bridge of Art," *CE* 2:225. This essay was first published as "Poetry, Fiction, and the Future" in the New York *Herald Tribune*, August 14 and 21, 1927.

47. Henry James, *The Ambassadors*, 1:43–44.

48. *The Letters of Henry James*, ed. Lubbock, 2:181.

49. Stephen Spender, *The Destructive Element*, 21.

50. See *The Destructive Element*, pp. 203–4, for Spender's brief comments on Woolf.

51. *The Letters of Henry James*, ed. Lubbock, 2:384. Woolf's reading notes on *The Letters of Henry James* include quotations from a related passage James wrote some months later. James wrote, "The subject-matter of one's effort has become *itself* utterly treacherous and false—its relation to reality utterly given away and smashed. Reality is a world that was to be capable of *this*—and how represent that horrific capability, *historically* latent, historically ahead of it? How on the other hand *not* represent it either" (*Letters of Henry James*, 2:446). Woolf noted, "the horrible interest—his world smashed up—what reality then? what new world wd have been possible for him?" (holograph reading notes, "Henry James. Letters," University of Sussex, Monk's House Papers B.2).

52. For comments by Woolf on James after "Phases of Fiction" not mentioned in the last three paragraphs (but including a few mentioned much earlier in this chapter or the preceding one), see *The Pargiters*, ed. Leaska, p. 163; *LVW* 5:142, 214, 392; *LVW* 6:478, 529 (letter of March 23, 1931); "The Novels of Turgenev," 885; *DVW* 4:241, 248 (where Woolf mentions reading *Alice James: Her Brothers—Her Journal*, ed. Anna Robeson Burr); *DVW* 5:28, 98, 357; "The Man at the Gate," 382.

Chapter Five

1. Harvena Richter, *Virginia Woolf: The Inward Voyage*, 6.

2. Quentin Bell prints this letter in *Virginia Woolf*, 1:208–10.

3. Louise A. DeSalvo, Introduction to *Melymbrosia*, xxxiv; Phyllis Rose, *Woman of Letters: A Life of Virginia Woolf*, 58.

4. In the present chapter, my quotations from *The Portrait of a Lady* are from the 1908 New York Edition revision that I believe Woolf read, whereas in the discussion of James Joyce, in chapter two, I used the 1881 text, the only one extant at the time of the composition of *Stephen Hero*.

5. Henry James, *The Awkward Age*, 383.

6. Rose, *Woman of Letters*, 73.

7. Alex Zwerdling, *Virginia Woolf and the Real World*; Rose, *Woman of Letters*, 72; Madeline Moore, *The Short Season between Two Silences*, 55.

8. Henry James, *The American*, 480, 49.

9. Denis de Rougemont, *Love in the Western World*.

10. Joseph Wiesenfarth, "A Woman in *The Portrait of a Lady*," 24. Of Ralph Touchett's death Wiesenfarth observes, "In the great tradition of romantic love, it is a *Liebestod*."

11. For a detailed comparison of *Daisy Miller* and *The Voyage Out*, see Paula Vene Smith, "The Library and the Tea Table." My reading of Professor Smith's dissertation—as well as talks we had while the dissertation was in progress—has informed the present discussion of *The Voyage Out* in a variety of ways, particularly with respect to the themes of the appropriate reading for young women and of the horror of prostitution.

12. Not everyone reads Daisy's disease as willed, but it is quite plausible to see her death as no less a "chosen suicide" than Rachel's. The illustrative detail is her last speech to Winterbourne, just before she comes down with her fatal illness, "I don't care . . . whether I have Roman fever or not" (Henry James, *Daisy Miller, Pandora, The Patagonia, and Other Tales*, 89). For a more detailed argument on this point, see my *Daisy Miller: A Dark Comedy of Manners*, 39–40, 84–85.

13. The phrase "undue temptation" is from a newspaper clipping in Woolf's notebooks for *Three Guineas* (University of Sussex, Monk's House Papers B.16). The newspaper was the London *Times;* the date is missing. The article is titled "Fifty Years, Society and the Season: The Age of Chaperonage." It is by Mary, Countess of Lovelace. The countess remarks, "for my sisters or me to go out alone into the streets would have been to defy the social taboo in its severest form." In *Three Guineas*, Woolf quotes the following sentence from the article (reprinted as "Society and the Season" in *Fifty Years: 1882–1932* [London: Thornton Butterworth, 1932]): "It was supposed that most men were not 'virtuous,' that is, that nearly all would be capable of accosting and annoying—or worse—any unaccompanied young woman whom they met" (Virginia Woolf, *Three Guineas*, 222).

14. Frederick Newberry, "A Note on the Horror in James's Revision of *Daisy Miller*."

15. A comparison between Rachel and Isabel Archer (which I relegate to a footnote because the full argument for it would be rather finespun) is that in the early versions of the novel Rachel was called Cynthia, a name that

would associate her with Artemis, the virgin huntress, just as Isabel is associated with Artemis (or Diana) by her name, *Archer.*

16. Virginia Blain, "Narrative Voice and Female Perspective in Virginia Woolf's Early Novels," 126.

17. Rose, *Woman of Letters,* 59.

18. Virginia Woolf, "Mr. Henry James's Latest Novel," 339; Virginia Woolf, "Henry James' Ghost Stories," 850.

19. Paula Vene Smith, "The Library and the Tea Table"; Leonard Woolf, *Sowing: An Autobiography of the Years 1880 to 1904,* 122–23; and for another commentator who has recognized Henry James in Fortescue, see L. L. Lee, "Woolf, the Times, the Provinces."

20. Virginia Woolf, "The Old Order," 497.

21. David Garnett, *Great Friends,* 124.

22. John Carlos Rowe, *The Theoretical Dimensions of Henry James,* ch. 3.

23. David Daiches, *Virginia Woolf,* 25.

24. For a discussion of Isabel Archer as one of Emma's daughters, see Elizabeth Sabiston, "Isabel Archer: The Architecture of Consciousness and the International Theme."

25. Woolf's notes include this sentence: "English have a moral sense that 'sends you up like a rocket'" (reading notes, "The Golden Bowl," University of Sussex, Monk's House Papers B.1a).

26. Henry James, *The Ambassadors,* 1:218.

27. Ibid., 1:217.

28. Henry James, *The Golden Bowl,* 2:250.

29. Rose, *Woman of Letters,* 96.

30. Harold Bloom, *The Anxiety of Influence,* 91.

31. Virginia Woolf, "Modern Novels," 189.

32. Ibid.

33. Virginia Woolf, "Modern Fiction," in *The Common Reader,* 189.

34. Virginia Woolf, "The Method of Henry James," 655.

35. James, *The Golden Bowl,* 1:3; Woolf, reading notes, "The Golden Bowl," University of Sussex, Monk's House Papers B.1a. Woolf makes similar use of Bond Street in "Mrs. Dalloway in Bond Street" and in *Mrs. Dalloway.*

36. Henry James, *The Complete Notebooks of Henry James,* 15; Virginia Woolf, "Henry James' Ghost Stories," 849. For an exemplary discussion of James as marking the transition from a metaphysics of presence to a metaphysics of absence (practically a cliché of James studies by the mid-1980s), see Sergio Perosa, *Henry James and the Experimental Novel.*

37. For a brilliant recent discussion of the political elements in *Mrs. Dalloway,* see Alex Zwerdling's chapter on the novel in *Virginia Woolf and the Real World.*

38. Rose, *Woman of Letters,* 99–102.

39. Carol Gilligan, *In a Different Voice,* 22, 16, 2.

40. James, *The Golden Bowl,* 2:236.

41. For a study that exemplifies the prosecutorial tone of many critics toward Maggie Verver (and Henry James), see Sallie Sears, *The Negative Imagination.*

42. See, however, for an illuminating discussion of *Mrs. Dalloway* and *The Portrait of a Lady,* Paula Vene Smith's "The Library and the Tea Table."

43. I am grateful to my colleague Michelle Massé for having clarified for me, in conversation, the gender-inflected narcissism found in the heroes of bildungsromans from *The Sorrows of Young Werther* through *A Portrait of the Artist as a Young Man* and beyond; see also on this topic *Narcissism and the Text,* ed. Lynne Layton and Barbara Ann Shapiro, especially Layton's essay "Narcissism and History: Flaubert's *Sentimental Education,*" pp. 170–91.

44. James, *The Ambassadors,* 1:81.

45. Ibid., 2:327.

46. Henry James, *The Notebooks of Henry James* (1947), 18.

47. Paula Vene Smith, "The Library and the Tea Table."

48. Zwerdling, *Virginia Woolf and the Real World,* 200; Henry James, Preface to *The Wings of the Dove,* in *The Wings of the Dove* (1909), 1:xviii–xix.

49. James, *The Golden Bowl,* 2:115.

50. James, *Notebooks,* 18, and Preface to *Roderick Hudson,* in *Roderick Hudson,* vii. For an argument that the aesthetic process of vision in James leads to "disinterested appreciation, which is, for James, the highest form of love," see my *Henry James and the Structure of the Romantic Imagination,* esp. 25–27, 47.

51. Carol Dole provides a good account of the ways in which Woolf's interiorized drama more closely resembles Henry James's in style and syntax than, say, that of James Joyce. See Dole's "Oppression, Obsession."

52. See *PL2* 2:164–65, 205; *The Ambassadors*, 2:256.

53. Holograph manuscript, "To the Lighthouse," Berg Collection, New York Public Library.

54. See Sandra Gilbert and Susan Gubar, *The Madwoman in the Attic*, ch. 1 passim.

55. One might also recall, at this juncture, Woolf's comparison of the powerful influence of Henry James to the nonexistent influence of Scott: "The most impressionable beginner, whose pen oscillates if exposed within a mile of the influence of Stendahl, Flaubert, Henry James, or Chekhov, can read the Waverley Novels one after another without altering an adjective" ("The Antiquary," 293).

56. I am grateful to Carol Dole for having pointed out the possible connection between Woolf's description of Henry James's "knife" and Mr. Ramsay's plunging "beak of brass"; see Dole's "Oppression, Obsession."

57. For a discussion of Woolf's treatment of Vita Sackville-West in *Orlando*, see Nigel Nicholson, *Portrait of a Marriage*, esp. pp. 200–203.

58. Henry James, *The Wings of the Dove* (1909), 1:150.

59. The phrase "turned her face to the wall" occurs at least five times in James's novel. See, for example, *The Wings of the Dove* (1909), 2:270 and 321.

60. The New York Edition, originally published as twenty-four volumes (1907–9), was extended to twenty-six volumes with the posthumous publication in 1917 of *The Ivory Tower* and *The Sense of the Past*. In New York, Scribners issued two editions of each of the posthumous novels—for each, a trade edition and an edition uniform with the volumes of the New York Edition. Thereafter Scribners always advertised the New York Edition as twenty-six volumes. The English publisher of *The Ivory Tower* and *The Sense of the Past*, however, issued only one edition of each title, which was not presented as an extension of the New York Edition. The Woolfs' copy of the 1917 *Ivory Tower* (London, W. W. Collins) survives at Washington State University; I do not know whether Virginia and Leonard Woolf may have owned at any time a complete set of the New York Edition. It seems quite probable that they did, however, because Woolf's holograph comment (in her unpublished fragmentary review of *Maud Evelyn* and *The Sacred Fount* [Berg Collection]) that the Macmillan edition of James (1922) was notable for making the "famous prefaces" available in an inexpensive form suggests that she already knew them in their only previous publication in the New York Edition—"this," she wrote, "is the first time that they

[the prefaces] have been detached from the expensive New York edition"; because the Woolfs' library was enormously reduced between 1928–29 (when there were more than 15,000 books) and the time of its appraisal after Leonard's death in 1969 (around 9,000 books); and because among the books sold shortly thereafter (and therefore not catalogued in the Washington State collection) were "the works of . . . Henry James," quite possibly a set of the New York Edition. I would suppose that Woolf was referring to this set when, in 1915, she wrote of James, "we have his works here" (*LVW* 2:67). See Holleyman, *Catalogue of Books from the Library of Leonard and Virginia Woolf,* 1–3 and the index.

61. Rose, *Woman of Letters,* 210.

62. Sandra Gilbert and Susan Gubar, *The War of the Words,* 193.

63. Like Henry James, Bernard collects observations in notebooks intended as aids to the writing of fiction. See *The Waves,* p. 26.

64. H. G. Wells, *Boon,* 106–7. Woolf may have read *Boon* at the time of its original publication in 1915. Wells's satire came out just a few months before she wrote to Strachey saying that she could find nothing in James but "faintly tinged rose water, urbane and sleek, but vulgar, and as pale as Walter Lamb" (*LVW* 2:67). If she did read *Boon* in 1915, then we might take retrospective note of some of the resonance between Wells's description of James and Woolf's language in the James essays she published in the teens. For instance, the opening of her review of *The Method of Henry James,* where she says that James is "to some an oppression, to others an obsession, but undeniably present to all" ("The Method of Henry James," 655), may be read as a recollection of Wells's "You see . . . you can't now talk of literature without going through James. James is unavoidable" (*Boon,* 98). The cathedral metaphor with which she begins her review of *The Letters of Henry James,* and the "altar" trope with which she closes, may similarly be a recollection of Wells's descriptions of the Jamesian novel as "a church lit but without a congregation" and of the "altar" contained therein (*Boon,* 106–7).

65. Susan anticipates this image earlier when she thinks, "I love with such ferocity that it kills me when the object of my love shows by a phrase that he can escape. He escapes, and I am left clutching a string that slips in and out among the leaves on the tree-tops" (*WV* 136).

66. Preface to *The American,* in *The American,* xvii–xviii.

67. When Charlotte demands that Prince Amerigo explain his disapproval of her contemplated purchase of the bowl, he replies, "Why it has a crack," and when she accuses him of being superstitious he exclaims, "Per Dio I'm superstitious! A crack's a crack—" (James, *The Golden Bowl,* 1:119).

68. Madeline Moore, "Nature and Community: A Study of Cyclical Reality in *The Waves*," 232.

69. Rose, *Woman of Letters*, 215. See Rose, pp. 213–17, for an account of the failure of *The Years* with which I substantially agree and on which I have drawn in the foregoing remarks.

70. Virginia Woolf, *The Years*, 323.

71. Woolf, *The Years*, 332; Henry James, *The Letters of Henry James*, ed. Lubbock, 2:384, 389.

72. Virginia Woolf, *Between the Acts*, 3, 209.

73. Henry James, *The Sacred Fount*, 99, 101.

74. David Adams Leeming, "A Conversation with Stephen Spender on Henry James," 128; Elizabeth Bowen in Joan Russell Noble, ed., *Recollections of Virginia Woolf*, 48.

75. Lyndall Gordon, *Virginia Woolf: A Writer's Life*, 268–69.

Conclusion

1. See on this point, for example, Nancy Chodorow, *The Reproduction of Mothering*, esp. ch. 8.

2. Christine Froula, "Naming and Renaming."

3. Janice Doane and Devon Hodges, *Nostalgia and Sexual Difference*, 92.

Bibliography

Armstrong, Paul B. *The Challenge of Bewilderment: Understanding and Representation in James, Conrad, and Ford.* Ithaca, N.Y.: Cornell University Press, 1987.

Atherton, J. S. "The Oxen of the Sun." In *James Joyce's* Ulysses: *Critical Essays,* edited by Clive Hart and David Hayman, 313–39. Berkeley: University of California Press, 1974.

Bell, Quentin. *Virginia Woolf: A Biography.* 2 vols. New York: Harcourt Brace Jovanovich, 1972.

Bell, Vanessa. *Notes on Virginia's Childhood: A Memoir.* New York: Frank Hallman, 1974.

Bennett, Joan. *Virginia Woolf.* Cambridge: Cambridge University Press, 1964.

Beveridge, W. I. B. *Influenza, the Last Great Plague: An Unfinished Story of Discovery.* New York: Prodist, 1977.

Blain, Virginia. "Narrative Voice and Female Perspective in Virginia Woolf's Early Novels." In *Virginia Woolf: New Critical Essays,* edited by Patricia Clements and Isobel Grundy, 115–36. London: Vision Press, 1983.

Bloom, Harold. *The Anxiety of Influence: A Theory of Poetry.* New York: Oxford University Press, 1973.

———. Introduction. In *British Modernist Fiction: 1920–1945,* edited by Harold Bloom, 1–18. New York: Chelsea House, 1986.

———. Introduction. In *Modern Critical Views: Virginia Woolf,* edited by Harold Bloom, 1–6. New York: Chelsea House, 1986.

———. *A Map of Misreading.* New York: Oxford University Press, 1975.

———. *Poetry and Repression: Revisionism from Blake to Stevens.* New Haven: Yale University Press, 1976.

Bowen, Zack. "Epiphanies, Stephen's Diary, and the Narrative Perspective of *A Portrait of the Artist as a Young Man.*" *James Joyce Quarterly* 16 (1979): 485–88.

Bradbury, Malcolm, and James McFarlane. "The Name and Nature of Modernism." In *Modernism: 1890–1930,* edited by Malcolm Bradbury and James McFarlane, 19–55. Harmondsworth, U.K.: Penguin, 1976.

Brown, Homer Obed. *James Joyce's Early Fiction: The Biography of a Form.* Cleveland: Case Western Reserve University Press, 1972.

Caramello, Charles. "Reading Gertrude Stein Reading Henry James, or, Eros is Eros is Eros." *Henry James Review* 6 (1985): 182–203.

Chodorow, Nancy. *The Reproduction of Mothering: Psychoanalysis and the Sociology of Gender*. Berkeley: University of California Press, 1978.

Collier, Richard. *The Plague of the Spanish Lady: The Influenza Pandemic of 1918–1919*. New York: Atheneum, 1974.

Colum, Mary, and Padraic Colum. *Our Friend James Joyce*. London: Victor Gollancz, 1959.

Cornwell, Ethel. *The Still Point: Themes and Variations in the Writings of T. S. Eliot, Coleridge, Yeats, Henry James, Virginia Woolf, and D. H. Lawrence*. New Brunswick, N.J.: Rutgers University Press, 1962.

Cousineau, Diane Levine. "Henry James and Virginia Woolf: A Comparative Study." Ph.D. dissertation, University of California, 1975.

Cunnington, C. Willett. *A Dictionary of English Costume*. London: Adam and Charles Black, 1960.

———, and Phillis Cunnington. *Handbook of English Costume in the Nineteenth Century*. London: Faber and Faber, 1970.

Curran, C. P. *James Joyce Remembered*. London: Oxford University Press, 1968.

Daiches, David. *Virginia Woolf*. Norfolk, Conn.: New Directions, 1942.

de Rougement, Denis. *Love in the Western World*, translated by Montgomery Belgion. Rev. and augmented. New York: Pantheon Books, 1956.

DeSalvo, Louise A. Introduction. In Virginia Woolf, *Melymbrosia: An Early Version of* The Voyage Out, edited by Louise A. DeSalvo. New York: New York Public Library, 1982.

———. "1897: Virginia Woolf at Fifteen." In *Virginia Woolf: A Feminist Slant*, edited by Jane Marcus, 78–108. Lincoln and London: University of Nebraska Press, 1983.

———. *Virginia Woolf's First Voyage*. London: Rowman and Littlefield, 1980.

DiBattista, Maria. *Virginia Woolf's Major Novels: The Fables of Anon*. New Haven: Yale University Press, 1980.

Doane, Janice, and Devon Hodges. *Nostalgia and Sexual Difference: The Resistance to Contemporary Feminism*. New York and London: Methuen, 1987.

Dole, Carol. "Oppression, Obsession: Virginia Woolf and Henry James," seminar paper, 1982, Cornell University. Revised version in *Southern Review* n.s. 24 (1988): 253–71.

Edel, Leon. "How I Came to Henry James." *Henry James Review* 3 (1982): 160–64.

———. *The Life of Henry James*. 5 vols. Philadelphia and New York: J. B. Lippincott, 1953–72.

———. *The Life of Henry James*. 2 vols. Harmondsworth, U.K.: Penguin, 1977.

———. "The Madness of Virginia Woolf." In Leon Edel, *Stuff of Sleep and*

Dreams: Experiments in Literary Psychology. New York: Harper & Row, 1982.

―――. *The Modern Psychological Novel.* Rev. ed. New York: Grosset Universal Library, 1964.

Ellmann, Richard. *James Joyce: New and Revised Edition.* New York: Oxford University Press, 1982.

Fleishman, Avrom. *Virginia Woolf: A Critical Reading.* Baltimore: Johns Hopkins University Press, 1975.

Fogel, Daniel Mark. *Daisy Miller: A Dark Comedy of Manners.* Boston: Twayne, 1990.

―――. *Henry James and the Structure of the Romantic Imagination.* Baton Rouge: Louisiana State University Press, 1981.

Froula, Christine. "Naming and Renaming." The *Woman's Review of Books* 5, no. 2 (1987): 20–22.

Garnett, David. *Great Friends: Portraits of Seventeen Writers.* London, Macmillan, 1979.

Gibson, Mary Virginia. "Event and Consciousness in Certain Novels of Henry James and Virginia Woolf." Ph.D. dissertation, University of Chicago, 1976.

Gifford, Don, and Robert J. Seidman. *Notes for Joyce: An Annotation of James Joyce's* Ulysses. New York: E. P. Dutton, 1974.

Gilbert, Sandra, and Susan Gubar. *The Madwoman in the Attic: The Woman Writer and the Nineteenth-Century Literary Imagination.* New Haven and London: Yale University Press, 1979.

―――. *The War of the Words.* Vol. 1 of *No Man's Land.* New Haven: Yale University Press, 1988.

Gilligan, Carol. *In a Different Voice: Psychological Theory and Women's Development.* Cambridge, Mass.: Harvard University Press, 1982.

Glasheen, Adeline. *Third Census of* Finnegans Wake: *An Index of the Characters and Their Roles.* Berkeley: University of California Press, 1977.

Goldman, Mark. *The Reader's Art: Virginia Woolf as Literary Critic.* The Hague: Mouton, 1976.

Gordon, Lyndall. *Virginia Woolf: A Writer's Life.* New York: W. W. Norton, 1984.

Gorman, Herbert. *James Joyce.* New York: Farrar & Rinehart, 1939.

Graham, Kenneth. *Indirections of the Novel: James, Conrad, and Forster.* Cambridge: Cambridge University Press, 1988.

Guiget, Jean. *Virginia Woolf and Her Works.* London: Hogarth Press, 1965.

Hoag, Gerald. "Henry James and the Criticism of Virginia Woolf." *Wichita State University Bulletin* 48 (1972), University Studies no. 92, pp. 3–11.

Hoehling, A. A. *The Great Epidemic.* Boston: Little, Brown, 1961.

Holleyman, G. A. *Catalogue of Books from the Library of Leonard and Virginia Woolf.* Brighton, U.K.: Holleyman and Treacher, 1975.

Hussey, Mark. *The Singing of the Real World: The Philosophy of Virginia Woolf's Fiction.* Columbus: Ohio State University Press, 1986.

Hyman, Virginia R. "Reflections in the Looking-Glass: Leslie Stephen and Virginia Woolf." *Journal of Modern Literature* 10 (1983): 197–215.

James, Henry. *The Ambassadors.* 2 vols. Vols. 21 and 22 of the New York Edition of *The Novels and Tales of Henry James.* New York: Charles Scribner's Sons, 1909.

———. *The American.* Vol. 2 of the New York Edition of *The Novels and Tales of Henry James.* New York: Charles Scribner's Sons, 1907.

———. *The Art of the Novel: Critical Prefaces by Henry James,* edited by Richard P. Blackmur. New York: Charles Scribner's Sons, 1934.

———. *The Awkward Age.* Vol. 9 of the New York Edition of *The Novels and Tales of Henry James.* New York: Charles Scribner's Sons, 1908.

———. *The Better Sort.* New York: Charles Scribner's Sons, 1903.

———. *The Complete Notebooks of Henry James,* edited by Leon Edel and Lyall H. Powers. New York: Oxford University Press, 1987.

———. *Daisy Miller, Pandora, The Patagonia, and Other Tales.* Vol. 18 of the New York Edition of *The Novels and Tales of Henry James.* New York: Charles Scribner's Sons, 1909.

———. *English Hours.* London: William Heinemann, 1905.

———. *The Golden Bowl.* 2 vols. Vols. 23 and 24 of the New York Edition of *The Novels and Tales of Henry James.* New York: Charles Scribner's Sons, 1909.

———. *Henry James Letters,* edited by Leon Edel. 4 vols. Cambridge, Mass.: Harvard University Press, 1974–84.

———. "Honoré de Balzac, 1902." In *Literary Criticism: French Writers, Other European Writers, The Prefaces to the New York Edition,* edited by Leon Edel and Mark Wilson, 90–114. New York: Library of America, 1984.

———. Introduction to *The Tempest.* Vol. 16 of *The Complete Works of William Shakespeare,* edited by Sidney Lee. London: George G. Harrap & Co., 1907.

———. *The Letters of Henry James,* edited by Percy Lubbock. 2 vols. New York: Charles Scribner's Sons, 1920.

———. *The Notebooks of Henry James,* edited by F. O. Matthiessen and Kenneth B. Murdock. New York: Oxford University Press, 1947.

———. "Notes for The Ivory Tower." In *The Ivory Tower.* London: W. Collin's Sons & Co., 1917.

———. *The Portrait of a Lady.* In *Novels 1881–1886: Washington Square, The Portrait of a Lady, The Bostonians,* edited by William T. Stafford. New York: The Library of America, 1985.

———. *The Portrait of a Lady.* 2 vols. Vols. 3 and 4 of the New York Edition of *The Novels and Tales of Henry James.* New York: Charles Scribner's Sons, 1908.

———. *The Princess Casamassima.* In *Novels, 1886–1890: The Princess*

Casamassima, The Reverberator, The Tragic Muse, edited by Daniel Mark Fogel. New York: Library of America, 1989.

——. *Roderick Hudson.* Vol. 1 of the New York Edition of *The Novels and Tales of Henry James.* New York: Charles Scribner's Sons, 1907.

——. *The Sacred Fount.* London: Rupert Hart-Davis, 1959.

——. *The Wings of the Dove.* Westminster: Archibald Constable and Co., 1902.

——. *The Wings of the Dove.* 2 vols. Vols. 19 and 20 of the New York Edition of *The Novels and Tales of Henry James.* New York: Charles Scribner's Sons, 1909.

Jameson, Fredric. "*Ulysses* in History." In *James Joyce and Modern Literature,* edited by W. J. McCormack and Alistair Stead, 126–41. London: Routledge & Kegan Paul, 1982.

Jones, Vivien. *James as Critic.* New York: St Martin's Press, 1985.

Joyce, James. *The Critical Essays of James Joyce,* edited by Ellsworth Mason and Richard Ellmann. New York: Viking Press, 1959.

——. *Dubliners.* London: Grant Richards, 1914.

——. *Letters of James Joyce,* edited by Stuart Gilbert (vol. 1) and Richard Ellmann (vols. 2–3). London: Faber and Faber, 1957, 1966.

——. *A Portrait of the Artist as a Young Man.* New York: B. W. Huebsch, 1916.

——. *Stephen Hero,* edited by John J. Slocum. Norfolk, Conn.: New Directions, 1960.

——. *Ulysses,* edited by Hans Walter Gabler. New York: Random House, 1986.

——. *Ulysses: "Circe" and "Eumaeus," a Facsimile of Placards for Episodes 15–16,* edited by Michael Groden. New York: Garland Publishing, 1978.

——. *Ulysses: "Telemachus," "Nestor," "Proteus," "Calypso," "Lotus Eaters," and "Hades," a Facsimile of the Pages Proofs for Episodes 1–6,* edited by Michael Groden. New York: Garland Publishing, 1978.

——. *Ulysses: "Wandering Rocks," and "Sirens," a Facsimile of Page Proofs for Episodes 10 and 11,* edited by Michael Groden. New York: Garland Publishing, 1978.

Joyce, Stanislaus. *The Dublin Diary of Stanislaus Joyce,* edited by George Harris Healy. London: Faber and Faber, 1962.

——. *My Brother's Keeper,* edited by Richard Ellmann. London: Faber and Faber, 1958.

Kelley, Alice van Buren. *The Novels of Virginia Woolf.* Chicago: University of Chicago Press, 1973.

Kenner, Hugh. *The Pound Era.* Berkeley: University of California Press, 1971.

Kirkpatrick, B. J. *A Bibliography of Virginia Woolf.* 3rd ed. Oxford: Clarendon Press, 1980.

Layton, Lynne, and Barbara Ann Shapiro. *Narcissism and the Text: Studies in the Literature and Psychology of Self.* New York: New York University Press, 1986.

Lee, L. L. "Woolf, the Times, the Provinces." *Virginia Woolf Miscellany,* no. 9 (Winter 1977): 1.

Leeming, David Adams. "A Conversation with Stephen Spender on Henry James." *Henry James Review* 9 (1988): 128–35.

Levin, Harry. *James Joyce: A Critical Introduction.* Rev. ed. New York: New Directions, 1960.

Leyburn, Ellen Douglass. "Virginia Woolf's Judgment of Henry James." *Modern Fiction Studies* 5 (1959): 166–69.

Love, Jean O. *Virginia Woolf: Sources of Madness and Art.* Berkeley: University of California Press, 1977.

Lovelace, Mary, Countess of. "Society and the Season." In *Fifty Years, Memories and Contrasts: A Composite Picture of the Period 1882–1932 by Twenty-Seven Contributors to The Times,* 24–30. London: Thornton Butterworth, Ltd., 1932.

Marcus, Jane. *Virginia Woolf and the Languages of Patriarchy.* Bloomington: Indiana University Press, 1987.

Minow-Pinkney, Makiko. *Virginia Woolf and the Problem of the Subject.* Brighton, U.K.: Harvester, 1987.

Moore, Madeline. "Nature and Community: A Study of Cyclical Reality in *The Waves.*" In *Virginia Woolf: Revaluation and Continuity,* edited by Ralph Freedman, 219–40. Berkeley: University of California Press, 1980.

———. *The Short Season between Two Silences.* Boston: George Allen & Unwin, 1984.

Newberry, Frederick. "A Note on the Horror in James's Revision of *Daisy Miller.*" *Henry James Review* 3 (1982): 229–32.

Nicolson, Nigel. *Portrait of a Marriage.* New York: Antheneum, 1973.

Noble, Joan Russell, ed. *Recollections of Virginia Woolf.* London: Peter Owen, 1972.

Novak, Jane. *The Razor Edge of Balance: A Study of Virginia Woolf.* Coral Gables, Fla.: University of Miami Press, 1975.

Oates, Joyce Carol. *See* Smith, J. Oates.

Orage, A. R. "Henry James and the Ghostly." *Little Review* 5 (August 1918): 41–43.

"Panel Discussion 2." In *Virginia Woolf: A Centenary Perspective,* edited by Eric Warner, 146–65. London: Macmillan, 1984.

Perosa, Sergio. *Henry James and the Experimental Novel.* Charlottesville: University Press of Virginia, 1978.

Pound, Ezra. "Mr. James Joyce and the Modern Stage." *Drama* [Chicago, Ill.] 21 (February 1916): 122–32.

———. "The Notes to 'The Ivory Tower.'" *Little Review* 5 (August 1918): 62–64 and (September 1918): 50–53.

———. *Pound/Joyce: The Letters of Ezra Pound to James Joyce, with*

Pound's Essays on Joyce, edited by Forrest Read. London: Faber and Faber, 1968.

Power, Arthur. *Conversations with James Joyce,* edited by Clive Hart. London: Millington Ltd., 1974.

Richter, Harvena. *Virginia Woolf: The Inward Voyage.* Princeton: Princeton University Press, 1970.

Rose, Phyllis. *Woman of Letters: A Life of Virginia Woolf.* New York: Oxford University Press, 1978.

Rosenbaum, S. P. "Three Unknown Early Essays by Virginia Woolf." *Virginia Woolf Miscellany* no. 26 (1986): 1–4.

———. *Victorian Bloomsbury: The Early Literary History of the Bloomsbury Group.* London: Macmillan, 1987.

Rosenman, Ellen Bayuk. *The Invisible Presence: Virginia Woolf and the Mother-Daughter Relationship.* Baton Rouge: Louisiana State University Press, 1986.

Rowe, John Carlos. *The Theoretical Dimensions of Henry James.* Madison: University of Wisconsin Press, 1984.

Ruotolo, Lucio P. *The Interrupted Moment: A View of Virginia Woolf's Novels.* Stanford: Stanford University Press, 1986.

Ryan, Judith. "The Vanishing Subject: Empirical Psychology and the Modern Novel." *PMLA* 95 (1980): 857–69.

Sabiston, Elizabeth. "Isabel Archer: The Architecture of Consciousness and the International Theme." *Henry James Review* 7, nos. 2–3 (1986): 29–47.

Sacks, Sheldon. "Novelists as Storytellers." *Modern Philology* 73, no. 4, pt. 2 (1976): S97–S109.

Schutte, William M. *Joyce and Shakespeare.* New Haven: Yale University Press, 1957.

Sears, Sallie. *The Negative Imagination: Form and Perspective in the Novels of Henry James.* Ithaca, N.Y.: Cornell University Press, 1968.

Sharma, Vijay. *Virginia Woolf as Literary Critic: A Revaluation.* New Delhi: Arnold-Heinemann, 1977.

Silver, Brenda R. *Virginia Woolf's Reading Notebooks.* Princeton: Princeton University Press, 1983.

Smith, J. Oates. "The Art of Relationships: Henry James and Virginia Woolf." *Twentieth-Century Literature* 10 (1964): 119–29. Rev. and rpt. in Joyce Carol Oates, *New Heaven, New Earth: The Visionary Experience in Literature.* New York: Vanguard, 1974.

Smith, Paula Vene. "The Library and the Tea Table: Virginia Woolf and the Fiction of Henry James." Ph.D. dissertation, Cornell University, 1987.

Spender, Stephen. *The Destructive Element: A Study of Modern Writers and Beliefs.* London: Jonathan Cape, 1935.

Stern, Carol Simpson. "Parties as Reflectors of the Feminine Sensibility: Woolf's *Mrs. Dalloway* Counters James's *The Wings of the Dove.*" *Communication Quarterly* 31 (1983): 167–73.

Sullivan, John. *G. K. Chesterton: A Bibliography.* London: University of London Press, 1958.

Thornton, Weldon. *Allusions in Ulysses.* Chapel Hill: University of North Carolina Press, 1968.

Tintner, Adeline R. *The Book World of Henry James.* Ann Arbor: UMI Research Press, 1987.

Todorov, Tzvetan. *The Poetics of Prose,* translated by Richard Howard. Ithaca, N.Y.: Cornell University Press, 1977.

Torgovnick, Marianna. *The Visual Arts, Pictorialism, and the Novel: James, Lawrence, and Woolf.* Princeton University Press, 1985.

Trombley, Stephen. *"All that Summer She was Mad": Virginia Woolf and Her Doctors.* London: Junction Books, 1981.

Warner, Eric. *See* "Panel Discussion 2."

Wellek, René. "Virginia Woolf as Critic." *Southern Review* n.s. 13 (1977): 419–37.

Wells, H. G. *Boon, The Mind of the Race, The Wild Asses of the Devil, and The Last Trump.* London: T. Fisher Unwin, 1915.

White, Allon. *The Uses of Obscurity: The Fiction of Early Modernism.* London and Boston: Routledge & Kegan Paul, 1981.

Wiesenfarth, Joseph. "A Woman in *The Portrait of a Lady.*" *Henry James Review* 7, nos. 2–3 (1986): 18–28.

Wirth-Nesher, Hana. "Limits of Fiction: A Study of the Novels of Henry James and Virginia Woolf." Ph.D. dissertation, Columbia University, 1977.

Woolf, Leonard. *Sowing: An Autobiography of the Years 1880 to 1904.* New York: Harcourt Brace, 1960.

Woolf, Virginia. "Across the Border." *Times Literary Supplement,* January 31, 1918, 55.

———. "American Fiction." *Saturday Review of Literature* 2, no. 1 (1925): 1–3.

———. "The Antiquary." *Nation and Athenaeum,* November 22, 1924, 293–94.

———. *Between the Acts.* New York: Harcourt Brace Jovanovich, 1969.

———. "Character in Fiction." *The Criterion: A Quarterly Review* 2 (1924): 409–30.

———. *The Collected Essays of Virginia Woolf,* edited by Leonard Woolf. 4 vols. New York: Harcourt, Brace & World, 1967.

———. *The Common Reader.* London: Hogarth Press, 1925.

———. *The Death of the Moth and Other Essays.* New York: Harcourt, Brace, 1942.

———. *The Diary of Virginia Woolf,* edited by Anne Olivier Bell. 5 vols. New York and London: Harcourt Brace Jovanovich, 1977–84.

———. *The Essays of Virginia Woolf: 1904–1912.* Vol. 1 of *The Essays of Virginia Woolf,* edited by Andrew McNeillie. London: Hogarth Press, 1986.

———. "Gothic Romance." *Times Literary Supplement*, May 5, 1921, 288.

———. "Henry James' Ghost Stories." *Times Literary Supplement*, December 22, 1921, 849–50.

———. *Jacob's Room*. New York: Harcourt, Brace and Company, 1923.

———. "Jane Austen at Sixty." *Nation and Athenaeum*, December 15, 1923, 433–34.

———. "Joseph Conrad." *Times Literary Supplement*, August 14, 1924, 493–94.

———. "The Letters of Henry James." *Times Literary Supplement*, April 8, 1920, 217–18.

———. *The Letters of Virginia Woolf*, edited by Nigel Nicolson and Joanne Trautmann. 6 vols. New York and London: Harcourt Brace Jovanovich, 1975–80.

———. "The Man at the Gate." *New Statesman and Nation*, October 19, 1940, 382.

———. *Melymbrosia: An Early Version of* The Voyage Out, edited by Louisa A. DeSalvo. New York: New York Public Library, 1982.

———. "The Method of Henry James." *Times Literary Supplement*, December 26, 1918, 655.

———. "Modern Novels." *Times Literary Supplement*, April 10, 1919, 189–90.

———. *Moments of Being: Unpublished Autobiographical Writings*, edited by Jeanne Schulkind. New York and London: Harcourt Brace Jovanovich, 1976.

———. *Moments of Being*, edited by Jeanne Schulkind. 2d ed. London: Hogarth Press, 1985.

———. "Mr. Conrad: A Conversation." *Nation and Athenaeum*, September 1, 1923, 681–82.

———. "Mr. Henry James's Latest Novel." *The Guardian*, February 22, 1905, 339.

———. *Mrs. Dalloway*. New York: Harcourt, Brace and Company, 1925.

———. *Night and Day*. New York: George H. Doran, 1920.

———. "The Novels of Turgenev." *Times Literary Supplement*, December 14, 1933, 885–86.

———. "The Old Order." *Times Literary Supplement*, October 18, 1917, 497–98.

———. "On Not Knowing French." *New Republic*, February 13, 1929, 348–49.

———. "On Re-Reading Novels." *Times Literary Supplement*, July 20, 1922, 465–66.

———. *Orlando*. London: Hogarth Press, 1928.

———. *The Pargiters: The Novel-Essay Portion of* The Years, edited by Mitchell A. Leaska. New York: Harcourt Brace Jovanovich, 1977.

————. "The Patron and the Crocus." *Nation and Athenaeum*, April 12, 1924, 46–47.

————. "Phases of Fiction." *The Bookman*, 69—part 1 (April 1929): 123–32; part 2 (May 1929): 269–79; part 3 (June 1929): 404–12.

————. *A Room of One's Own*. New York and London: Harcourt Brace Jovanovich, 1957.

————. "The Russian Point of View." In *The Common Reader*. London: Hogarth Press, 1925.

————. "Speech before the London/National Society for Women's Service, January 21, 1931." In *The Pargiters: The Novel-Essay Portion of The Years*, edited by Mitchell A. Leaska. New York and London: Harcourt Brace Jovanovich, 1980.

————. "Thomas Hardy's Novels." *Times Literary Supplement*, January 19, 1928, 33–34.

————. *Three Guineas*. New York: Harcourt, Brace and Company, 1938.

————. *To the Lighthouse*. New York: Harcourt, Brace, 1927.

————. *Virginia Woolf and Lytton Strachey: Letters*, edited by Leonard Woolf and James Strachey. New York: Harcourt, Brace, 1956.

————. *The Voyage Out*. New York: George H. Doran, 1920.

————. *The Waves*. London: Hogarth Press, 1931.

————. "Within the Rim." *Times Literary Supplement*, March 27, 1919, 163.

————. *The Years*. New York: Harcourt, Brace and Company, 1937.

Zlotnick, Joan. "Influence or Coincidence. A Comparative Study of 'The Beast in the Jungle' and 'A Painful Case.'" *Colby Library Quarterly* 11 (1975): 132–35.

Zwerdling, Alex. *Virginia Woolf and the Real World*. Berkeley: University of California Press, 1986.

Index

marriage themes in, and VW,
126
Master, appellation for and
legend of, 13–14, 44
modernism and, 2–3, 44–46
morality of care in, compared
with VW, 142–44
New York Edition of Novels
and Tales of, 155–56,
185–86 n. 60
prefaces to, 78, 89
Proust, HJ trailblazer for according to VW, 110–12,
114
reading of by VW, catalogued,
78–79
renunciation in and VW, 135
seventieth-birthday tribute to,
84, 177 n. 9
VW, HJ's remarks on, 54–57,
69, 174 n. 1
VW's "Modern Fiction," in
background of, 138–39
VW's *Night and Day*, association with Fortescue in,
130–33
VW's *Orlando*, covert presence
in, 155–56
VW's *To the Lighthouse*, resemblance to Lily Brisco
in, 147
VW's unease about writing
after reading him, 107
VW's *The Voyage Out*, resemblance to Hewet in, 130
VW's *The Waves*, association
with Bernard in, 157–59,
186 n. 63
see also Joyce, James; Woolf,
Virginia; *and individual
titles by HJ*
James, William, 92
"James Clarence Mangan" (JJ),
35, 172 n. 12
Jameson, Fredric, 171 n. 27
Joyce, George, 30

Joyce, James
anxiety of influence, freedom
from, 2, 51–53, 165
epiphanies in, 35
and Henry James
admiration for HJ's *Portrait
of a Lady*, 27, 29,
172 n. 4
anti-Jamesian fictional strategies, 44–45
burlesque of style of, 7,
22–25
compared unfavorably with
by VW, 100
derides Stanislaus Joyce for
enthusiasm for, 28, 39,
173 n. 19
dislike of HJ's "tea-slop,"
and VW, 87
imitation of in *Stephen
Hero*, 29–34
"kick in the arse" for, pre-
scribed by JJ, 19–20,
171 n. 20
lessons of late fiction of, in
Dubliners and *Portrait
of the Artist as a Young
Man*, 34–44
misreading of, 45–46
point of view in JJ's fiction
and, 40–41
reading of, 26–29
recognition of as father of
modernism, 54
relation with, compared with
VW's, 164–65
trope of HJ/Beaufoy in *Ulysses*, 7–15, 46–53
literary and biological creation,
connection of, 47–50
Meredith, George, compared
unfavorably with by VW,
100
Shakespeare theory, date of,
171 n. 25
Ulysses, schoolboy theme on, 50